A Silent Siren Song

D1714050

A Silent Siren Song

The Aitken Brothers' Hollywood Odyssey, 1905–1926

Al P. Nelson and Mel R. Jones

Cooper Square Press

Published by Cooper Square Press
An Imprint of the Rowman & Littlefield Publishing Group
150 Fifth Avenue, Suite 911
New York, New York 10011

Distributed by National Book Network

Library of Congress Cataloging-in-Publication Data

Nelson, Al P.
  A silent siren song : the Aitken brothers' Hollywood odyssey, 1905–1926 / Al P. Nelson and Mel R. Jones.
    p. cm.
  Includes bibliographical references and index.
  ISBN 0-8154-1069-7 (alk. paper)
    1. Aitken, Harry E., 1870–1956. 2. Aitken, Roy E. 3. Motion picture producers and directors—United States—Biography. 4. Mutual Film Corporation—History. I. Jones, Mel R. II. Title.

PN1998.3.A4324 N45 2000
791.43'0232'092273—21
[B]

00-031781

⊗™ The paper used in this publication meets the minimum requirements of American National Standard for Information Sciences—Permanence of Paper for Printed Library Materials, ANSI/NISO Z39.48-1992. Manufactured in the United States of America.

To Harry and Roy Aitken, whose vision and faith helped shape the movie industry. And to Al P. Nelson, who paved the way for overdue recognition of their achievement.

First you shall meet with the Sirens, who capture the minds
Of all whom they can acquaint with their attractions.
Whoever shall approach them unforewarned
And heed their song will never again turn
His affection home, and will despise
His wife and children, as they gather to greet him—
The Sirens will so enchant him with their song,
Shrill, and yet powerfully sensual.

Homer, *Odyssey*, Book 12, lines 39–44

Contents

Preface

L ike most odysseys, this one began with a dream. Two farm boys, one already a budding entrepreneur and the other exhibiting the soul of a poet, left Goerke's Corners, Waukesha, Wisconsin, and before the twentieth century was a decade old, Harry E. and Roy E. Aitken were movie moguls. While still in their thirties, the Aitken brothers established the first silent movie empire by owning film production companies, a major film exchange system, and a number of major theaters in the Midwest. In brief, the Aitkens controlled what pictures were made, how they would be distributed, and where they would first be shown. Others followed this producer–exchange–theater owner pattern and became giants in the industry. Men like William Fox, Carl Laemmle, and Louis Mayer gained fame and fortune through participation in the Aitken formula, but the brothers themselves returned to Wisconsin after a long, hard-fought, bittersweet movie career.

Shortly before he died at age seventy-eight in 1956 in Chicago, Harry Aitken summed up his and his younger brother's movie odyssey: "That career of ours—that delirious decade—I still can't believe it. The nickelodeons, the exchanges and studios, the huge salaries, the fabulous stars, the millions of dollars that passed in and out—things moved so fast, so crazily—sometimes the whole experience seems to be a huge kaleidoscopic fantasy—grotesque, incredible."

Roy, freed of the mantle of leadership that weighed so heavily on his brother's shoulders, viewed their movie odyssey in far less burdensome terms. The younger Aitken was able to turn anxiety and uncertainty aside through his complete trust in Harry combined with a boyish sense of adventure that never deserted him. To Roy, Hollywood and the movies were just another part of the world to wear like a stylish garment, or better yet to drive through in one of his fancy cars.

None of this should imply that Roy was a playboy. He worked too hard at every task assigned or undertaken on his own to be so categorized. Rather, it is the cheerfulness with which Roy engaged his work that made him the perfect complement to Harry's genius for organization. Nowhere is this more evident than in Roy's own summation of the brothers' sojourn as movie moguls:

> What a thrill it was for two green farm boys to leave home and start the ball rolling in the movie business. The happiness in boyish enthusiasm we brought to the task never subsided. Like kids at a circus, or Disneyland today, we lived in a trance. Movie fever! We got it and spread it. It was like strong drink to us. Although we never knew what lay ahead, it was a thrill to send people to Hollywood and let them rent space and build platforms and start cameras rolling to take pictures of people doing antics which would later be seen in theaters around the world. The best names and the best minds flocked to our magnificent adventure. It became Aitkenland, fantasyland, Disneyland, the circus rolled into one. What a blessing it was for us and those who shared the dream.

Contrast Roy's fun-filled statement with Harry's kaleidoscopic, grotesque comments cited earlier, and it's obvious each brought his own perspective to the lifelong partnership. They drew from each other, and the composite gave the brothers' enterprise its passion, strength and durability as they answered the call of a silent siren.

As the survivor, it was left to Roy, Harry's junior by four years and eight months, to chronicle the elder Aitken's genius and his own charming personality so that their legacy could endure. Together they had lured directors like David Wark Griffith, Thomas Ince, and Mack Sennett to work from scripts produced by Irvin S. Cobb, Richard Harding Davis, Anita Loos, Booth Tarkington, and Mary Robert Rinehart. Similarly, the stars the Aitkens developed created a galaxy that Hollywood will never forget: Douglas Fairbanks Sr., Mary Pickford, Gloria Swanson, Charlie Chaplin, Norma and Constance Talmadge, William S. Hart, Lillian and Dorothy Gish, Wallace Beery, and Roscoe "Fatty" Arbuckle. So when he was in his late eighties, Roy Aitken, who cherished his brother like no other man, set out to tell how they produced some 2,500 silent films including the classic *Birth of a Nation*. In Al P. Nelson, this writer's father-in-law, Roy Aitken found a voice to match his and his brother's spirit.

I can still see two elderly gentlemen pouring over papers and photographs at a table at the Red Circle Inn, Nashotah, or in Roy's home in Waukesha as the former silent film tycoon and the down-home Wisconsin writer collaborated on their first book together, *The Birth of a Nation Story*. The roots of *Birth* (the book) reach deep into the moviemaking careers of the Aitkens. These young, idealistic men produced one of the most controversial films in history. Some have labeled it the greatest movie ever made. Others see it as a bigoted and twisted saga that glorifies the Ku Klux Klan during the South's Reconstruction period. Everyone agrees it was a colossal moneymaker for its time, grossing $15 million and earning more than ten times what it cost to make in 1915.

Written as a memoir, Roy Aitken and Al Nelson's first collaboration began and ended with the making of the *Birth* movie. Missing from the earlier book is the rich background and character of two midwestern youths who fought a valiant struggle against the iron grip that immigrants from Eastern Europe later gained on Hollywood. Had the Aitkens been allowed to throw in their lot with a support network like that of the Warners, the Goldwyns, the Mayers, the Zukors, the Thalbergs, the Scharys, the Schulbergs, and even the Laemmles from the brothers' home state, the outcome might have been markedly different. Today—along with Warner Brothers, MGM, Fox, and Universal—*Majestic*, *Reliance*, and *Triangle* would be household words linked to the Aitken brothers. Roy Aitken and Al Nelson knew there was more to the story, so they set out to write a sequel to their *Birth* book. Unfortunately, Roy Aitken died in Waukesha in 1976 at age ninety-four. Sixteen years later, Al Nelson died. He was ninety-one and left behind at his home in Delafield an unpublished chronicle entitled "The First Silent Movie Empire."

My involvement came when my brother-in-law, Bill Nelson (Al's only son and a writer in his own right), encouraged me, with the support of his sisters, Barbara Nelson and Marian Nelson Jones, to tackle the nearly twenty-year-old project. I began by changing the title, since the saga of Harry and Roy Aitken has been repeated throughout history as young men and women follow one silent siren song or another in their march toward what Aristotle called the complete life. In this sense, the Aitken brothers' story is universal, yet also unique, in their reaction to fame, fortune, and reversals of the same. As now presented, the Aitken story is a new, yet continuous and hopefully judicious, mixture of the strange and the familiar. Under similar circumstances, each of us would react differently, but we share the wisdom of the ancients who said that a man's or woman's life should be measured by the opposition it takes to discourage that person from acting virtuously. Some stumble sooner than others, and some fall and never get up. On a number of occasions in history, single individuals stood upright throughout their entire lives. But the Aitkens were more like us than Socrates, Buddha, Christ, or any past or current philosopher or great historical figure. These brothers followed the glitz and glamour to the end of the rainbow and discovered, almost too late, that the brighter light shines within, where false siren songs are never heard. Still, the Aitkens are guides for those of us too fearful to run the good race that includes handling success all the way to the finish line and beyond. But most of all, the Aitken brothers are revolutionaries with a vision who own a place in history for the many beneficial ways they shaped the movie industry.

While retaining Roy Aitken's point of view, I changed what was compiled as another "as told to" memoir to a biography of the two Aitken brothers and their impact on the early film industry. This approach gave more leeway to flesh out the interesting characters the Aitkens encountered on their odyssey and at the same time unshackle Al Nelson from Roy Aitken's zeal to compensate for the lack of recognition the brothers received during Harry's lifetime. Adding a great deal of material Roy had left out of his memoir but I discovered in the Aitken brothers' papers and official records allowed for a rounded synthesis that integrates and interprets the lives of Harry and Roy for every generation. This new biography, then, is anchored in fact as interpreted by material evidence and not on Roy's memory alone. Resources for this biography include interviews with Roy E. Aitken conducted by Al P. Nelson over a ten-year span and a vast amount of Aitken papers, photographs, and other supporting documents currently in the coauthor's possession.

Where appropriate I have tapped outside sources to augment the materials Aitken and Nelson assembled for future use. To those authors who granted permission to quote from their published works, I am indebted beyond measure. They are aware, as I am, that the Aitken brothers did not operate in a vacuum. By juxtaposing the Aitkens' experience against that of their contemporaries, a clearer picture of the early movie industry emerges as each mogul, director, star, or writer has enriched an evolving fabric by weaving in a good measure of diversity and insight.

I am grateful for the opportunity to demonstrate what I have learned from Al Nelson, the master craftsman. At his funeral, I tried to put into words the feeling thousands of his beneficiaries, like me, felt at his passing: "This is not *The End*. The spirit of your byline is stamped on all who knew you as a complete, virtuous, upright and steadfast, beloved *friend*."

I am also grateful to the host of early movie stars, directors, scriptwriters, producers, and friends of Roy Aitken, most of whom are now deceased, who provided insights and facts. I want to recognize two members of the Al Nelson family without whom this work would have remained dormant. First in this writer's heart is Marian Nelson Jones, my wife of more than thirty years, and like her mother, the best researcher, copyeditor, critic, and agent a writer could ever hope for in one lifetime. Then there's Mildred F. Nelson, Al's ninety-four-year-old widow, who lived with us in the sunset of her life. Although she suffered from

Alzheimer's disease, Mildred's passing this year is a gentle reminder of her once vibrant life, so characteristic of that shared by others like the Aitken brothers, their associates, and all those who forged ahead in a tumultuous century.

I would also like to acknowledge our son, Captain Mark R. Jones, United States Air Force, for the many hours he spent during precious leave time away from his flying duties scanning vintage photographs and performing other computer wizardry. Among the cards welcoming Mark into the world after his birth is one signed "Uncle Roy." Thirty years later, our son was happy to assist in the preparation of the Aitken brothers' story in recognition of his grandfather, father, and honorary "Uncle Roy" Aitken.

Finally, I need to thank Otterhounds McDuke and Mandy, since their antics rival a Mack Sennett Keystone Kops comedy routine, providing a great deal of humor in our lives since our children Beth, Grace, Mark, and Matthew departed the nest.

1

Yearning for Adventure

A year or two after the stone house was demolished in 1973 to make way for a Holiday Inn, Roy E. Aitken stood at the front entrance to examine a marker placed there by the Waukesha County Historical Society on March 16, 1974. People going in and out of the busy motel ignored both the ninety-two-year-old, well-dressed gentleman and the plaque erected to commemorate the Aitken brothers' humble origins and later movie careers.

The sounds of heavy traffic descending on Goerke's Corners drove the old man inside the motel to rest his fragile ears and collect his thoughts on the very spot where his family's comfortable farm home had stood. He slumped into a chair in the lobby and laid a battered brown briefcase across his knees. He allowed a sad nostalgia to sweep through his mind, ironically carrying exhilarating images of his and his brother Harry's movie experiences between 1905 and 1926. It had been a glorious parade culminating in the production of 2,500 silent movies in an eight-year span. Harry and Roy Aitken's drum majors were David W. Griffith, Thomas Ince, Mack Sennett, and other renowned directors hired by the brothers to produce movies. And produce they did, including the world-known daddy of all silent films, *Birth of a Nation*, as well as *Intolerance*.

If indeed the great directors became the drum majors in Harry and Roy's Hollywood parade, then the majorettes and soloists were the stars. The Aitken brothers launched into stardom Lillian and Dorothy Gish, Gloria Swanson, Mae Marsh, Douglas Fairbanks Sr., Wallace Beery, Henry Walthall, Monte Blue, Norma Talmadge, Bessie Love, Alma Rubens, Edna Purviance, and a host of others.

Eighty years later, sitting at the Holiday Inn waiting for his sister, Roy Aitken found the odyssey unbelievable. Unbelievable, too, were the dances in the Beverly Hills Hotel ballroom with Mary Pickford, America's Sweetheart, whose saucer eyes, porcelain-like features, and golden curls captivated a whole generation of admirers. Then, too, there were rollicking beach parties in which Harry and Roy led vivacious Mabel Normand, Teddy Sampson, and many other movie lovelies in playful chases across the hot sands.

All this occurred while the brothers were young men, and Roy took it as proof that almost anything can happen in America, even to farm boys, if they are willing to dream and work. Since Harry's death at age seventy-eight in 1956, Roy admitted that he had done more dreaming than working. Outings like the Holiday Inn excursion gave him the opportunity to sit alone and harvest memories. His sister, Gladys Aitken Armitage, wondered why at his age, Roy didn't just buy a rocker and sit at his home in Waukesha, near hers, and fill his mind with fanciful thoughts of Hollywood. He knew that she had his safety in mind, but no one, except perhaps Harry, could see the importance of returning to that once peaceful place where the dream began.

Both Harry and Roy were born before the turn of the century—Harry Elvin on October 4, 1877, and Roy E. on June 13, 1882. In their youth, of course, no airplanes, no automobiles, no trucks, no expressways, no Holiday Inns marred the tranquil beauty of Goerke's Corners. The only sounds resembling noise were the tinkling of cowbells and the occasional shout of a farmer trying to hurry his horses over the rutty, twisting road.

It is five o'clock on a cold January morning in the year 1893, and a thin eleven-year-old boy sits on a wooden stool milking a cow in a cold, drafty barn in southern Wisconsin. Roy Aitken is so sleepy his eyes refuse to stay open. A small tin pail is pressed between his bony knees, and as he wearily squeezes and pulls on the cow's fat teats, a stream of warm milk rattles against the tin. The noise helps him stay awake.

Seated at the next cow is his sixteen-year-old brother Harry, followed by the boys' father, Elvin Aitken, who milks the third cow in line. There are six more cows, two for each milker, waiting their turn. In the kitchen of the stone farmhouse, the family matriarch, Sarah Hadfield Aitken, checks baked apples in the oven and a pot of steaming oatmeal, fried eggs, and coffee cooking on the burners. The milkers can smell their breakfast, and a sense of urgency to complete the chores spurs the older boy into action.

"How are you getting along, Roy?" calls Harry as he gets up to empty his full milk pail into a large metal milk can.

"I can't get my fingers warm," the younger boy shouts.

Harry laughs, empties his pail, and comes back. "Let me milk your cow for a few minutes while you warm your hands at the lantern," he says.

Roy smiles at his brother and crouches over the lantern. More than his hands are warmed, for in his heart he knows that Harry always looks out for him. He also resolves not to milk cows all his life. He has shared with Harry his desire to do something different, something more adventuresome, a job where he can sleep later in the morning.

The Aitken boys were not pampered in their youth. The milking scene at five in the morning was repeated at least two hundred or more days a year. Their Scotch-English father believed in teaching his children, especially his sons, the value of work. Elvin Aitken passed on to Harry and Roy the values he got from his own father, John Aitken, who had migrated from Scotland with his parents, Andrew and Jane, and six brothers and sisters in 1835. Later, the marriage of John and Jane Aitken produced only one offspring, Elvin. John operated a large farm near Quincy, Illinois, on the Missouri border about a hundred miles northwest of St. Louis.

In 1866, the year Reconstruction was in full swing in the former Confederate states, Elvin's father packed up the family and moved to a farm near Waukesha, Wisconsin, intent on wresting a bountiful living from the rich northern soil by virtue of hard work. Elvin worked on his father's two-hundred-acre farm for many years, plowing, cultivating, threshing, milking cows, and pitting his eager, young strength against the inevitable exhaustion of farm life.

One day at church in Waukesha, Elvin Aitken met a pretty young woman seated on the piano stool. Sarah Jane Hadfield lived on a farm east of the city with her parents, Joseph and Sarah Hadfield, one sister, and nine brothers. Her father had migrated from Derbyshire, England, in 1842 at the age of twenty-seven with his bride Harriet, who died in 1844, leaving an infant son named Joseph. Remarriage in 1845 resulted in ten more offspring. Several of Sarah Jane's nephews would later follow her sons Harry and Roy into the film exchange and theater operation business as Aitken associates. When Elvin met Sarah, she had just returned from a college for women in Pennsylvania where she studied music. They fell in love and were married on December 16, 1874, in Pewaukee, Waukesha County. The happy young couple moved into the big, square stone farmhouse with Elvin's father, who was grateful for his son's assistance in his old age.

In 1875, John Aitken decided to retire from farming. He turned the farm over to Elvin, and he and his second wife, Agnes, bought a house in downtown Waukesha, where they led a rather leisurely life in what was then called Spa City. Roy recalls that many southerners came to the small community of Waukesha every summer to escape the heat and the political situation in their own communities. The tourists stayed in rambling, commodious hotels, drank the healthful waters, and danced well into the warm nights.

Many years later, in his posthumously published book *Notes from Little Lakes*, Mel Ellis, Wisconsin's foremost nature writer, would say of the crystalline waters of Waukesha County:

> It is doubtful the water from the springs that form the ponds here at Little Lakes, our home place, has any special healthful ingredients. Once, however, many years ago, these bubbling blue-green springs had something of a fountain of youth reputation, and a half million dollars was spent to pipe the sparkling flow to Chicago so visitors to the 1893 world's fair might slake their thirst. Chicagoans evidently did not like the water, and little wonder. It had to travel through eighty-seven miles of pipe before it arrived. The project was a stupendous undertaking for the 1890s. Labor was imported and the pipeline was laid in ditches dug with pick and shovel. The company went broke, and now nothing remains except the bricked-in spring and pieces of pipe in which bullheads hide when the sun lights up the depths of the crystalline waters. (5)

Nonetheless, young Harry and Roy Aitken marveled at the various schemes to bottle and ship Waukesha water all over the nation. They enjoyed the national publicity the city was getting for its healthful lifestyle. So every chance they got, the two boys and their sisters, Jessie, Mabel and Gladys, would head for their grandparents' home in Waukesha to participate in the exciting city life.

On these weekend visits, the children's first stop was always Grandmother Aitken's huge cookie jar and the cupboard where a coconut-topped cake or an apple pie awaited them. If it was a Saturday night stay-over, Roy took his sweets and headed for the Soo Line tracks less than a quarter of a block away from the house. The ever-watchful Harry went along to keep an eye on his little brother. Together they sat cross-legged in the tall grass beside the tracks, hands cupped behind their ears, listening for the trains that thundered by several times daily. At night, Roy would lie in a cold upstairs bedroom and shiver as the lonesome wail of the trains trailed off in the distance.

"I'd feel a vague discontent, as if I wanted to travel somewhere, but I never knew exactly where," he confided later to Harry.

Despite Roy's inner longing for fast-moving machinery that could take him to other places, the Aitkens were a happy family on the farm. What with nutting and threshing time, and a visit to the old mill, the Aitken children had plenty of fun chores to occupy them in the early 1890s.

When the hickory nuts were ready to pick, Elvin hitched up his old mule named Jenny to the stone boat and drove to the nearby fields with his four children Mabel, Jessie, Harry, and Roy. Jenny was a gentle, kind, and faithful animal, so Elvin entrusted his children to drive or ride her on these special occasions. Once he got them to a spot where the nuts were plentiful, Elvin would walk back to the barn and work on the black cherry furniture he made for the home. As the eldest son, Harry was left in charge of Jenny and the nut-gathering expedition, but first his father cautioned him about overdoing things.

"Jenny has enough to do pulling that heavy stone boat without you riding on it, too," Elvin said.

A gravel pit opened wide near the hickory trees, and during a break in the nutting chore, Harry and the rest of the Aitken children drove Jenny to the edge where they built a fire out of fallen wood against a large rock. When the rock was hot, they cracked the nuts between two smaller stones and spread the curly meats on it to roast. "They taste so good out in the nippy October weather," said Roy, summing up the sentiments of his brother and two sisters.

After this break, the Aitken children returned to the hickory grove and gathered what nuts they could from the ground. But most of them still clung to the branches and had to be knocked down with a piece of rail fence or by striking the base of the shagbark tree with a big rock to jar the trunk.

At dusk they made their way home with several bushels of nuts, some of which Elvin set aside to sell in Waukesha. The rest were kept for a winter treat of freshly popped corn, hickory nutmeats, and juicy apples.

"Nuts were for eating, not baking," said Roy.

Gathering and eating nuts was fun all right, but in Roy's estimation, it still took a backseat to threshing time. When he heard the whistle of the engine signaling the neighbors in Goerke's Corners to prepare for several days of threshing, Roy was the first boy on the road. Even the horses and colts grazing in the fields came to the fences to watch the engine pulling the separator move slowly up the road, followed by a team of horses hitched to a water wagon. Soon the sound of barking dogs and cheering children greeted the threshers with the same excitement given to a circus parade.

During operation at the Aitken farm, Roy watched as the men went right to work carefully placing the stacks of oats and barley so that the separator would fit in between the stacks. They would pitch the bundles onto a sort of table where another man stood with a knife to cut the twine that held the grain together. Of course, the twine was saved to tie up corn stalks later in the fall. Each man hefted a bag of grain on his shoulder and carried it to the barn, where it was dumped into bins of the granary. In later years, Roy said he could always spot a thresher, since one shoulder drooped lower than the other from carrying grain bags on that side.

The highlight of the operation for young Aitken came when the water wagon, supplying water for steam for the engine, had to be refilled. "I would generally ride with the driver to Poplar Creek, where water was pumped into the cart," Roy explained. "A large hose with a screen was dropped into the stream and water pumped through it by hand. The streams were the best places to get the supply of water rather than the wells on the farms."

Another favorite activity of the Aitken brothers, especially Roy, was to stand beside Deissner's five-story mill along the river as the family's grain was ground into grist. He and Harry laughed at the miller and his helpers, covered head to foot in dust, looking like ghosts as they churned out 125 barrels of flour a day. But the sixteen-foot fall of water, which turned the cast iron turbine, captured Roy's attention, and he begged his father to take him inside. The train, the threshing machine, and now the mill run by a system of wooden gears further whetted his appetite for what was to become a lifelong fascination for machinery.

Elvin was more philosophical, however. He told his sons that water flowing over the race had come from Pewaukee Lake, going through the mill on its way to the Fox River in Waukesha.

"Life's like that," he said, "coming from one place, working in another, then moving on changing direction."

Sarah Aitken was a talented piano player and a good singer who had beliefs to match Elvin's when it came to raising children. She often played the piano on weeknights and sometimes on Sunday after church services. Everyone, except Elvin, joined in the singing. He'd sit in his broad chair reading farm journals or figuring his farm accounts while his wife and children sang their favorite hymns—"Onward Christian Soldiers," "Rock of Ages," "Jesus Lover of My Soul," and "Lead Kindly Light." They sometimes filled the stone house with the popular songs of the day, smiling happily at one another, weaving closer the bond of family fellowship. They looked forward to these singing sessions, some more than others. Yet, Roy believes love of music was one of the factors that led Harry and him into the production of silent movies that depended so heavily on the piano to set the mood for what was shown on the screen. But he also noticed that Harry, like their father, could take it or leave it and preferred quiet, hard work to group singing, although he, too, occasionally liked a little glamour and excitement. Roy, on the other hand, was willing to sing and dance at any time, which immensely pleased his mother. He liked to be with people and yearned to travel.

At about the same time, a young Russian Jew, the same age as Roy and whose mother was, coincidentally, also named Sarah, had already gotten a belly full of travel. Louis B. Mayer's family moved from Minsk to New York City, then to Saint John, New Brunswick, Canada, to escape famine and persecution. Unlike Roy E. Aitken's pastoral upbringing, Mayer's early years coincided with a period of upheaval and cruelty in

Russia, especially for Jews. The minister of religion for Czar Alexander III proposed a violently anti-Semitic solution to what he termed the Jewish problem: force one-third of them to emigrate, convert another third to Christianity, and make the final third "disappear."

Of course, the Mayer family chose the first alternative in 1888 when they managed to scrape enough money (about $30 per person) to buy a one-way, steerage-class ticket from Europe to New York. In the new country, Sarah Mayer, like Sarah Aitken, could lead her family in singing folk-songs and renditions of the holy music without fear. This freedom and first brush with the fine arts had a tremendous impact on the future head of Metro Goldwyn Mayer and the great Hollywood studio that later bore his name and personal stamp.

Since Elvin Aitken raised Jersey cattle and sold the cream to a Milwaukee company, Roy got his chance to satisfy both his gregarious nature and the yearning to travel. Each morning on non–school days, he and Harry would hitch up the team and accompany their father to the yellow brick Waukesha railroad station where they unloaded metal, cream-filled cans and placed them on a train nicknamed the Milk Special. Other dairymen got their product to market the same way, so there was always time to gossip or swap baseball stories.

On one of the trips, Elvin handed his youngest son the reins. "I hope we make it in time. The ruts in the road are filled with lots of water and will slow us up," he cautioned. Roy got the team and wagon to the train with only three minutes to spare. Harry never would have cut it so close.

The boys also helped their father with the haying and lent a hand filling the big barn while their sisters aided Sarah with the housework. In no time, the girls learned to cook as well as their mother did, which set fine with the Aitken brothers. Harry spent most of his spare time absorbed in a book or studying his school lessons. Roy preferred to play baseball, although living on a farm in those days limited his opportunities. So he would often take walks down to Goerke's Corners to see if there was a pickup game in progress. If not, he went fishing for trout in the noisy brook that ran through the meadow.

One summer day the boys broke off their activities to greet their father, who had a surprise for them. Elvin had taken one of his young, prancing colts to a small bicycle factory west of Waukesha and traded it for two shiny white bicycles. Harry mastered the two-wheeler almost immediately, then taught Roy how to ride. Soon they were pedaling the three miles to Waukesha on Saturdays and Sundays, waving to all their envious and less fortunate friends.

They knew how much their father loved horses, and to repay him for the sacrifice he had made, they took extra care to see that the two or three other colts left on the farm got proper exercise. Although they had saddles, most of the time they rode bareback the way Elvin had done growing up in Illinois.

"I grew up with horses, and I always liked them," he said, "so I want you boys to have some of the fun I had."

Elvin Aitken was like a boy with a new wagon at colt-breaking time. When it was rumored around the neighborhood that one of the Aitken colts was to be hitched up to a wagon, almost everybody found excuses to come over to watch.

On their regular visits to a Waukesha quarry owned by their maternal grandfather, Joseph Hadfield, the boys alternated between horsepower and pedal power. Hadfield had founded a large limekiln at the quarry, had built a short-line railroad in Wisconsin, and owned considerable real estate. By anyone's standards, he was a very influential and successful man. Harry also found him inspirational. Years later in a letter to a friend who planned to write a history of the Aitkens, Harry wrote:

> Until a better idea is found, I suggest that my weekly visits with Grandfather at the quarry be the start of the book. I asked Grandfather Hadfield if he brought from England the money to build his enterprises.
>
> He said he earned it himself by making shoes and walking 17 miles to Milwaukee to get the leather. He explained that in this country you could do anything if you worked to supply what people wanted. I, then, in a like manner, considered Grandfather John Aitken and how he and his father got the money to pay for the farm. They worked hard and practiced thrift. I then discovered that every Aitken relative going from the farm started enterprises, such as a blacksmith shop, a store, a factory, a real estate business, etc.
>
> There seemed to be no limit to what the Aitken–Hadfield families could do. The thought became a conviction to me that if they could do that, then I, the product of both families, could also accomplish a great deal.
>
> Many years later, after building a movie empire with the help of my brother Roy, and creating many stars and directors, I found that certain elements were out to break me.

Commenting on this letter to his own collaborator, Roy said it left little doubt in his mind that Harry got the impetus to become a financier from his two grandfathers. In John Aitken and Joseph Hadfield, Harry had found confident and determined models for success. He had found something else that would serve him well: resolve when confronted with a difficult business problem.

"Harry was never one to pass up opportunity for lack of money," said Roy.

This trait manifested itself in the grade school that the boys attended. Harry was popular among teachers and pupils for his thrifty habits and willingness to assume a leadership role. Since Harry was Roy's senior by four years, he was midway through the one-room Goerke's Corners school when the younger Aitken entered first grade. Then in a flash Harry finished grade school and moved on to the next level, leaving Roy to fend for himself for the first time.

"I felt rather sad that I could not follow him for another four years," Roy lamented.

But at age twelve, Roy struck out on his own with the help of Elvin Aitken, who took his youngest son to Chicago in 1894 to visit Uncle Bert Hadfield, Sarah's brother. He was in the coal, lime, and cement business on the West Side, and, as a hobby, Bert Hadfield operated a small animal circus. It consisted of a few ponies and dogs that Uncle Bert housed in a barn at the back of his large lot.

In a spacious yard, the part-time ringmaster had pitched a tent of considerable size. Inside were tiers of wooden seats such as one encounters in a real circus. Uncle Bert's wife sold the tickets and acted as usher to the parents and their small children, who arrived at close of business each day.

Bert Hadfield, like his father, was a very distinguished gent. Clad in a Prince Albert coat and shining top hat, with his brown mustache precisely clipped and waxed, he was an imposing figure to young Roy Aitken. The boy saw that he put a lot of time into training his dogs and ponies. The dogs jumped on and off the backs of the circling ponies at just the right time at the proper stations. Roy and the other spectators, mostly children of his age, cheered at the many tricks the animals performed.

"Stay another day or two, Roy, and you can see the show again, in the evening after work," Uncle Bert invited.

But Elvin shook his head, took his son by the hand, and headed for the train station. He told his brother-in-law that he could not afford to spend another day away from the farm and that he didn't want Roy to have to travel back home alone. Besides, he protested, with Harry buried in his books and schoolwork, he needed every available hand on the farm.

On the train to Waukesha, Elvin dozed while Roy fidgeted in the seat next to him. The boy's mind was on Uncle Bert's showmanship and flair for natty clothes. He wished that in some way he could take part in a performance like the one he had seen in Chicago.

Later that same year, in response to Roy's constant urging, the Aitken father and son made the same trip again. Only this time, they attended Buffalo Bill's Wild West Show on the Chicago lakefront. William F. Cody had organized his rodeo-style circus a decade earlier, in 1883, at the time the Brooklyn Bridge was opened. But for young Roy Aitken, no engineering feat could match the sight of an erect Buffalo Bill riding his rearing black stallion and the masterful way in which he held the reins. When the great showman doffed his wide-brim hat to the crowd after a saunter, exposing his thick gray thatch of flowing hair, Roy was certain he had been singled out for recognition. Then, on cue from the old cowboy, Bill's out-riders leaned down effortlessly and scooped up kerchiefs from the ground without breaking stride. Roy let out a gasp of admiration, and Elvin could see that his son, smitten with this full-of-thrills show business, would soon find farming a dull life.

A continent away, while Roy dreamed about show business, sixteen-year-old Schmuel Gelbfisz, who was Harry Aitken's age, made his way alone on foot across Europe, leaving his native Poland behind to fol-low his dream in a new country. Later, the immigrant youngster would change his name to Goldfish and slip across the Canadian border to Gloversville, New York. But when Harry and Roy encountered him years afterward in Hollywood, Samuel Goldwyn (as he was legally renamed) had joined other moguls in establishing a movie dynasty of his own.

This time on the roaring Soo Line back to Waukesha, Roy pretended he was astride a bronco as the train rocked over the rough roadbed, send-ing fears of derailment through the minds of the other passengers. That night he lay awake in his bed determined to be a part of a life such as Uncle Bert and Buffalo Bill lived. But he had no idea how and when this might occur.

On the morning following his Chicago trip, Roy saddled up the fam-ily's red filly, mounted her, took a turn around the front of the stone house, and then casually dropped a white handkerchief on the ground. After getting the prancing mare warmed up, as he had seen Buffalo Bill's riders do, Roy approached the spot where the handkerchief lay. Although the mare moved at a slow gallop, the twelve-year-old rider lost his grip on the saddle horn as he leaned down to retrieve the handkerchief. He missed the target and took a few unexpected turns around the yard hang-ing half-in and half-out of the saddle. Scared that he would spend the rest of the day in this awkward position, he tried to climb back into the sad-dle. He could hardly make it because his back ached so much. Laughter echoed from a window in the house, and he looked up to see his father, mother, Harry, and sisters enjoying his attempt at circus riding.

The Buffalo Bill wanna-be quit for the day. Yet he seemed determined to master the handkerchief trick. The next day he tried again. Still no luck, but his back didn't take such a pounding this time, although the ribbing from his folks and siblings continued unabated.

"Guess you're not cut out to be a cowboy, Roy," his mother chided.

But, within a week, he was able to pick up a handkerchief from the ground at full gallop with what he considered a graceful flair. While still not as professional a showman as Buffalo Bill and his men, or even Uncle Bert, he had done it on his own, and few triumphs in his life would give

Roy Aitken greater satisfaction. He wanted desperately to share this thrill with Harry, but his older brother had other uses for the red mare.

After finishing high school, Harry attended Carroll College in Waukesha, a Presbyterian institution founded in 1846, making it Wisconsin's oldest center of higher learning. Elvin Aitken permitted his eldest son to use the red mare and Sunday buggy to make the daily trip of about four miles. Harry would put up the horse at Grandfather Aitken's barn on Hartwell Avenue or sometimes in the barn of a friend. Then he would walk the seven blocks to the Carroll campus, nestled in the midst of one of Waukesha's oldest residential areas.

From the upstairs window in the old stone house, Roy watched his brother until the gleaming buggy was out of sight. He envied Harry. How wonderful it must be to drive the rig to a prestigious school named in honor of Charles Carroll of Maryland, a statesman in America's formative years and a signer of the Declaration of Independence. Roy couldn't wait for his turn to come. But events dealt a severe blow to his plans.

In the 1890s, both Aitken grandparents died. They were in their late seventies, but nonetheless their deaths plunged the family into deep sorrow. Harry and Roy recalled how close the family had been and at times reminisced on into the night about the many Sunday afternoons at Grandfather Aitken's, dining and singing and enjoying life. Even the youngest children felt the deep sense of loss.

Upon John Aitken's death on February 15, 1895, the farmer who had started out in Quincy and moved to Goerke's Corners, then to Waukesha proper when he retired, left more than a vacant place in the hearts of his grandchildren. He also left an empty house in the city built near the Fox River, which runs through the town. The house remained unoccupied for about two months. Then one day Elvin gathered his family around the fireplace at the farm and announced, "I think we ought to move to Waukesha and live in grandfather's home. I can operate the farm just as well from the house in town, and the children will have the opportunity to go to better schools and make more friends."

And so for the second time in a generation, John Aitken relinquished a fine homestead for his son Elvin and his family. The Aitken clan, including Sarah, was stunned by Elvin's proposal. For the children, the move to Waukesha meant more playmates, walks along the lighted streets at night, and an opportunity to attend parties and still get home by Elvin's 9 P.M. curfew hour. For Sarah Aitken, the move would enable her to visit her own aging parents, the Hadfields, more often and cut down on her travel time to church, where she still served as pianist. Roy, thirteen, and Harry, seventeen, expected to do far less farmwork once they were in the city. Elvin, who had recently hired a good man to help him, would certainly lighten up on their chores.

The first white settlers once called Waukesha, which is an Indian name meaning "By the Little Fox," Prairieville, and then later referred to as the "Saratoga of the West" owing to the resorts that grew up around its mineral springs. For Harry and Roy Aitken, it was the "center of the universe" with Milwaukee (eighteen miles to the east), Chicago (one hundred miles south) and Madison (sixty miles west). And, of course, four miles north near Goerke's Corners stood the old Aitken farm that Elvin traveled to every morning. He ate his noon meal with the hired man and his wife and then hitched up the horse and buggy for the return trip to Waukesha, where Sarah had supper waiting for him at six o'clock sharp. During the school year, this was the only time the children spent with their father because playmates or club activities filled their afternoons and evenings.

"At times it seemed we were busier than we had been at the farm, but even so, city life was more exciting," said Roy.

During summer vacation, he and Harry did odd jobs to earn spending money. A former neighbor from Goerke's Corners who now owned a lumberyard in town approached Roy.

"Come work for me, Roy," pleaded Henry Gëttner, "I have lots of work for a young fellow like you."

One day as Roy piled lumber in a shed, Gëttner walked over to him and pointed to a big steam engine parked in the yard. "We want to move that darn thing into another corner of the yard. It's in our way where it is. What can you do about it?" he asked.

Roy examined the harvesting machine abandoned by Gëttner's predecessor. It reminded him of the steam engine the threshers brought to the farm at Goerke's Corners. He had spent hours watching the men work it over the fertile soil, paying particular attention to how the belts and levers operated. Occasionally, when the farmhands weren't watching, Roy climbed up on the platform near the engine just to feel the heat from the firepot on his legs.

Until Gëttner's invitation, that's as close as Roy came to operating a steam engine, although in his fantasies mastering a powerful machine ranked equally with performing like one of Buffalo Bill's outriders. He decided to give it a try, knowing full well that the engine in Gëttner's yard hadn't been started in a long time. Some of the other workers ran over to the pump to get water. They came back with the pails and emptied the contents into the boiler. Another man struck a fire in the engine. They urged Roy to climb aboard and start the machine. But he could see they were as scared as he was and fully expected to see a wild steam engine thunder around the big lumberyard with a frightened farm boy unable to stop it.

"I got up on the platform and studied the levers, my heart thumping," said Roy. "To gain time and build up my courage, I fiddled lightly with one of the levers, then finally pulled back a lever as I had seen one of the threshers on the farm do when starting the engine."

The old engine stuttered a little, but then to everyone's surprise, the machine crept forward. The men cheered, and from his lofty position on the platform Roy spotted a grin sweeping across Gëttner's broad, sweaty face. Carefully, he steered the machine to the exact spot Gëttner had indicated, and when Roy shut off the lever, a wave of satisfaction swept over him as well.

"I was at home with an engine," said Roy. He repeated this exact sentiment many times in the future as he sped around France, England, New York, and California at the wheel of one fancy foreign car after another. Most often he had a starlet or film celebrity at his side and enough money in his pocket to buy a new vehicle at each location.

At the lumberyard, Roy tinkered with the engine whenever Gëttner would give him a break. In the evenings at their Waukesha home, the Aitkens kept up their music and family songfest under the direction of Sarah, who immediately recognized that her son Harry had developed a fine tenor voice. It was so good, in fact, that he won a place of honor in the Carroll College chorus. Roy's voice was only passable and certainly not on a par with either Harry's or his sisters'. But none of them could make a steam engine sing. Yet, Roy Aitken believed that with all the musical talent exhibited in his family, some of them were destined for the show business career he still yearned for in his heart.

2

Fancy Cars, Pink Balls, and Southern Exposure

In high school, Roy met the Welch brothers, who became his close friends. Charles and William Welch filled the void left by Harry's attendance at Carroll College. Their father owned White Rock Springs, noted for its fine water shipped all over the nation from Waukesha.

The Welch family received other notoriety as well. They were among the first of Waukesha's citizens to buy an automobile. Manufactured in Detroit, the Northern car was an open model sporting a tonneau at the rear. It steered with a tiller, had kerosene lamps, and had to be cranked to start.

Two persons could sit comfortably in the front seat and perhaps three slim people in the tonneau. The crank turned hard, and Roy did most of it after he and Charles Welch formed a date pursuit patrol. On their frequent drives around town on the roads made of brick or wooden blocks, the two teenagers searched for young women to impress. When they reached the rutty, thinly covered gravel roads out in the countryside, Charles turned the tiller over to Roy for a driving lesson. In a matter of weeks, young Aitken mastered the task, and soon Welch let him do most of the driving, especially if there was a date along for Charles to snuggle next to in the tonneau.

On weekends, the two boys and their dates headed for Oconomowoc, a picturesque city nestled near three lakes, about twenty miles northwest of Waukesha. The city got its name from the Potawatomi Indians who considered "Coo-no-mo-wauk" (waterfall in the vicinity) the best fur-trading post in the area. Locals shortened the name and referred to the town as "Cooney." Like young men of the times, Roy Aitken and Charles Welch no doubt regaled their dates with tales about the place that bore no resemblance to fact. Proof that a story need not be true to be a good story, legend held that Oconomowoc got its name when an old Indian chief trekking across America stopped on the spot, bathed his sore feet in one of the lakes, and declared, "O-Can-No-Mo-Walk." The young ladies would have been more impressed, however, had Roy and Charles driven them past Seavern's Farms, whose cottages once served as summer homes to Allen Pinkerton (founder of the detective agency bearing his name) and H. H. Higenbotham (president of the Chicago World's Fair).

En route back to Waukesha, Charles would inevitably turn and signal Roy, seated in the tonneau next to a young women dressed in flowing skirt, billowy blouse, and wide-brimmed hat. "How about driving for me, Roy?" he'd ask.

Roy nodded eagerly. Then Charles would occupy the tonneau with his girl gripping her own wide-brimmed hat as she swapped places with her companion who moved to the front seat with Roy. Charles often chuckled and said, "It was so handy to have a friend who could drive." But the date pursuit patrol was short-lived.

Roy Aitken didn't finish high school. Highly nervous, he often had indigestion, and Sarah and Elvin constantly worried about their son's thinness. In early winter 1897, he agreed to go see Dr. Albert J. Hodgson, who had married Sarah's sister, Laura Belle Hadfield, on May 1, 1890, when Roy was eight years old. At about that same age, Dr. Hodgson had lost his left hand in a sugar cane shredder. Roy's cousin, Vivian Hodgson Jacobson, described her father as a strong and courageous man who "despite his handicap was an excellent surgeon, operating and suturing skillfully with only one hand."

Standing more than six feet tall, Dr. Hodgson towered over most of his patients, and those not intimidated by his stature were soon overwhelmed by his powerful personality. At Carroll College, he stood out as a firebrand, but later he settled down and established a hospital for treatment of diabetes and Bright's disease, his two specialties. Roy's Uncle Albert also served on the medical staff of Bethesda Springs Resort, which brought him into contact with a lot of southern women who summered in Waukesha. Dr. Hodgson was known to refer to his female patients, regardless of age, as "girlie," although the consultants he imported from Chicago for a second opinion were more circumspect.

Following the examination, the physician told his apprehensive young nephew, "Roy, you are very nervous and run-down. I also think you have a touch of diabetes. I suggest that, if possible, you go south for the winter to see if a change of climate will help you."

Shocked, Roy hurried home to tell his parents. They, too, were stunned. As usual, Harry eased anxiety out of the situation. "Why can't all of us go south for the winter, Father? We could go as a group. I'll be glad to make the arrangements," he offered.

Not only was this characteristic of Harry, but Roy thought it indicated his brother's aptitude for promotion, an ability that later would help them build the first silent movie empire.

Elvin mulled over the suggestion, glanced at his wife, and then turned to face Harry. "Well, go ahead and see what you can do, Son. I suppose we can afford it. The farm has been doing well the last few years. And now I've got two good hired men I can trust to take care of the cows."

Within a day or two, Harry reported back that he had visited a railroad agent and had been informed that if he could get a party of twenty to twenty-five people to make the trip, they could rent a railroad coach at an attractive round-trip rate.

"Oh," said Sarah, "that should be fun."

Within another few days, Harry had visited Aitken friends and relatives trying to sign up enough interested people so he could charter a railroad coach to Biloxi, Mississippi. Sarah Aitken's brother, Wesley Hadfield, his two sons and three daughters, and Mrs. Hadfield's sister and her husband were among those to take him up on it.

Excitedly, the Aitkens packed their bags, and one gray January day in 1898, they boarded a Soo Line coach at Waukesha for Biloxi via Chicago. At the stopover in the Windy City, Elvin bought a newspaper and read to the family how Admiral George Dewey, commander of the U.S. Asiatic Squadron based in Hong Kong, had prepared his forces should war break out with Spain.

At Biloxi, Harry located a home owned by a man named MacDonald. The frame house was quite large and had a hall, which ran the length of the entire structure. The many bedrooms angled off the hallway, just like a hotel, so there was room for the Aitken and Hadfield families. The rest of the Waukesha people in the party found quarters elsewhere. Soon all the northern tourists in Harry's group strolled along the Gulf Coast, coats strung over their shoulders, enjoying the temperate weather.

The children soon found schools in which they were readily accepted. In a spirit of good nature, the southern pupils laughed and turned to look at the Yankee kids whenever one of the visitors spoke up in class. "I suppose our northern accent was as strange to them as their southern accent was to us," Roy observed.

Notwithstanding the language barrier, some of the Waukesha families liked the area so well they bought homes in Biloxi after retirement. The Aitken family continued visiting Biloxi long after Harry and Roy went into the movie business. Even after Elvin died in 1908, Sarah and her surviving relatives were often able to go to the Gulf Coast for a month or six weeks. Harry and Roy sometimes joined them for a week or so.

Less than a decade before his own death, Roy visited the area one last time to relive pleasant memories of the city by the Gulf. He reminisced that despite the changes, he still liked the area a great deal. "I stayed at an old colonial type inn with spacious rooms, and was served wonderful meals in a sedate, high-ceilinged dining room by gracious waitresses. Life is still lived leisurely in many sections of the South today, and thank heaven for that."

When the Aitken family returned to Waukesha that March, Roy had regained a portion of his health, and Harry resumed his studies at Carroll College. But the sojourn in Biloxi had stirred the old promotional urge. Harry wanted to get into some type of business where he could make some money.

One day Elvin's oldest son said, "Dad, I've met a student at Carroll whose home is in Wausau. His name is E. B. Jones, and he says there is much land available up there for one dollar per acre. He believes it would be a good investment, because the land will be settled some day and sell for considerably more. Jones wants me to go home with him on Easter vacation and look at the land."

Elvin Aitken smiled. Although a hardworking farmer, he was very practical and liked to see evidences of initiative in his sons. "Go ahead," he encouraged. "Look at the land, find out about it, and report to me when you get back."

Elvin eventually bought one thousand acres of this land for Harry, and Harry held it as an investment. Each year he tried to pay back part of his loan. It was a valuable lesson for Harry.

Sarah had her own investment plan under way that actually started the day the family moved from the farm to Waukesha. Suspending her strict Methodist upbringing, their mother insisted that Harry and Roy learn to dance like other sons in respectable families had done. Their sisters agreed, so the two boys reluctantly enrolled in an evening dance class operated by a charming, dark-haired woman in her midthirties. After instruction, they would go home and practice the steps they had learned with their willing sisters as partners.

Since the home on Hartwell Avenue stood only a block or so from the famous Park Hotel, a leading summer spot in those days, opportunities for socializing were plentiful. The hotel offered a casino and little theater, run by the staff, to which the southern families using the Silurian Springs across the street used to flock in the evening. Mrs. Horning, a friend of the Aitken family, managed the Park Hotel, and her pretty, brunette daughter Mitty assisted her.

"Harry," called Mrs. Horning as the boys passed her on the street one day, "why don't you and Roy come over on Saturday night to our weekly dance? We need partners for the pretty southern belles who are staying with us. They get so lonely sometimes."

Flattered and a little bashful, Harry and Roy accepted the invitation. Each Saturday night thereafter, the Aitken boys slicked down their blond cowlicks and went straightaway to the Park Hotel if they could manage it. In a span of two weeks, they succumbed to the charms of their southern dance partners and made the Park Hotel a regular destination.

Soon a competition arose among the management of all the summer hotels in Waukesha to see who could attract "gentlemanly young men to come to help entertain these gracious young ladies, under the watchful eyes of their mothers, of course."

It took the Aitken brothers no time at all to discern the reason for a preponderance of females at these hotels. Their southern husbands and fathers, who had businesses or professions to tend to, remained in the South most of the summer, although some occasionally came to Waukesha for a week or two to stay with their families. Thus, Harry, Roy, and many of their male Waukesha friends reaped a bonanza. They not only danced with the single southern girls but also glided across the floor with their equally charming mother-chaperones.

Roy usually went alone to the Fountain House, a much larger hotel that held a Wednesday night dance. Harry was too busy reading and planning his business career to accompany his younger brother more than once a week, so Roy used the extra dance session to get better acquainted with the girls and their mothers. At Harry's suggestion, he jotted down the names and addresses of the southern families in the remote likelihood that the brothers might visit Dixie again in the immediate future. When they did swing through the South some years later as beleaguered movie moguls, they called on many of the families they had met at Waukesha dance parties. For Roy, at least, the visit helped while away some otherwise lonesome hours.

Many of the southern girls returned to Waukesha summer after summer, so Harry and Roy got to know them quite well. According to Roy, no serious romance was involved, although neither he nor Harry denied that flirting added to enjoyment of the dances.

Whatever other activities were in progress, the Aitken brothers made it a point to position themselves at the head of the line during the Park Hotel's annual Pink Ball. For that event, all the girls dressed in lovely pink, powdered their hair with assorted scents, and painted little black spots on their cheeks. "They were absolutely stunning," claimed Roy, who thought of the Pink Ball years later when he and director D. W. Griffith selected ushers for the opening of the *Birth of a Nation* motion picture at the Liberty Theater in New York City. "We chose many pretty girls and directed them to powder their hair and wear hoop skirts," said Roy.

For the Pink Ball in Waukesha, the men were required to wear pink ties. Roy wore one and danced well into the night until the lapels of his coat were saturated with powder. When he got home, Sarah greeted him at the door. She expressed shock at the white powder and scolded her sixteen-year-old for dancing too close.

The Aitken's eldest daughter, Jessie, never learned to dance. She loved music but somehow did not seem to have the coordination or grace. In later years, after Harry and Roy got into the movie production field, they often went to dance parties with D. W. Griffith, Douglas Fairbanks Sr., Mabel Normand (whom Sam Goldwyn fell in love with despite her addiction to drugs and alcohol), and others. As Roy danced with vivacious movie stars, he was grateful for the lessons he had taken in Waukesha and for all the practice with the southern belles at the summer hotels.

Harry was not a good dancer. He could two-step a little and that was about all. Mabel, the middle sister, was a fine dancer. She learned at high school. Gladys, the youngest Aitken, was the most splendid of all and very light on her feet. She and Roy used to waltz around the house on Hartwell before, during, and after chores.

Meanwhile, Harry continued to prepare for a career in business. As graduation and the inevitable hunt for a job neared, he had little time for those activities that gave Roy such great pleasure.

3

Keeping Pace in a
Sales-Oriented World

By the turn of the century, the war with Spain had come and gone. Admiral George Dewey, proclaimed the "hero of Manila," received a ticker-tape parade in New York City in 1899. He had destroyed the Spanish fleet without the loss of a single American life, and Dewey's picture appeared in all the newspapers. Harry Aitken, recently graduated from Carroll College, shared the news with his seventeen-year-old brother, who needed a morale booster himself. Roy had learned that Harry had applied for a job as a seed salesman and that soon their lives would take separate paths again.

Harry's first employer was T. H. Cochrane, a farm supplier in Portage, Wisconsin. Harry worked at the job for about two years and got along with his boss so well that Cochrane later became a loyal friend and a partner in many of the Aitken brothers' movie enterprises.

On a visit to Waukesha one weekend, Harry met a friend of the family. "Why don't you try selling insurance?" the friend counseled. "Selling farm seeds is a good business in Wisconsin, but an energetic young man like you could make more money in the insurance business."

Taking the advice, Harry applied for a job with the Federal Life Insurance Company in Chicago. After a short training period in Illinois, he was assigned to Milwaukee as Wisconsin state manager. In a short time, he hired a number of agents to sell insurance and supervised their activities. Some months afterward, Harry stepped out of the managerial position and began to sell insurance himself. In a year or so, he became the largest personal producer in the insurance company.

Roy remembers that it was the success of this first individual effort that convinced Harry that he had a distinct flair for convincing other people that his views were right and proper and should be adopted. Harry once told Roy he credited his success as an insurance salesman to the experience he previously had selling farm seeds with T. H. Cochrane in Portage. He also said that both experiences prepared him well for a much larger selling job: the creation of a silent movie empire.

Similarly, several hundred miles east in Gloversville, New York, young Sam Goldfish (Goldwyn) was also on the move. He had risen from a floor sweeper in a glove factory to the city's star glove salesman at age twenty-two. In addition, Louis B. Mayer cited a similar transition from a door-to-door peddler of household supplies, to a junk dealer, to a sales partnership with his father in a New England salvaging operation. He later branched into the operation and distribution of movies in Haverhill, Massachusetts, where his sales skills helped convince the population that they could enter a nickelodeon without suffering public disgrace.

Although he maintained an office in Milwaukee, Harry lived at the family home in Waukesha with his parents and the other Aitken children. He made his daily trips to Milwaukee by commuter train. Whenever he accumulated spare cash, he would pay off $100 or more on the land loan he had secured from his father. Harry did not wish to have Elvin bear the financial responsibility of that land, and the old man was very pleased to see how businesslike his son had become.

Meanwhile, Roy accompanied his father on frequent visits to the farm in Goerke's Corners. Together, they would mend fences and help the men who had rented the place. Because of his southern vacation and the outdoor farmwork, Roy's health improved, and he went back to his old high school, although he remained a year or more behind his classmates. Aware of his little brother's struggle to keep pace, Harry suggested, "Roy, you could begin to earn your living by getting into the insurance business like I did. Interested?"

To Roy, this seemed like a graceful way out of the doldrums that catch-up schoolwork had thrust upon him. Harry had been in the life insurance business for eighteen months, and everything had worked out well for him, Roy reasoned. He decided to give it a try. Harry outlined the type of training Roy would require for insurance work. He then contacted the Chicago office, and his superiors recommended that Roy travel in Wisconsin as an apprentice and companion to an elderly insurance representative named G. W. Vanderhoff, who retained his residence in Chicago.

Vanderhoff was a very successful salesman, even though blind. His wife had been his secretary and traveling companion for many years, but she had now reached the point where she thought he ought to have someone else for such duties.

Harry arranged for Roy to board the Milwaukee Road train at Waukesha for Janesville. There he met the afternoon train from Chicago and looked for Vanderhoff. Harry had told his brother that Vanderhoff used a cane, had thick gray hair, was a very neat dresser, and could be mistaken for Admiral Dewey.

When Roy got on the train at Janesville, he repeated this description for the conductor. "Oh Vanderhoff, he's down in the middle of the first coach," the trainman responded. "Everybody knows him."

Walking along the aisle, Roy spotted an elderly gentleman alone in a coach seat, his head held high, chin thrust forward like Admiral Dewey's, so that his full white mustache was the first feature that caught the eye. "Mr. Vanderhoff," the young man said softly, "I'm Roy Aitken."

The blind man's handsome face ignited in the afternoon sun that poured in from the train window.

"Roy! Roy! I'm glad to know you. Sit down! Sit down!"

On their first stop at Monroe, Wisconsin, the boy and the old man obtained quarters at a boarding house where Vanderhoff and his wife had previously spent the night. The beds were clean and the food wonderful. It was served family-style, which especially pleased Roy—he was able to fill up his plate as often as he wished.

As he traveled with Vanderhoff, Roy grew to respect him more each day. A courageous, kindly, hard worker and always courteous, Vanderhoff never spoke about his disability. He just continued working. And he sold a great deal of insurance. There was an air of dignity and integrity about the man that prospects were quick to sense. They knew he would take care of their best interests when selling them policies. Roy never heard a complaint about Vanderhoff's methods.

On these journeys across Wisconsin, they slept in separate beds in the same room. When Vanderhoff would undress in the evening, he would sit on a chair, take off his shoes, and place a sock over each shoe. The other pieces of clothing he would place on the chair, so he would know exactly where they were when he awakened the next morning.

Roy usually got up first. He'd wash, shave, dress, and then go downstairs and wait for his mentor. They would eat breakfast together, and the blind man would ask, "What have we got here, Roy?" If they had bacon or ham, Roy would cut it for him.

At the evening meal, the routine was the same. Roy would cut his meat and tell him what else was on the table. Vanderhoff made a selection, and Roy would place it on the old man's plate.

With the help of Roy's compasslike directions, Vanderhoff knew where each item was located. Without further assistance, he would eat his meals very neatly, and rarely did he spill anything or entangle food in his mustache.

Later, faced with difficult phases in his own life, Roy Aitken harked back to these moments with Vanderhoff, whom he considered a walking billboard for what could be accomplished through patience coupled with a calm and competent approach to any problem. Admittedly, Roy only occasionally succeeded in matching Vanderhoff's demeanor. But he tried.

Still, theirs was a mutual partnership in which each person gained. Roy provided considerable assistance to Vanderhoff, guiding him down unfamiliar streets to the offices he wished to visit. Once inside, the old man took over as Roy observed how he greeted customers and prospects and how he persuaded them to buy insurance policies. Charm carried the day then and later when Roy dealt with some of the biggest egos in Hollywood.

Since Vanderhoff had sold numerous insurance policies in these towns and cities for many years, he knew many people. He would first call on policyholders, visit with them for a few minutes, and then ask them whether they knew some other men or women who might consider buying insurance. Rarely did he fail to get one or more leads on almost every call.

"When I can walk into a prospect's office and tell him I know his friend or relative and that he has one of our policies, this is an important advantage for me, Roy," Vanderhoff pointed out. Working from leads saves so much time and increases sales."

The insurance company paid their travel expenses, of course, and Roy obtained a small percentage of the sales Vanderhoff made. Roy found the work interesting and the arrangement profitable from the experience standpoint. "Meeting people and handling them diplomatically helped me considerably later on when Harry and I entered the movie business where we had to sell ourselves and our ideas to businessmen, bankers, and movie stars," he said.

After three weeks traveling the Wisconsin circuit, Vanderhoff headed back to Chicago for several weeks' rest. Roy returned to his home in Waukesha until it was time to go on the road again. During one of these rest periods, Roy's Aunt Laura Belle Hadfield Hodgson died on June 12, 1902, at the age of thirty-five due to hemorrhage after a miscarriage. Roy tried to comfort his mother at the loss of her only sister. All the Aitkens remembered Aunt Laura as a "kind, gentle woman, well loved by everyone." Roy's cousins, Harold and Vivian Hodgson, also needed his and Harry's support and sympathy. As for Dr. Albert J. Hodgson, he coped with his grief by building a car he called the "Red Devil" from parts he ordered made at a Waukesha blacksmith shop. Despite his missing hand, he wielded a wrench with the same dexterity as a scalpel and even played championship baseball on a local doctor's team.

In time, the Aitken brothers drifted apart from the Hodgson side of the family following Laura's death. Thereafter, Dr. Hodgson had two more wives and his eccentricity became a favorite topic for gossip in the community. For example, he was known for his large, unconventional parties that rivaled anything Harry and Roy ever attended in Hollywood. At one affair, Dr. Hodgson was reported to have lectured members of the Waukesha County Medical Society on the use and abuse of drugs as they sat at tables in a darkened room "gazing at illuminated skulls and crossbones sporting jeweled eyes."

After his aunt's death, it wasn't long before Roy was traveling again, going to places like Oshkosh, Wisconsin, which Vanderhoff ranked as his favorite stopover since he sold many policies there. On one of their visits to this town seventy-five miles north of Milwaukee in the heart of leather and textile territory, they met a stocky, clothing store manager at the Continental Clothing House. He was pleasant and kind, with a wonderful smile that filled his round face.

But he didn't buy any insurance. He told the two salesmen he already had many policies and didn't need any more. This was Roy Aitken's first encounter with a man he would see many times during his movie production career. His name was Carl Laemmle. The next time they'd meet would be in Chicago, where Laemmle, having left Oshkosh, established his first nickelodeon.

After a year or so, Vanderhoff, because of advanced age, decided to quit and retired to his home in Chicago.

"Now you can go selling insurance on your own, Roy," Harry Aitken reminded his brother. "You've had fine training under Vanderhoff."

So Roy began to travel the Wisconsin circuit alone. He visited many of the towns where Vanderhoff and he had stopped and called on some of the same prospects. The best part of being on his own was the spare time that allowed him to linger at the depot. The railroad agents not only bought policies in some instances, but they furnished Roy excellent leads in between chats about baseball, hunting, and fishing.

Louis B. Mayer had his own early brush with sportsmen that led to nasty name-calling. About the only out-of-home entertainment he had growing up in Canada was watching the other kids play baseball. One day, he asked whether he could join them. Someone shouted, "Baseball's not a Yid's game." Another youth pointed out that the Jewish kid didn't even own a glove. A few weeks later, after saving his money, Mayer turned up with the best baseball mitt money could buy, which he paraded in front of his tormentors.

After six months of selling insurance on his own, Roy Aitken realized that this was far afield from his dreams and not something he intended to do for a lifetime. One weekend, when he returned to Waukesha, he found a letter from Gil Clark awaiting him. He had met Clark in Biloxi, and the two young men had continued a sporadic correspondence. Now

Clark was in Chicago. "Why don't you come here and get a job at the place where I work, Montgomery Ward?" wrote Gil. "They pay from $10 to $15 per week."

This was all the encouragement Roy needed. He immediately packed his bag.

"Be careful, Roy," Sarah Aitken cautioned in her motherly fashion. "Don't get into trouble. Chicago is a big city for a young man."

He assured her he would heed her advice. Then he set her mind at ease by telling her he would have a roommate.

Roy stayed with Clark in his room on Wabash Avenue near the Illinois Central railroad station. Getting his first taste of big city life as an adult, Roy walked along lighted Michigan Avenue that first night and, as precursor to the lyrics of a yet unwritten song, decided "it was his kind of town."

The next morning, he ate a leisurely breakfast and then strolled along Michigan Avenue again, this time looking for the employment office of Montgomery Ward. It was then that he spotted a shiny new automobile in a showroom.

Roy halted in his tracks, for the car displayed was a Northern, the make of the vehicle owned by the Welch family of Waukesha. He entered the auto agency for a closer look at the beautiful automobile that brought back memories of weekend drives to Oconomowoc with Charles. Inside, he approached a rather neatly dressed, heavyset man seated at a desk.

Aitken gave the salesman his name and told him he had learned to drive a Northern car at Waukesha several years earlier and wondered whether he needed an employee. The dealer looked at Roy critically for a few moments and then asked questions about his family and where he was staying.

Roy's answers seemed to satisfy him, for he said, "I'm just getting started here myself. I have one other young man working for me, but if you want to do some soliciting, I'll give you some names. If you can find prospects for new cars, of which I have a few, I can pay you $8 per week."

"I'll take the job," Aitken said. "When do I start?"

"Tomorrow," he said. "I'm anxious to work this territory hard."

The young man from Wisconsin did some quick calculations in his head. After paying Gil Clark a share of the room rent, Roy would have about $3 left for meals. Even though the pay was small, he was thrilled. "To think," he told himself, "that a green farm boy like me had a white-collar job in the big city, selling the fancy Northern automobiles." He could hardly wait until the folks back home, Charles Welch, and the girls they used to drive around heard about this.

Roy's friend, Gil Clark, was displeased, however. "Eight dollars per week!" he exclaimed. "Why, Roy, you might get $12 at Montgomery Ward!"

"I know," Aitken replied. "But I like the automobile business. It's in my blood." Later, Roy used this same sanguine argument over and over again to explain how he and Harry became attracted to the movie business and the huge outlays of money for real estate and salaries that it required.

Forgotten, too, was the lesson of the Potawatomi Indians that Roy Aitken had seen practiced during his drives around his hometown in that first Northern car. Their philosophy was simple to grasp. A man could buy, trade, or own only that which he could carry with him. Water, land, and trees belonged to everyone.

Meanwhile, Jewish Americans like Sam Goldfish, Louis B. Mayer, Marcus Loew, Adolph Zukor, and Lewis Selznick also sought to improve their capital. Goldwyn left Gloversville in 1904 to seek more money as a glove salesman with a larger territory. He was soon earning $15,000 a year selling gloves throughout New England, often traveling by interurban trolley to meet his customers.

Mayer, too, was on the move, buying a run-down burlesque house in Haverhill and converting it to a theater he named the Orpheum. The Gem, or "The Germ," as locals once referred to it, then became a respectable theater.

Since they shared a common heritage and, more important, covered the same territory, whether as glove salesmen, junk dealers, or jewelers, it was inevitable that these former immigrants crossed each other's paths. When they started acquiring property to create the new theaters for projecting motion pictures that the public had found so fascinating, they began to forge partnerships.

In an article in the *Saturday Evening Post*, November 23, 1907, Joseph Medill Patterson reported that not a single nickelodeon, or theater, devoted to moving picture shows existed in 1904. However, in 1907, he noted that between four and five thousand such theaters had developed across America and that the number increased rapidly.

Patterson went on to report that the nickelodeon had tapped an entirely new stratum of people and was developing a section of the population into theatergoers that formerly knew and cared little about drama as a fact of life:

> In cosmopolitan city districts the foreigners attend in larger proportion than the English-speaking people do. This is doubtless because the foreigners, shut out as they are by their alien tongues from much of life about them, can yet perfectly understand the pantomime of the moving pictures.
>
> As might be expected, the Latin races patronize the shows more consistently than Jews, Irish, or Americans. Sailors of all races are devotees.
>
> Whatever the locality, children make up about thirty-three percent of the crowds. For some reason, young women from sixteen to thirty years old are rarely in evidence, but many middle-aged and old women are steady patrons, who never, when a new film is to be shown, miss the opening.

During his first week at the Northern car dealership, Roy Aitken called on about twenty-five people, most of them business and professional men in what is now the Loop area of Chicago. He didn't sell any cars that week, but many of the prospects listened to his enthusiastic sales talk, modeled after Vanderhoff's, and showed interest in this new, strange vehicle, the automobile. Several promised to come to the display room and see the Northern car. Of course, the manager had hired him to drum up traffic at the auto agency.

At the end of the second week, his boss said, "Roy, I like the way you've applied yourself. I have to go to Detroit for about a week to straighten out some business arrangements with the Northern people. Will you manage the place for me while I'm gone? I'll raise your pay to $15 per week."

"I certainly will," said Aitken, elated by the fast promotion.

When told of the pay hike that night, Gil Clark offered no criticism. In fact, Roy spotted what looked like a flash of envy and awe in his roommate's eyes. "Wow, you're a Horatio Alger!" Clark gasped. "Your salary doubled in two weeks. Take me out on Michigan Avenue and buy me an ice cream soda. This calls for a celebration!"

Aitken's boss returned from Detroit the following week and began working two prospects his temporary manager had secured for him. As the potential buyers entered the showroom, they expressed interest in the Northern car. Roy felt pleased. On many calls during the past week, he had often had the door slammed in his face, so to speak. But when someone smiled and listened to him, he remembered a blind insurance salesman's patience, and the effort was worthwhile again.

He gained respect for the salesmen of this world as he tried to sell cars in Chicago. "No one who has not tried to sell knows the persistence, the courage, and the daily whipping-up of faith in oneself that it requires," Roy remarked.

One day while out making calls on Harrison Street for the Northern agency, Roy noticed a line of people gathered in front of a dingy store. Approaching, he saw gaudy posters near the entrance and a mustached barker in a black derby, black coat, and sharply pressed pants. The pitchman looked straight at Aitken and shouted, "See *The Great Train Robbery*! It's dramatic! It's thrilling! It will send shivers up and down your spine! See a bunch of bold robbers hold up a train! Hurry! Only five cents!"

Excited by the new art, Roy joined the line, paid his five cents, and entered the nickelodeon. He noticed that many of his fellow movie patrons were workers. Some carried their lunch buckets as they went into the theater.

The place was small and quite smelly. Patrons sat on hard folding chairs. Glass slides were exhibited on a white bedsheet hung on the wall. In *Star Maker: The Story of D. W. Griffith*, Homer Croy, a contem-

porary of Roy Aitken's, describes how nickelodeon slides went in for
humor in a heavy way:

DON'T SPIT ON THE FLOOR.
REMEMBER THE JOHNSTOWN FLOOD.
READ THE TITLES TO YOURSELVES.
YOUR NEIGHBORS CAN PROBABLY READ.
IF YOU LIKE THIS PICTURE, TELL YOUR FRIENDS.
IF YOU DON'T, PLEASE KEEP YOUR MOUTH SHUT.
LADIES WILL TAKE OFF THEIR HATS.
WOMEN WILL LEAVE THEM ON.
LADIES DON'T SMOKE. SO WHY SHOULD YOU? (23)

A favorite of the time was a drawing of a flirtatious young man tickling
a horrified maiden under the chin. The caption read, "If annoyed when
here, please tell the management" (24).

After the last slide, a heavy-breasted woman seated at a piano pounded
out a marching song. Then the lights clicked off, followed by the whir of
a projector somewhere behind Roy, instantly plunging him into a new
world that rivaled Buffalo Bill's exploits in this very same city.

Roy forgot who he was or where he was. He became part of a moving
picture on a screen. He found himself transported to a speeding train
whose passengers were held at bay by masked robbers dramatizing their
demands. "This was tremendous," he thought. "I wanted more and more.
But the show was over all too soon."

Even after he left the theater, a silent siren song stirred within him, and
he couldn't bear to shatter the mood by calling on any more Northern car
prospects that day. Instead, he went to his room and wrote a letter to
Harry. To his brother he described his movie experience in glowing terms.
Then he invited Harry to come to Chicago to see a nickelodeon show.

Several days later, quite unexpectedly, his older brother knocked on the
apartment door. "Well, Roy," said Harry, "let's go see this marvel you
wrote about. If it isn't interesting, I've lost a day selling insurance and the
expense of the trip down here."

The Great Train Robbery also impressed Harry Aitken. He immediately
grasped the potential of the new media for combating illiteracy, since
phrases could be interspersed with the moving pictures to help audiences
follow the story. In *Star Maker*, Croy cites these typical examples from a
nickelodeon in the early 1900s:

THE NEXT DAY.
AN HOUR LATER.
CAME THE DAWN.
NO ONE KNEW THE SECRETS OF HER HEART. (24)

After *The Great Train Robbery* showing, the Aitken brothers walked to the railroad station to meet Harry's train for Waukesha. Just as they had done on the knoll near Grandpa Aitken's place as youngsters, they talked about trains and shared dreams. Then Harry brought up the subject most on their minds. "Nickelodeons are exciting," he said enthusiastically. "If we can scrape together some money, how about starting one down here as partners?"

A dumbfounded Roy replied, "Well, why not? People flock to see these shows. They open in the afternoon and run until midnight. This is a business with a future, Harry."

4

★

"If You Like Our Nickelodeon, Tell Your Friends"

Harry Aitken went back to Waukesha and Milwaukee to try to raise money. Most of his own funds were earmarked to repay Elvin's loan, and he hated to defer those payments for the land purchased in Wausau. Harry had committed the rest of his money to a few real estate deals elsewhere, and so he, like his younger brother, was temporarily short of cash.

Harry had instructed Roy, however, to look for an empty store in downtown Chicago and to inquire about a movie projector, film, folding chairs, and a few other rentals. His parting words had been, "Keep your job, Roy. Do all this scouting in your spare time."

Roy's mind had wandered away from Northern automobile prospects to thoughts of the new nickelodeon enterprise. He strolled up and down State Street and finally discovered a small building at the intersection of State and Congress that met Harry's specifications. Rent listed at $30 per month. The place had been a former museum of anatomy, but the last renter had skipped, owing four months' rent. A few buildings away stood the popular Seigel-Cooper store. Roy researched the rental of a projector and films from the Chicago Film Exchange, owned by Max Lewis, and then sent all this information to Harry and awaited a reply.

Within a week in March 1905, Harry was back in Chicago. "I've taken a month's leave from the insurance business," he said eagerly. "In that time we'll know what we can do in this nickelodeon field. My friend, J. V. Ritchey, lent us $100. He made lots of money in a department store in Burlington, Iowa, and is looking for new fields in which to invest. I can put in $100, too, and that ought to get us started."

30

The Aitken brothers rented the store building and folding chairs and hired a carpenter to build a wooden projection booth eight feet off the floor. A ladder permitted the operator to crawl up into this enclosure. The carpenter also built a ticket booth at the store entrance.

"Roy, you'd better ask the film exchange owner to give you some lessons in operating a projector," Harry advised. "Then hire a young man and teach him how to run the machine. Perhaps you can also relieve him in the evenings. I'll stay up front and sell tickets."

They did hire a teachable, eager young man as a projectionist, and Roy taught him how to operate a machine. Daytime, Roy worked for the Northern auto agency until 4:30 in the afternoon, and then he went to the nickelodeon to help however he could. The first night he turned the crank on the Edison projection machine for a one-reeler, the excitement exceeded that which he felt the day he moved the big harvesting machine around Gëttner's lumberyard. For his first film, though, he had conducted a dry run earlier, but with an empty house.

The Aitkens' nickelodeon began operations at 11 A.M. and ran right through until 11 P.M. About fifty to sixty people came in for each fifteen-minute show at five cents per ticket. Roy usually operated the projector from seven in the evening until closing time, except at five o'clock each afternoon when he gave the full-time operator a half-hour break.

During that first week, the Aitken brothers took in $328 in nickels. After paying their bills, they had a $175 profit. Analyzing their expenses, Harry and Roy discovered that film rental costs amounted to $25 per week. This bought them two changes of one-reel programs per week. Later, they got three changes per week. Each one-run film was about nine hundred to one thousand feet and consisted of several subjects. Films with briefer story plots ranged in length from three hundred to five hundred feet.

Chicago's large population enabled the Aitkens to run one show for three days and get a profitable attendance every day. Workingmen and shoppers would circulate in the downtown area, read the theater posters, and choose a show they hadn't seen. Some even came back a few days later and paid a nickel to see a favorite show the second time. A few laborers would view three or four shows a week after working hours and still get home in time for a hot dinner. Harry and Roy found themselves surrounded with carnival and show people, some from the worst districts of Chicago. This was quite a departure from the small-town farm and Methodist church crowd with whom they had been associated at home in Waukesha.

One of the early films the Aitkens rented from the Chicago Film Exchange was Pathé Brothers' *Allah's Holiday*. This was a three-hundred-foot film that had been tinted by a special process to give a pleasing color effect. Audiences loved it. Harry and Roy could run this film several times per month and still attract crowds.

Fifty to sixty dollars per day gross was considered a profitable take for a small nickelodeon such as the Aitkens'. This meant at least fifty people per show for twenty-four, fifteen- to twenty-minute shows, twelve hours every day.

Police officers often dropped in to see a show but were never charged admission. This courtesy ensured that patrol officers gave the Aitken nickelodeon an extra look or two while walking their beats.

One day, Roy's boss at the Northern auto agency called him over to his desk. "I don't think your heart's in the automobile business any longer. It's in that nickelodeon you and your brother are operating. I suggest you go to work there full-time."

Young Aitken paled a little at the thought he was about to lose his guaranteed weekly salary. However, he knew the auto agency manager had a point. Roy had found a new love, one that was to last for the rest of his life and lead him through hazardous, thrilling, yet satisfying adventures.

"Well," said Harry when Roy told him he had lost his job, "we can use you full-time here. Now we can think about starting another nickelodeon. We have limited capacity in this one. People are just wild about the movies."

Within a month (it was now May), the Aitken brothers had opened two more nickelodeons in downtown Chicago. One was located at Halsted and Madison Avenue, the other on Milwaukee Avenue. Roy had multiple jobs. He helped set up the theaters, taught young men how to become projectionists, and relieved them during a busy schedule. The rest of the time he bartered at the Chicago Film Exchange, made and distributed programs, and handled many other duties. By this time, too, they had hired two women, one as ticket taker and the other to play a rented piano. Harry and Roy shared supervisory duties.

One day, while in the Chicago Film Exchange, Roy met Carl Laemmle. The enterprising merchant who had turned down Roy's insurance sales pitch had come from Oshkosh to open his own clothing store. A friend persuaded him to open a nickelodeon as well. So, Laemmle slapped a coat of white paint on an old building and got into the theater business by accident, as did many other people. An Aitken nickelodeon was located four blocks from Laemmle's film emporium, which was called the White Front, on Milwaukee Avenue. In the building he had rented to show movies, Laemmle had found considerable theatrical equipment already in place.

Compared to the Aitken brothers and Carl Laemmle, Jesse Lasky, Sam Goldwyn, Cecil B. De Mille, and Louis B. Mayer got a much later start in the movie business. Goldfish-Goldwyn didn't walk into his first nickelodeon until a summer afternoon in 1913. He saw a cowboy named "Bronco Billy" leap from his horse to a moving train and decided then and there that he wanted to be a part of the whole new exciting world of "flickers." Goldwyn got his chance later as he and his brother-in-law, a former vaudevillian named Jesse Lasky, linked up with a minor actor and playwright of little note named Cecil Blount De Mille. The three men formed a motion picture production company for filming recent stage successes. That same year, Louis B. Mayer, the exhibitor in Massachusetts, decided that a better future in film lay with either production or distribution. He stepped a rung up the ladder by moving into distribution, which brought him to the door of Goldwyn, De Mille, and Lasky. Except for the latter partner, the others had no experience in theater, so they signed Mayer to distribute the films they were to produce under a company that was to become Metro Goldwyn Mayer.

Only a few film exchanges existed in Chicago in 1905, and the Chicago Film Exchange operated by Max Lewis and his sons was probably the most prosperous. Lewis had lost a leg in an accident and in a settlement with his employer received enough money to start a film exchange.

The idea of a film exchange dated back to 1904, just a year before Harry and Roy opened their first nickelodeon in Chicago. It was the brainchild of Harry J. Miles. He saw clearly the burden of the exhibitor who, under existing conditions, had to purchase films outright from manufacturers and often found himself with many surplus films at the termination of runs.

Miles realized that such films were salable to other theater men, but an exchange plan would be needed. So, he began purchasing prints from producers and then started to lease them to theater owners for a week at a time. He charged less than half the purchase price of the films, which pleased exhibitors. At the end of the exhibition period, the films were shipped back to Miles, who would then lease the films to other exhibitors. As the films got older, the leasing price dropped to bargain levels.

A few days after the Aitkens opened their second nickelodeon, Roy met with the Chicago Film Exchange owner. "You boys are promoters," Lewis said, arching his black brows and thrusting his head forward until it nearly collided with Roy's chin. "I like to see people get ahead. Keep at it."

Since the Aitkens had three nickelodeons within a short time and procured all their film from Lewis, he often gave them preference when he could. However, demand for new film was terrific, and it was scarce. There just were not enough film-producing companies in the nation at the time.

Through patience taught to him by Vanderhoff, Roy was often able to get first-choice new film for the brothers' State Street nickelodeon, show first-run pictures, and then fill out the program with older films. Of course, they had to pay a higher price for first-run films than for third or fourth run. This approach is still in force in the movie business today.

"I cannot overemphasize how much the film exchanges contributed to the growth of the motion picture industry," Roy said. "They facilitated the marketing of film, so that all theaters would have a varied supply of the films that were available. Without such programs, we in the theaters could not have held our audiences."

Before the advent of the film exchange, it took time for theaters to procure film from producers, but when exchanges were established, this permitted film to be stocked, repaired, rented, shipped, and received in convenient locations all over the nation. Thus, a big burden was lifted from nickelodeon operators. They still had to fight for an adequate supply of films, but the fight was in their own backyards.

Each time Roy went to the Lewis exchange for a change of film subjects, bedlam ensued. Theater men like him stood in line, talking and cussing, while waiting their turn to get a film supply.

"Not that one, Max!" a theater owner would wail. "I had that two weeks ago. I want something different, or my customers will kill me. OK, OK, I'll take it for the second picture if you give me a new film for the top spot. Damn this business anyway. Why did I ever get into it?"

Max Lewis and his sons apparently had iron nerves—or perhaps no nerves at all. Outwardly they were calm and went patiently about their work to try to supply customers with a limited amount of film that they had not already shown. New or old, most films in those days were substandard compared to what was offered less than ten years later. The acting, the photography, the lighting, and the story lines were from poor to average. But most of the theatergoing public in 1905 didn't care too much. They were still fascinated by anything that moved on a screen or, rather, a bedsheet.

If Lewis had no new films for the Aitkens, he would urge them to use old stock from the shelves. "Roy," he would plead, his hands outstretched, "better to use the old film, even if you used it weeks ago, than to go on repeating your present program. At least it will show you're trying hard to please the customers."

Often he was right. Lewis knew he had important problems in trying to satisfy all customers. Harry and Roy were to face these same problems within a short time, for they, too, were destined to open film exchanges.

The Aitkens sought the friendship of E. H. Montague, the Pathé Brothers' representative in Chicago. He was a tall, well-mannered Englishman, and it was his duty to distribute Pathé movies to film exchanges. Lewis was one of his best customers. Montague wanted a place to view the new films he received from Pathé, and Roy suggested he use the State Street nickelodeon, now named the Tourist Theater, to exhibit them during morning hours before the Aitken shows began.

"That's wonderful of you, Roy," Montague beamed. "Your theater is close to my office, too."

Later in their movie careers, Harry and Roy often met Montague at conventions and elsewhere, and he always greeted them warmly. He put in a good word for the enterprising brothers whenever he could. In New York City, Roy frequently had lunch with him.

One problem constantly in the Aitkens' minds was the danger of flammable film. Made of a nitrate base, this film would burst into flame very easily when overheated. This fear of fire clutched at the heart of every projectionist and theater owner, especially in fire-conscious Chicago, still reeling from the Iroquois Theater fire and panic of December 30, 1903, itself second only in severity to the tragic fire in that city of October 8, 1871.

Carbons in the early Edison projectors, too, could not always withstand the varying current in the power lines, and sometimes the carbons would overheat and burn out.

To minimize this problem, many projectionists made their own rheostats. These homemade affairs consisted of loops of coiled wire, which often would get red hot as the electric current passed through them. Roy always hung these coils of wire on the walls of the projection booth, away from the machine and the flammable film. Often he tried to keep one eye on the hot, coiled wires and another eye on the projection machine, while he cranked to bring a jumping, flickering motion picture to focus on a distant bedsheet. Sometimes when the fragile film broke, Roy had to improvise while an impatient audience hooted and made shadow puppets on the screen. "One never got bored on that job," he said.

While cranking the noisy Edison in their State Street nickelodeon on a late spring day, Roy smelled smoke in the stuffy projection booth. Alarmed, he looked at the projector. A yellowish flame was leaping inside the machine, mixing weirdly with the glaring white lights of the carbons. For a moment he was stunned, but he continued cranking. There was only one thing to do: get the audience of fifty or more out of the building quickly.

Suddenly, he stopped cranking, breaking off the sequence of the picture. The screen went dark. Roy flashed on the dim floor lights and climbed halfway down the wooden wall ladder. "Folks," he said as calmly as he could, "I suggest you leave the theater as soon as you can."

There was a quick scraping of feet. With alarmed cries, people rushed for the entrance that was the only exit. Trembling, Roy stood and watched them push, shove, and clamor. Luckily, all of them got into the street without injury.

In the meantime, the alert woman ticket taker saw what was wrong and called the fire department located nearby. When the firefighters arrived a few minutes later, smoke poured into the theater from the booth. The film was aflame, but the fire was still confined to its starting point.

A couple of confused firefighters who had never dealt with a film fire before climbed into the booth. One of them somehow pried the flaming reel out of the projector and tossed it through a small window into State Street at the feet of some of the startled onlookers. A possibly disastrous fire was thus averted. Despite the lingering odor of burnt celluloid, another rented projector and film put the Aitken brothers back in business a few hours later.

By midsummer 1905, the heat in Chicago's poorly ventilated nickelodeons was intense, and attendance began to dwindle. All the theater owners began to complain about poor business. Survival depended on how much money nickelodeon operators were prepared to spend to last out the summer until cool fall weather appeared.

"Roy, we'd use up all our profits if we stayed in business until fall," Harry said, "and then we'd have no assurance that business would be as good as it has been since we started in March. Max Lewis told me that thirty nickelodeons have been started in Chicago this year, and they'll all be scrambling for business."

"You mean we ought to quit?" Roy asked incredulously.

Harry nodded. "Let's pull out while we are still ahead. Both of us like the movie business, but let's get back into it later on in a different way. If you own a film exchange, for example, you can rent film and get cash from those who stay in business, and you'll get your money regularly. It's an easier and more profitable way to make money."

So, regretfully, the two Aitken brothers closed their three Chicago nickelodeons and left the field to hardy souls like Laemmle and others who would stick it out through the humid weeks of summer and hope they could hold on until autumn's breeze brought a renaissance in business. Harry and Roy knew that the movie fever was in their blood and would prod them to renewed action before long. So, they went back to the family home at Waukesha to think things over and to lay plans for the future in the movie field.

Those plans, although neither Aitken was aware of it at the time, would bring scores of future movie stars under their direction within five years.

These would include the famous Keystone Kops director, Mack Sennett, and actors Charles and Sydney Chaplin, Chester Conklin, Harold Lloyd, Charles Murray, fat Mack Swain, Slim Summerville, astute but comic Ford Sterling, roly-poly Fatty Arbuckle, and many others. Keystone bathing beauties Olive Thomas, Gloria Swanson, Mabel Normand, Louise Fazenda, and other fun-loving actresses would join them.

5

Near Death Far from Home

Harry had given up insurance sales while the brothers operated their nickelodeons, and he did not want to reenter that field at age twenty-eight in 1905. He knew that if he did, he might never get back into the movie business. While both Aitkens kept the idea of a film exchange in mind, they felt that the time was not yet ripe to start one.

Meanwhile, Harry owned those thousand acres of land in northern Wisconsin, and he wanted to translate it into cash. "I think now is the time to sell the land at a good price," he told Elvin. "Northern Wisconsin is settling rapidly and land prices are up. Why couldn't Roy and I capitalize on our movie experience, put on some free shows in Illinois, for example, and then, between reels, talk to the audiences about the land we have to sell?"

"That might be a good idea," his father responded. "The shows ought to be able to stir up some interest."

"We could get some pictures of the land before development, before cutting, after cutting, and some of it as it is now after houses and barns are built," Harry went on. "We could show such slides to our movie patrons."

Harry took the train to Wausau the next day to consult Mr. E. B. Jones, his real estate partner. Jones agreed to go along with the traveling show idea and bear part of the expense. Harry then went to the Chicago and Northwestern Railroad and the Chicago, Milwaukee, and St. Paul Railroad and told officials about the Aitkens' proposed land sales plan.

"If we can sell northern Wisconsin land to Illinois farmers, it will help your freight and passenger volume," he pointed out. "Perhaps you'd be interested in giving us a couple of passes to help out."

He got the passes without any difficulty.

The brothers then hired a Chicago operator who owned a projector, rented a few one-reel comedies and other films from the exchange, and picked out Dixon, Illinois, as a starting point for the land sales program. Later, Dixon would go down in history as the boyhood home of Ronald Reagan, fortieth president of the United States.

Harry and Roy met a real estate man in Dixon, discussed their idea with him, and finally rented the town hall. Establishing headquarters at a rooming house, they advertised the show and got ready for the opening. To move things along, they sold tickets to local merchants at a low rate, and they in turn gave them to their best customers. It appeared to be a sure-fire deal all around, and both Harry and Roy were elated about the prospect.

Roy acted as ticket seller and taker, and he beamed as scores of people entered the rental hall. Harry gave a short talk welcoming the audience and then told of the wonderful land-buying opportunities in northern Wisconsin.

The people were a little impatient. They wanted to see the show, not listen to a land-selling pitch, but, of course, they had no choice. Finally, they showed several short one-reel movies, and they made a hit. The audience laughed and looked highly pleased. Between each reel, Harry gave another short talk about land opportunities in northern Wisconsin.

They didn't sell a single acre that night, although they secured a few prospects. However, they pressed on somewhat discouraged but undaunted. The Aitken brothers traveled to eight other Illinois towns. Harry sold some acreage, but they both finally realized that their land promotion via movie shows was a long-range deal that would take more financing than they could get at the moment. So after one week Harry and his twenty-three-year-old brother packed their bags and went back to Waukesha. From Roy's perspective, the Illinois land venture hadn't been a total bust. The experience revealed a side of Harry they both knew was itching to find expression. Harry was steadily becoming more interested in sales promotion. He apparently liked this type of work much more than selling life insurance.

After a brief visit in Waukesha with Elvin, Sarah, and his sisters, Roy made a trip to Chicago to see Max Lewis of the Chicago Film Exchange. He needed a job and the money it would bring, and he preferred to work in the movie business.

For once, Harry moved at a slower pace. He remained at home for several weeks, since he already had money put away from his insurance job.

Max smiled at the youthful face that greeted him. "Hello, Roy. What brings you to Chicago?"

"Max," he replied, "you know I'm familiar with films and projectors. Do you need a hardworking, eager salesman to travel around Wisconsin getting new business for you?"

Chuckling, Lewis regarded the young man quizzically. Roy could almost feel the man thinking. "Yes, we could use a good man," Lewis said finally, "and maybe you could fill the bill. We do get some mail and express business from Wisconsin, but with personal selling, we might get more. Who isn't trying to expand these days?"

Roy waited.

"We'll give you a small salary, say $25 per week, plus moderate expenses and a thousand-mile railroad travel book."

Young Aitken must have smiled too eagerly, because Lewis added cautiously, "For three months, Roy, if it works out for me."

Thrilled about his new job, Roy visited nickelodeon theaters in Milwaukee, where he generated initial sales renting old and whatever new films Lewis had available. Theater owners appreciated this personal service and often tipped Aitken off to places he might be able to sell film accounts.

"I'm glad you're doing so well selling films," Harry told Roy one day. "You're getting experience that will help us a great deal when we finally start our own film exchange."

In those days, as did successful gentlemen of the times, Roy wore dark suits, a black derby, and polished, high-button shoes. He tried to dress well, and most of his spare cash went into haberdashery items. He always liked fashionable clothes, and this attention to sartorial splendor paid off many times in his movie career. He traced this fastidiousness back to his observing firsthand how well Uncle Bert Hadfield and dashing Buffalo Bill dressed.

Milwaukee streets in 1905 were either brick or wooden block. Once in a while Roy would take a hack when he called on theaters, but most of the time he went by streetcar. He always tried to help his accounts arrange film programs, and they appreciated this.

After a few months of selling in Milwaukee, Roy ventured out in the state to sell film and equipment. In Madison he stayed at the Park Hotel on the Square across from the state capital. In striking up a conversation with the hotel manager and guests, he soon established a reputation as being closely connected with that glamorous, newfangled business, the flickers. In fact, stopping at leading hotels, whenever he could afford it, became one of Roy's favorite techniques. He secured many leads for new theaters just from tips given to him by hotel managers and others. "Lobbies are a great place to get information about a town or city," he surmised.

Another tall, thin farm boy who would make his mark on the movies after he had joined the Aitken brothers struggled in 1905 just to survive or get a roof over his head. David Wark Griffith in his autobiography (edited and annotated by James Hart as *The Man Who Invented Hollywood*) shared Roy's view that lodging places not only teemed with information, but they became training grounds for performers of every stripe. Griffith wrote of one such New York City experience in 1905:

> Finding a lodging house on Thirty-seventh Street that was cheap but far superior to my former Bowery abodes, I stepped into my happiest days as an actor. It wasn't so lonely this time; I had one or two pals here . . . and I was beginning to quiet my heretofore growing alarm at the prospect of starvation.
>
> This lodging house was the home of none but stage people, and what a place it was! From its many rooms accordions groaned, guitars tinkled, voices trilled the scales as one and all rehearsed over and over the popular tune of the day. Day and night you could hear the tapping of hoofer's routines and the mighty voices of Shakespearean actors rehearsing their lines. Fat actors liked this place. There was so little chance to sleep that they reduced as a matter of course. (62)

Many men who went into the nickelodeon field in the early days, 1905 to 1909, were like Jesse Lasky, Louis B. Mayer, and Sam Goldwyn who had other businesses, retail, wholesale, or manufacturing. Some were professional men. Like all entrepreneurs, they were looking for places to invest spare cash profitably, and the exotic, but not yet lush, movie business had pronounced appeal. These men could work their businesses or professions during the day and then supervise nickelodeon operations at night. No respectable woman would lend her name to a business many regarded as pornographic, so it began as a man's world and stayed as such until Harry Aitken later ushered in the star system that gave movies respectability.

Max Lewis was pleased with the orders sent in by his Wisconsin representative. Besides orders for film, Roy Aitken also sold a projector here and there. Much of the film Lewis was shipping Roy was old, of course. It had exhausted its exhibiting appeal in Chicago and suburbs, where it had been shown five to ten times. Nonetheless, it had never been shown in Wisconsin, and so Lewis got extra mileage from the films rented through Roy.

"We'll continue the arrangement for another three months," Lewis told Roy when he arrived in Chicago to discuss his future. "I never knew we could rent so much film in Wisconsin."

Roy charged theaters whatever the tariff would bear in those days. If a theater used two one-reel films for two days, the asking price was $25. Sometimes owners wanted three changes of film a week, which meant $50 to $65 in film rentals from each theater. It took a lot of nickels and dimes to gross film rentals, but the movies attracted crowds no matter what was exhibited.

After all, those were the days before automobile, travel, radio, television, and airplanes. Movies meant excitement in little cities and towns in the first part of the twentieth century where previously the big events were church suppers and long passenger trains stopping at the local station.

Roy saw the roller skating craze as the only serious competition to the movies in 1905 and 1906. Rinks were springing up all over the nation. A roller rink was the popular place to take your best girl without getting in trouble with her parents.

To retain interest in the movies, film exchanges set release dates for all new films rented. This made Aitken a czar, deciding what he would rent to whom since competition was still very limited in the film exchange field.

"Give me new films, Roy," the bigger theater owners would plead each time he called.

He had to explain that prints of new films were scarce because there were not enough producers in the field to supply the demand. Most film exchanges could afford to buy only two to five prints of each new film and then make these cover as wide a territory as possible. Later, of course, film exchanges became better financed and more prosperous and could buy as many prints of new films as they wished and rent them simultaneously on a set fee in their territory.

One of Roy's nettlesome problems was to show new theater owners how to work out a balanced program. Few had any idea how to handle such a task. If a cowboy picture satisfied the audience, some owners decided to use a second western film, too, thinking this would please the customers. Aitken argued that a change of fare, one cowboy film, for example, and then a one-reel comedy, was wise. In many cases his advice was accepted.

He would also show theater operators how to use a new film as a main feature, and then work in an older and shorter film as the second feature. The old film cost less, the new film more, so this approach balanced financially, too. He drove home the point that if one film didn't please the customers, the other probably would.

One weekend upon returning to Waukesha, Roy found Harry packing his traveling bag. "Roy," he said eagerly, "I had lunch in Milwaukee with E. B. Jones today, and we agreed that I ought to go to Texas and try to sell our Wisconsin land to Texans. They might like a Wisconsin retreat in the hot weather. Some of that land, too, is wonderful for cattle."

"It'll be expensive traveling down in Texas," Roy warned.

Harry chuckled. "Jones says he'll advance my expenses. He can't get away from his job, but I'm free to go for a while."

Roy studied his brother carefully. Something in his voice indicated that Harry welcomed a second party on this trip.

"Don't count on me to sell tickets this time," Roy said. "I've got a good-paying job, and I'm starting to make some real money."

Harry smiled and strapped his traveling case. "I don't expect you to come to Texas with me now. But if the land sells fast, I may offer you more money to help me than you are now earning."

So Harry, the promoter, ever optimistic and in high spirits, went to Texas by rail, and Roy went back to selling film and other theater supplies in Wisconsin.

Winter came and passed, and Roy had covered his home state quite well. Many of the theaters were so well established now that they could order their weekly film supplies by mail direct from Lewis. Roy had also trained theater owners how to plan attractive film programs, and now they didn't need him for that.

He again boarded a train for Chicago to discuss the situation with Max Lewis. "I'd like to go south and visit Harry in Texas," Roy told the head of the Chicago Film Exchange. "I've covered Wisconsin quite thoroughly and have sold many steady accounts for you. Would you consider hiring me to see what I could do for you down south?"

Lewis's eyebrows lifted at this suggestion of possible further expansion of his trade area. He considered for a moment, then grinned. "I didn't lose money on you in Wisconsin, Roy, so maybe I'll go for this southern deal. It's a little far afield, but there aren't many film exchanges south of St. Louis as yet. Maybe you could pick up some good accounts. I'll go along with you on that for three months."

So once again Roy received a thousand-mile railroad travel book, as well as $25 in weekly expenses and a $25 drawing account against commissions. After he had made the deal and gone back to Waukesha, he became a little uneasy about the matter. "You've never been south selling in what is strange territory compared to Wisconsin, where you felt very secure," he reminded himself. But then the old confidence returned. He shrugged off his fear and prepared to pack.

As usual, Sarah Aitken hated to see her youngest son leave home, even though she knew she should let him try his wings in a venture that appealed to him.

"Write real often, won't you, Roy?" she counseled. "Be a good boy and go to church on Sundays."

"I'll try, Mother," he said, kissing her good-bye.

His first stop to solicit business was at Dyersburg, Tennessee. Roy knew a southern family there. The address was in his black notebook that he had used at those summer hotel dances in Waukesha some years earlier. He was to refer to that notebook many times on southern trips.

By scouting around, Roy learned that a local man wanted to open a nickelodeon. He had rented a store building for a theater, purchased a machine, but did not know how to operate it.

The southerner cordially welcomed the young man from up north when Roy called on him. Roy sold him a weekly film program and taught him how to operate the projector. In fact, he stayed in Dyersburg for three days helping this man get started "on the right foot," as he put it. The new theater operator was very grateful. "I'll certainly tell others what good service you and the Chicago Film Exchange give," he promised.

This first sale down south cheered Roy greatly. He telephoned a southern family whose name appeared in his notebook. They invited him out for dinner that evening to celebrate.

"So you are now in the movie business," the hostess said, her eyes shining. "How exciting, Roy."

His next stop was at Memphis where he sold some film. Then he went to Nashville and on to Columbia. At Columbia he met a man who was proposing to open a nickelodeon, and he was very happy to see Roy. He gave the proprietor hints on film programming, admission prices, and advertising techniques, and he liked that.

"Will you stay and help me open?" he asked.

"Yes, if you'll buy a projector and film from me," Roy said.

"It's a deal," he said.

Roy wired in the projector and film order and asked Max Lewis to ship down *Allah's Holiday*, if possible, because he thought opening night patrons would like the tinted film.

Three nights later the new nickelodeon opened. *Allah's Holiday* was a hit, and the theater owner was very pleased. He had a full house of about 150 patrons, and he ran two shows. Later, he planned some matinees.

Roy had spent five days with this theater man and felt the time and effort were well rewarded because of the sale of a projector and a steady weekly order for films.

"Now I can teach my wife to operate the projector," said the theater owner. "I can also get someone to take Helen's place in the ticket office while I collect tickets and check on the rowdies."

Quite often Roy made a point to stay at well-recommended boarding houses in the southern towns. They were cheaper than hotels and usually had wonderful food. He was fond of fried chicken, candied sweet potatoes, and cherry pie—often served family-style.

At a boarding house table, too, the regulars would persistently ask questions until they discovered how a newcomer earned a living. In one town, after Roy described how he sold movie equipment and film, a comely widow laid aside her evening meal and squealed, "Oh, Mr. Aitken! The movies! How romantic!"

There certainly was romance in the South—plenty of it, if a bachelor were so disposed, thought Roy. "Boarding houses abounded with pretty single women and shapely dressed-up widows with wandering, eager eyes," he recalled later.

But young Aitken felt he was already married to a demanding movie career. However, he did take time at night to go to a roller rink, where he met many charming girls who wanted a skating partner. He never refused an invitation.

At various cities along his route, he checked general delivery at the Post Office for Sarah Aitken's letters. His mother related so much news about home that he often became very homesick. Resolutely, he shook off this feeling by making extra calls to keep busy. Invariably Sarah ended her letters with the admonition, "Be sure to go to church on Sundays."

As Lewis's checks came in, sometimes very late, Roy began to spend a little money for clothes, better shirts, and nattier ties. He had his suit pressed more often and his shoes shined by a porter, and he put a fresh linen handkerchief in his coat breast pocket every morning.

He soon learned that most people expected someone representing the movie industry to be better dressed than most, scrupulously neat, up-to-date, and worldly wise. He'd never forgotten this lesson and how the practice of it gained attention and respect.

From Tennessee, Roy went to Georgia, stopping at Americus, then to other cities. He continued to get more business, including the sale of several projectors.

Lewis was delighted with the steady flow of business from a territory he had not previously tapped. But he was irritatingly slow, now and then, in sending Roy his $25 weekly salary. This often meant strict budgeting for the young salesman and a longer stay in some towns and cities awaiting a check.

Though frequently dejected when his money ran low, Roy did not give up. The excitement of this new movie business never left him. He felt as the pioneers did when they opened the virgin West. He was thrilled to be taking part in a business that he was certain would sooner or later capture the interest of millions of Americans.

When delayed in a city, Roy would open his address book of southern families courted in those long summer evenings at Waukesha and start telephoning. Often he was invited to dinners.

Years later, people would ask Roy whether he had been born in the south or in England, where he also lived for a while. He took this as a sign that certain customs of the south and the British Isles had made quite a lasting effect on his speech and manners. This may have been a contributing factor as to why he and D. W. Griffith got along so well during the production of *Birth of a Nation*.

Born in Kentucky on January 22, 1875, seventeen miles from Louisville, to a father hailed as a hero in the Civil War, Griffith regarded himself as an aristocrat. Questions still exist whether the large Griffith farm near Crestwood, Kentucky, in Oldham County ever reached plantation status as D.W. often claimed. Yet, his mother's people, the Oglebys, unlike the family of his father, Colonel "Roaring Jake" Griffith, ran a large plantation and were slave owners at one time.

Young Griffith was a gangly boy growing up on the farm and, like Roy Aitken, did his chores dutifully but put his formal education aside at a young age. Roy was by far the better looking of the two dreamers, since David had a large, bony nose. He wore a wide-brimmed floppy hat pulled down over his forehead to conceal what he called his "Duke of Wellington" nose. Later, as an eccentric movie director, he switched to an old straw hat with the top removed to admit sunlight, which he believed would prevent hair loss. Harder and more bitter to swallow, however, was the loss of his family's prestige and their impoverished state following the Civil War. D. W. Griffith seemed never to forget the injustices piled against his family by the northern carpetbaggers and their allies during the supposed excesses of Reconstruction. Later in their own movie careers, Harry and Roy Aitken unintentionally provided this brilliant but perhaps unforgiving southerner the instrument to wreak his revenge.

When Roy reached Mobile, Alabama, he received a letter from his mother with alarming news. "Harry is ill with typhoid fever in a hospital at San Antonio, Texas," Sarah wrote. "Please wire the doctor."

Roy sent a wire immediately, and the doctor answered quickly. Harry's illness was not serious at present, but he asked the younger Aitken to please keep in touch with him.

Two days later, the anxious brother again wired Harry's attending physician. This time the return wire was marked urgent. "Your brother very ill. Come at once."

6

Back to the Flickers
with a Film Exchange

A worried Roy Aitken packed his bag, checked out of his hotel, and took the night train for San Antonio. He arrived many hours later to find Harry sleeping. The duty nurse directed Roy to a chair near Harry's hospital room, and the tired traveler collapsed in a state of anxiety at the thought of losing his only brother.

The next day Roy cautiously approached Harry's bedside. The patient recognized his little brother and smiled weakly. "I never figured on this, Roy," he mumbled.

"You'll soon be better," Roy encouraged. "Then we'll go home."

Harry nodded and went back to sleep.

While he waited for Harry to recover, Roy telephoned Major Richard Jacob, who was stationed at Fort Sam Houston. An old school chum of Roy's, the major had renewed their acquaintance in Milwaukee one day when the two chanced to meet. Upon hearing that his friend was posted in Texas, Roy jokingly told him that he might "get down south some day."

"If you do, look me up, Roy," the major had said.

When Roy phoned him from the hospital, Jacob was delighted. He invited Aitken to stay with him several days at the army post and guaranteed a good time.

Roy checked on his brother, saw that Harry had now improved enough to be left on his own, and accepted Jacob's invitation. At the sprawling post, Jacob and his fellow officers greeted Roy like a celebrity and insisted he tell them about the movie industry.

"I think I made movie patrons of them after that talk," said Roy.

Since Fort Sam was a cavalry post, the conversation naturally drifted toward horses and horsemanship. The officers complained about the mounted artillery troopers, whose mules and colts required a tremendous amount of breaking to get them used to pulling wagons and caissons. Inevitably, on parade, it was a wild-horse-drawn vehicle that marred the occasion by throwing mud or dust all over the dignitaries on the reviewing stand as the wagon or caisson passed in review.

Major Jacob said he thought the "Redcaps," as the artillerymen were called, faked this out-of-control maneuver just to embarrass their gold-trimmed fellows in the cavalry. Aware that these men, like his father, loved horses, Roy told the story of how Elvin used to break colts back in Waukesha, when almost everybody in Goerke's Corners found an excuse to come over to the Aitken farm and help or watch the fun. He covered everything from the moment his father backed the kicking, stomping colt out of the stall until it was hitched to the wagon next to an old reliable horse.

"Now came the real test to see how the colt responded to pulling its part of the load," said Roy, pointing out that everybody waited for this moment.

"When Father said 'Get up!' the old horse would start, but not the colt. There was always the chance that as the colt felt the weight of the wagon on its collar it would balk. Then the two horses seesawed back and forth until they began to pull evenly.

"But this didn't always work just that way," Roy continued, thrilled that the officers listened attentively to every word. "There was a lunging and kicking, with the man at the head of the colt still hanging on but keeping out of the way of the excited animal. Finally, the team got in motion and headed out of the yard. After crossing the road and getting through the gate, the men hopped into the wagon. It took a couple of turns around in the field until the team began to pull with some evenness.

"As the team made its way back to the barn, least happy of all was the broken colt. It did not like the bit in its mouth, or the hames and collar around its neck, or the harness on its back.

"Father had a satisfied look on his face, the neighbors had enjoyed a great afternoon, and the colt had the beginning of a new experience. But the old horse only looked disgusted," said Roy who capped his tale with references to his own horsemanship.

As it happened, Roy's new army friends were preparing for a parade honoring a royal patron of the cavalry during his visit. The officers expressed their camaraderie with young Aitken by arranging for him to participate in the parade.

"You'll wear a United States Army uniform but without the insignia," Jacob said. "You'll be an outrider to the queen."

"What kind of horse?" Roy inquired.

"Just one of the army horses, Roy. But don't use your spurs."

It was the next best thing to being in Buffalo Bill's Wild West Show, and Roy had a wonderful time. He rode the horse well and had no trouble. He felt as if he were home on the farm riding his mare through the tall grass of the meadow, with the mare's tail flying in the wind and his father looking up approvingly from his work. Of course, in the parade, he didn't go that fast, and, instead of Elvin, he rode past the quizzical gaze of an army colonel already covered in dust from a passing caisson.

Roy's stay at the post eased his mind about Harry, whom he visited every day at the hospital. He found his brother's physical condition improving but his spirit lower than a newly broken colt. "The doctor says you'll be here at least another week," he told Harry, "so I think I'll try to sell some film in the city. We'll need money."

"I can believe that," Harry agreed sadly. "The land deal didn't work out, Roy. We'll just have to hold our acreage in Wisconsin for the future."

"Don't worry," Roy said. "I've still got a few dollars in my pocket."

He rented quite a few films in San Antonio. It was a long way to ship film from Chicago, but southern theaters then were not getting the quality of films out of New Orleans and St. Louis that Max Lewis could furnish. So Roy had a real sales angle to push.

Finishing his calls in San Antonio, Roy made sales stops at Houston, El Paso, and other Texas cities. He was pleased by the film orders he booked.

When Harry was well enough to leave the hospital, his younger brother took him to a recommended boarding house at Austin for further rest. A kindly woman whom the Aitkens had met at a summer hotel in Waukesha owned the home, and she was glad to see the boys from Spa City.

While Harry rested at the boarding house, Roy canvassed the theaters in Austin. He had to, because after the hospital and doctor bills were paid, he had very little money left, in fact, not enough for two train fares to Waukesha. And the coupons on Roy's second thousand-mile rail book were almost gone.

"Strong enough to start for Waukesha tomorrow morning?" Roy asked Harry one afternoon.

His eyes lit up. "I think so."

They figured that the remaining mileage tickets would get them as far as St. Louis, about seven hundred miles short of their destination. Cash in hand was $10—not nearly enough to cover train fare the rest of the way to Waukesha.

"Well, what do we do now?" Roy asked as they munched on sandwiches at a railroad restaurant in St. Louis.

Harry had been quite glum, but suddenly he looked up smiling and asked Roy to pass him the address book. He searched through the ledger and selected Allen Martin, a St. Louis businessman who had come to

Waukesha summer after summer with his family. Harry and Roy remembered dancing with Martin's lovely wife and daughter at the Park Hotel.

They went to Martin's office in a downtown building, apologizing for interrupting his work. Martin said he was surprised to see them and asked what had brought them to St. Louis. With considerable embarrassment, they related the whole story about Harry's illness, their lack of funds, their film-selling business, and most of all their need for a small loan to pay for the railroad fare to Waukesha.

Martin listened very attentively and then said, "Certainly I'll be glad to loan you enough money to get back home. I'm sorry you had such tough luck."

On the train a few hours later, listening to the clickity-clack of the whirring coach wheels, Harry said, "It pays to have friends, doesn't it?"

Roy smiled and just nodded.

Back in Waukesha, they wasted no time in repaying the loan and sent a letter of appreciation along with the money. A year or so later, they pointed to Allen Martin's kindness as one of the deciding factors that drew them to St. Louis to set up their second film exchange.

Harry was in need of further rest at Waukesha to recuperate from the debilitating illness that had made him so weak and thin. However, Roy had the restlessness of a healthy twenty-four-year-old. He didn't want to stay idle.

"I think I'll go back and see Max Lewis," he told Harry one night as the Soo Line train whistle echoed in the distance beyond John Aitken's old house on Hartwell. "Perhaps I could work awhile for the Chicago Film Exchange in Wisconsin again."

"Yes, stick to the film business," Harry advised. "You like it, and you have much valuable experience to contribute. We'll need that when we open a film exchange."

"Still thinking of that?" Roy asked.

Harry nodded. "Give me a month or more to get better, and I'll work on it."

Max Lewis was agreeable to Roy's traveling the Wisconsin territory again and gave him another thousand-mile ticket book, plus expense money.

Following his trip south, he had returned to find that more nickelodeons had opened in Wisconsin cities and that these were additional outlets for Lewis's old films. He was amazed that so much silent movie activity had developed since he last worked the territory.

A month later, Harry's health had improved sufficiently for him to venture to Milwaukee for a meeting with energetic John R. Freuler, an imposing, stocky man with heavy jowls that nevertheless enhanced his handsome Teutonic features. He was a businessman with lots of drive.

Roy had sold Freuler a film service the previous year and had often mentioned him to Harry as a "comer."

In 1905, Freuler, a real estate man with offices in the prestigious Matthews Building on West Wisconsin Avenue, established Milwaukee's first permanent motion picture theater on the south side of town. Like so many other Aitken contemporaries, Freuler got into the movie business by accident. He learned that an ex-policeman had a portable projector and two reels of film worth $450 in his Milwaukee basement. Freuler matched that investment, and they opened the Comique Theater at 2246 S. Kinnickinnic Avenue. Freuler had not told his wife that he owned the theater, because he feared she might not think it a suitable sideline business for a man of his standing.

As Freuler watched the nickel admissions pour into the box office of the Comique, however, he became enamored with the movie business, and his sporting blood was stirred.

The older Aitken brother and Freuler liked each other at once. Each recognized in the other a driving energy and a desire for promotion and moneymaking. Harry was more adventurous than Freuler, who was inclined to be cautious, but this difference didn't seem to create any obstacles at the moment.

In their conversation, Harry told Freuler that there was an opportunity to open the first film exchange in Wisconsin and that the profit possibilities were promising for an investment of a few dollars.

Freuler's heavy eyebrows lifted. "How much?" he asked. "A hundred dollars?"

"No," Harry said. "I think it can be done for less."

Harry next took a trip to Chicago to call on Max Lewis. There he made arrangements with the exchange owner to rent the Aitken brothers and their new partner reels of old film for $10 each for one week.

"I wish you boys luck," Lewis chuckled, scratching his stubby beard. "I guess there's business for all of us the way the public is yelling for movies. But stay in Wisconsin! Don't try coming into Illinois or else!" He drew his finger across his throat, and Harry got the message.

Harry then visited three theaters in the Fox Valley cities of Appleton, Kaukauna, and De Pere in Wisconsin. He agreed to furnish the owners with three changes of one reel each per week. For this, each was to pay him $25 per week, and each, in turn, promised to ship the film after the last show to the next theater, so that the owner would receive it the following day in time for his next show. The expense involved in this procedure cost Harry $37, and he in turn could collect $75 from the three theaters.

Harry had proved his point to the delighted Freuler, who was glad to advance $75 for start-up expenses, and thus the Western Film Exchange was organized. The partners rented space on the third floor of the Enterprise

Building in Milwaukee on the corner of West Michigan and North Second Street. The building was a block and a half from the big Chicago, Milwaukee, and St. Paul Railroad Company, with its high-peaked brick tower.

Because of his experience, Roy was asked to do a number of jobs at the new film exchange. He began by assembling equipment, checking film, and setting up attractive film programs and also training theater owners in many phases of their operation. Harry and Freuler handled the administrative duties of the exchange, the first in the Midwest outside Chicago and St. Louis.

One day when Harry and Roy were alone in their tiny office, Harry swung his swivel chair around. "Roy!" he exclaimed, "We're in the movie business again, and this time I'm sure it's permanent!"

"I'm sure, too," Roy responded. "I know we can grow with this fast-expanding business!"

The Aitken's film exchange grew so rapidly that Harry and Roy were often exhausted at day's end. But they didn't mind because this movie business always stirred their imaginations. Something about it made even the most commonplace office tasks glamorous. One could always think, "This film I'm checking will be seen tonight by a delighted audience and the next day by audiences in another town."

Many theater owners visited the Aitkens at their small exchange. After all, to visit the state's only film exchange and get information firsthand on what films to schedule to make more profit delighted the small-town theater businessmen.

Harry and Roy often took their clients to lunch at the world-famous Schlitz Palm Garden. It was located on North Third Street between Michigan and Grand, barely a block from the exchange office.

In this high-ceilinged palm garden, a squadron of black-mustached waiters hurried to square wooden tables with trays of big, foamy beer steins and ham or cheese on rye sandwiches.

The din of gemütlichkeit in the Palm Garden was usually deafening, as people drank beer and talked. In the background, a group of long-whiskered musicians played the melodious tunes of the day—"Kiss Me Again," "Wait 'til the Sun Shines Nellie," "Everybody Works but Father," "Where the River Shannon Flows," "Mary's a Grand Old Name," and many others. Those who ventured downtown in Milwaukee on business or shopping in the daytime or to the Davidson or Pabst theaters at night nearly always arranged to meet friends at the Schlitz Palm Garden. That's where the important and the not quite so important people came together.

Later duties for Roy in the film exchange centered on management responsibilities. He supervised the receiving, inspection, and shipping of films. As the films came back from theaters after first, second, and third runs, he checked them for damage and saw to it that they had been rewound. A cranking device was used to pass the film from one reel to another. Roy's job was to nip any rough edges with scissors and also to patch broken films with special cement made of banana oil and ether. The older the film, the drier it became from running through projectors. Since the film was celluloid, it would gradually dry out from the heat of the bright light in the machine shining on it each time it went through. This meant a short life for many films. Once inspected and repaired, the film was placed back in its metal container for reshipping.

A pressing problem emerged for the Aitkens of how to keep their stock of films circulating to theaters in order to acquire the revenue to pay expenses and to buy new films to improve their inventory. Roy came up with the solution. He trained a young man to inspect film and assigned a young woman to handle office work and help the trainee. He then went to his partners and told them that he was ready to go on the road again, "to rent out more films and sell projectors."

"Good," said Freuler, who came in now and then from his real estate office to check on operations at the exchange. "Get as much business as you can, Roy. We won't turn it down." He laughed heartily.

Harry agreed Roy should go out and sell, too. He had journeyed to De Pere, Wisconsin, because of a tip and helped a new theater owner get started. He had also sold him a projector and a regular film supply. However, Harry preferred administrative and promotional work and was glad to leave the outside selling to his younger brother.

Freuler could not help them with sales very much, because his real estate business and the Comique Theater on Kinnickinnic Avenue absorbed a great deal of his time. The theater proved quite profitable, and from it over the years Freuler financed the Atlas on North Third Street, the Whitehouse near downtown Milwaukee, and the romantic Butterfly Theater.

One day Freuler told Roy, "There's a man in La Crosse who wants to open a theater. Why not go to see him?"

Aitken packed his bag and arrived at the right time in La Crosse. "He wanted to open a theater all right and had rented a building, but he had not bought a projector as yet," said Roy, who sold him one on the spot and also ordered a supply of film for him.

The projector came within a few days direct from Chicago, and Roy helped the theater owner set it up in the projection booth, which a carpenter had already built to specifications. But when Aitken tried out the lens, the trouble began. There wasn't enough room in the projection booth to position the machine properly to get the right focus, so Roy had to order a different lens by telephone from Max Lewis.

With the show scheduled to open at seven o'clock the next evening and the ads already published in the newspapers, Roy began to get nervous. Sitting in the stuffy projection booth, he could do nothing but fuss since he could not show the film on hand with that lens. He estimated later that he lost five pounds until minutes before show time, when the manager came rushing from the railroad station express office. He crawled up the ladder to the projection booth out of breath.

"I've got it, Roy. I hope it works."

It did work, and a packed house of movie patrons was unaware of the crisis that might have postponed the show.

From La Crosse, Roy journeyed to Wausau where his cousin, Bert Hadfield, and a friend, Harry Hall, wanted to start a theater. They, too, were glad to see him, and Roy helped them launch their enterprise. Harry Hall, who spent his last years in a nursing home in Waukesha, developed a very efficient rheostat while operating the Wausau Theater in 1906. It was much better, the Aitkens thought, than the rough version they had used in their own Chicago nickelodeons.

As he lay dying, Hall loved to reminisce about the early days of the movies when Roy came to visit him at the nursing home. Inevitably, movie information one or the other had not heard before surfaced at these sessions.

Hall once told **Roy** that in an early-day theater where he worked, the only source of **heat cam**e from a big potbellied coal stove. On cold nights in winter, the air became extremely hot, stuffy, and odorous. To try to overcome the smell, the theater owner mounted electric fans ten to fifteen feet high along the walls. Ribbons saturated with perfume were attached to the fans and helped alleviate the odor.

Ray Hadfield, another cousin on Sarah Aitken's side, opened a movie theater in Duluth, Minnesota, a year after his brother Bert had started one in Wausau. Ray expanded and within six months opened a second theater in Superior, Wisconsin. Years later, upon hearing that Roy was gathering material on the Aitken's movie career, Ray Hadfield wrote at great length in a letter about his own experience. Said Hadfield:

> *The Great Train Robbery* was the first one-reeler that I can remember viewing. I was so thrilled I could hardly leave the theater at the end of the show. At that time, the film was the longest on one subject in the world—1, 000 feet! A picture machine sold for $135 and had no top or bottom film boxes. They were a terrible fire risk, as the film was very flammable.
>
> The performance would start and after the theater filled up, the operator would run the film to the end, and if he got the signal from down below he would call out, "That completes the performance. All those who have not seen the entire show may remain for the next!"
>
> A barker was considered a necessity in those days because the patrons were mostly workingmen who passed on the street, and our pitch was to the men. I used a barker in both my picture shows at Duluth and Superior for awhile but finally discovered it was better not to have one. This came about

because one of my barkers was taken sick one night, and while he was in the hospital, business picked up a great deal, for women and children started attending the theater. That lesson ended the male-pitch barkers for me, and I saved money.

A large phonograph was used by some theaters as the musical part of the entertainment and often was blaring out a gallop during a heartrending part of a picture. But since the price of a ticket was only five cents, who would dare kick? We raised the price of admission to ten cents a year or two after opening and never changed it during the life of the theaters. One theater, the Savoy in Superior, cleared $26,000 in twenty-six months during its heyday. That was big money in those days.

Another friend of Roy Aitken's, the late Tom Evans of Delafield, Wisconsin, related his boyhood experience as an avid movie fan. Evans lived in Wilkes-Barre, Pennsylvania, and as an eleven-year-old, he and his friends raced down to the theater after school. The first boy to reach the movie house was given the job of sweeping out the place. In return, he received a free ticket to see the show.

It was the code of honor with Evans's pals that whoever the lucky boy was, he was expected to sit near the exit door and open it to admit the other lads after the house lights were dimmed for the show. Many a penniless boy got to see the show in this manner. Sometimes, Evans said, an usher or the local constable would see the flashes of daylight as the side door opened and closed, and then the freeloaders would get caught and rushed back out of the theater. If the constable questioned the boy next to you and he was a special pal, your ticket stub covered him, because the cop never thought to see yours. According to Evans, the audience in the theater increased far beyond what the ticket receipts showed, especially on afternoons and nights when Keystone Kop pictures were shown.

Charles James, who traveled through the United States and England selling trailers for movie screens from 1910 to 1920, also shared anecdotes with Roy Aitken about experiences with early-day nickelodeons. Wrote James in a letter:

> We called the New York dream houses "Oderums" because they were poorly ventilated. No matter how gripping the picture, you were always aware that someone had been eating plenty of garlic, or onions, or both, and some had apparently skipped several bath nights.
>
> Patrons sometimes reached the snoring point, especially if the stuffy air put them to sleep after a hard day's work.
>
> Some of the theater owners equipped their places with a peephole or two in the front entrance partition, so the prospective customers could look through and sample the show. However, the scheme had its drawbacks now and then. A kid would sometimes stand at a peephole and look too long.

Thereupon the ticket taker would walk over and kick him in the pants and point to the box office.

Another slight defect in such joy-inspiring amusement houses in the early days was that they used wooden benches instead of individual seats. The benches served the purpose until a fat woman would walk in and sit down in the middle of the bench and squeeze kids off on both sides.

Sarah and Elvin Aitken and the rest of the family were glad to have Harry and Roy home every night. Usually the brothers arrived in Waukesha on the evening train and went back to Milwaukee at seven the following morning.

The Aitkens' Milwaukee film exchange grew so fast that within five months it was operating smoothly and profitably enough that Harry became restless. "Roy," he said one late November day in 1906 as the two brothers rode the train from Milwaukee to Waukesha, "do you think we could talk Freuler into agreeing to help us open a branch exchange, perhaps in St. Louis?"

Roy let out such a loud whistle that a banker from Nemahbin Lakes spun around in the woven straw seat ahead of them and shook his *Sentinel* newspaper in their faces.

"Do you think it would pay?" Roy asked in a dubious whisper.

"All of us can't continue to live on Western Film Exchange earnings all our lives," Harry pointed out. "We need to grow, to reach out. With two film exchanges, we could swap film from one city to another by fast express and make it earn more for us. Old film in Milwaukee might be new film to some of the theaters in St. Louis and the rest of Missouri."

Roy brightened. "We've got a friend in St. Louis, too," he said, "Allen Martin, who lent us money to come back to Waukesha from Texas."

"I know," replied Harry. "That's one reason I picked St. Louis. I think the people down there are friendly and nice to do business with."

A few weeks later, over a big lunch and foamy beer steins at the Schlitz Palm Garden, the Aitken brothers persuaded John Freuler to back their idea for the St. Louis exchange.

"I can see that you boys are restless," Freuler said. "You like to take chances, but I'm different. I take it slow. I think a long time before I do anything. But, since the Western Film Exchange is making money, I'll go along with you for six months. If it doesn't pay by that time, then we'll close it and pull in our belts and plan to stick to Milwaukee for a long, long time."

Harry and Roy were left with little to say. After all, not only was Freuler a partner in the exchange, but he was the only partner with some spare cash, in case the Aitkens needed it.

On the train back to Waukesha that evening, Harry chuckled as he returned to the subject. "Well, Roy, we've got six months. That's an awfully long time."

As soon as they could arrange to turn over the affairs of the Milwaukee exchange to Freuler's capable hands, the two brothers packed up and headed for St. Louis. They had little surplus cash after buying their railroad tickets, but Freuler had promised to send them a stipulated amount every week after they had established an office in the new territory.

7

Midwest Expansion
Energizes the Aitkens

While the St. Louis area was new to the Aitkens, it came as no surprise to them that a film exchange was already operating in the city. A man named Bill Swanson owned it. He was reputed to be an aggressive businessman.

"We'll battle him for business," Harry said determinedly. "After all, he can't supply all the theaters, and he can give first runs to only one theater in the downtown area. Otherwise, he'll run into trouble. We'll try to service a few of the other downtown theaters."

No matter how anxious they were to tackle the competition, Harry and Roy's first task was to look for a suitable office. They wanted to be near the central business district as well as convenient to the railroad station where most of their films would arrive. They found two suitable rooms with a steel vault in the Century Building on North Seventh Street and discovered that the superintendent of the building had some surplus desks and chairs. The office equipment was included in the modest monthly rent, which pleased the brothers.

Now they were ready to notify Freuler to ship old and new film, as well as rewinding equipment and inspection blocks. The next step was to visit a quick-service printer and get cards and stationery printed with their St. Louis address. They kept the name Western Film Exchange, the same as the Milwaukee office.

"Let's go to dinner at that fine restaurant down the street," Harry said. "We should celebrate the expansion of the Aitken brothers into the film exchange business in St. Louis."

From the glint in Harry's eyes, Roy knew his brother looked forward to building this film exchange and would not shrink from any battles to secure business. He also realized that once the St. Louis film exchange prospered—and somehow he sensed that it would—Harry would have other ideas to develop. That was the way he was. He was the planner, the risk taker, while Roy was the more cautious brother. This made them an excellent team, for they seemed to subscribe to the idea that if partners always agreed, one of them wasn't necessary.

Both were pleased, however, that their St. Louis exchange had a suitable steel vault in which to store films. In fact, a steel storage vault was on its way to becoming a requirement for all film exchanges. Police and fire commissioners had discovered the danger of handling flammable celluloid film, as a hazard was always present when those who inspected or projected film would smoke during the procedures. Fire department heads also grumbled if films were allowed to remain on the floor of offices following inspection. Therefore, many states passed laws requiring exchanges to store films in steel vaults at night.

The danger of fire from film is almost nonexistent today, since the industry uses nonflammable film. But Roy points out that even modern exchanges will not tolerate the presence of old nitrate-type film (even precious collector's items) in their buildings. Practically no theater built after 1950 would exhibit a nitrate film no matter how rare.

With hindsight, Roy expressed amazement at the laxity of fire commissioners in American cities in the early days of the industry concerning flammable film. "It took those chiefs a long time to enforce better film safety measures," he said.

Three years after Harry and Roy set up their film exchange in St. Louis, two young girls fast approaching adolescence had joined their mother in East St. Louis. Lillian and Dorothy Gish had been performing on stage since age five, and Lillian, the oldest by only a year, had begun to grow out of the children's parts she played. To support her destined-to-be-famous daughters, Mary Gish had saved enough money from her own stage career to open an ice cream parlor next to a nickelodeon in East St. Louis. One afternoon when business at the sweet shop was slack, the Gish sisters made their way into the world of fantasy where a D. W. Griffith picture called *Lena and the Geese* was being shown on the white sheet that served as a screen. The lead peasant girl's saucer eyes, engaging smile, and long, blond tresses caught the Gishes' attention. It was Gladys Smith (publicly known as Mary Pickford), a friend from New York, acting in the flickers!

This was the high point during the Gish family's sojourn in East St. Louis. Later Lillian fell ill with typhoid fever, the same malady that had stricken Harry Aitken in Texas. While she was convalescing under her mother's care, Lillian learned that the nickelodeon next to the ice cream parlor had burned to the ground, taking Mary Gish's little shop with it and leaving the family penniless.

The job of securing business for the St. Louis branch film exchange began as soon as the Aitken brothers received printed stationery and calling cards three days after their arrival. Proud of their printed credentials, Harry and Roy went to visit the owner of a presentable downtown theater. The man's main line of work was in optical supply, but he had invested his surplus cash in a theater. Like so many of his counterparts, he worked in his regular business by day and at night supervised the operation of the theater. "This was the true entrepreneurial spirit of the era," said Roy, who remembered the optical man as bald, round-faced, and very well dressed.

He inspected the Aitkens' calling card and looked the two well-dressed young men over just as critically. "Well," he said finally, "my competitor, a block south, is getting first-run film service from Swanson. I've had to get my first-run films wherever I can. And it's been tough. If you fellows can deliver regularly, I'll take one first-run film per week plus some older films at least for a while. When can you start?"

Harry was perfectly cool, as he always managed to be in exciting situations. "I'll wire our Milwaukee exchange first thing in the morning and see how soon we can deliver," he promised.

They agreed on a price of $65 to begin with. This would give the theater man one new film, and about five older films per week. The new film could be run only three days before it would have to be rerouted.

Jubilantly, Harry and Roy walked out of the theater.

With one contract for $65 per week film service under their belts, the two brothers tirelessly rode streetcars and visited every small and large theater in the St. Louis area. Many of the theaters were small nickelodeons, and they were entitled only to what could be termed older films.

A few of these nickelodeons were downright stuffy places, even for farm boys used to sitting down near a manure pile to milk the cows. The worst type of nickelodeon had only a front and back door for ventilation, and these were seldom open. Many of the workingmen came to the theater in their work clothes, and sometimes the air in the theater smelled worse than a barn in the heat of summer. Waiting to see the theater owner about a film program, Harry and Roy would now and then take a seat and watch the show. The air almost made Roy sick on several occasions.

"Let's get out of here," he would suggest to Harry.

But ever patient Harry would urge his younger brother to stick it out until they saw the owner. In fact, Roy said to one nickelodeon owner, "Why don't you air out your theater a little?" The owner smiled and replied. "The customers like it this way."

Roy never ceased to marvel at the contrast between those stuffy early-day theaters and the big, comfortable, air-conditioned theaters that came along later.

By working twelve-hour days, Harry and Roy soon had the St. Louis film exchange up to $250 a week income, which was a hefty sum of money in the early 1900s for anyone, much less two men under thirty. In the following months, income rose steadily. Within a relatively short time, they serviced sixty to seventy theaters weekly and got an average of $35 to $45 per week from each for film service.

However, theater owners kept crying, "Give us more new film! More new film!" Thus, the Aitkens always had a supply problem. Producers were cranking out new films as fast as they could, but still the demand exceeded the supply. Many of the films had poorly developed stories, the photography was foggy, and the acting was amateurish, but the theatergoing public didn't appear to mind. They were still fascinated with any kind of moving pictures on a screen.

To shorten the gap between available new film in the system versus that under production, the Aitkens hit upon a workable scheme. Downtown Milwaukee theaters got a first run on a new picture for two nights. After the last showing, the Aitken film exchange operator in Milwaukee packed the film and rushed it to the express company for placement on a train to Chicago. One more transfer in Chicago to a train bound for St. Louis, and by the following afternoon the film arrived there.

Harry or Roy would meet the train and rush the film by streetcar or by foot to a theater that had contracted for a first-run picture. Several days later, they'd rent the same film to a theater on the outskirts of St. Louis for the second run of two days and then maybe to another suburban theater for the third run. After this, they'd reverse the procedure and rush the film back to Milwaukee for second and third runs in theaters there.

The new films cost the Aitkens about ten cents per foot for a 740- to 1,000-foot film. By renting one several times each week, they practically recovered the entire cost of one new film in a week.

Both the Milwaukee and St. Louis exchanges were in a position where each could buy outright a print or two of a new film each week, instead of renting them from producers as they had formerly done. The Milwaukee exchange usually bought new films of different titles than those purchased in St. Louis. Thus, by exchanging films, an impressive stock of new films gradually developed between the two exchanges, and this setup placed the Aitken brothers in a very competitive position.

"I think we are one of the few film exchanges in the nation that has more than one regional office," Harry told Roy one day. "I wonder if that means something for the future?"

Roy didn't know what he meant at that time, but less than a year later, Harry again demonstrated his ability to plan ahead.

Harry and Roy took turns visiting the theaters in the St. Louis area to solicit new business and to keep the owners happy. Both of them discovered that personal contacts helped increase business friendships, which made it so much more difficult for competitors to keep pace or lure customers away from the Aitkens.

The time-consuming delivery by streetcar was the major drawback in the system. One morning Roy suggested an alternative.

"Wouldn't it be more profitable in the long run if we purchased a secondhand electric car to use in getting around to theaters?"

Harry feigned surprise. Then he smiled. "Roy, that's a pretty good idea. Let's have a look."

They shopped around for days and finally settled on a natty, black electric car in good condition. It sold for $300. After the brothers finished their theater calls at night, a garage man took the car to a station where he charged the batteries and made the car ready to roll the next morning. They enjoyed driving around St. Louis and felt rich—which, of course, they were not.

"A few months ago when we came to St. Louis to open an office, we didn't have one account buying film," Roy opined as Harry and he drove to a neighborhood theater. "Now we service over sixty theaters in this area and can afford to buy an electric car."

For a moment, Harry said nothing and then, "Wish we had stayed in Milwaukee?"

"No. You were right—it was time for us to expand. You saw it, and I didn't."

For two former farm boys, driving the noiseless vehicle over brick or wooden block roads and streets in greater St. Louis not only enabled them to service more customers but also garnered them a great deal of prestige as well. Owning an electric car in those days, even a used one, automatically brought with it a certain social status, and in the movie business, one needed all the upward mobility available.

As the weather got colder, Harry and Roy moved to the Buckingham, one of the better St. Louis hotels. They considered the move in keeping with the rising importance and prosperity of the St. Louis film exchange. They often took theater clients to dinner at the fine restaurant in the hotel.

Another step in their rise was to buy matching black hats and long black overcoats with fur collars. Both young men were quite tall and made a rather striking appearance as they stepped out of the car to call on theater owners.

One theater owner in the outskirts begged the Aitkens to come often and park the electric car in front of his theater. "It's good for business," he said. "It'll help us get the carriage trade."

There is little doubt their electric car and stylish clothes gave the impression that they were more prosperous than their competitors. The Aitken brothers fostered this image, convinced that their business grew still more rapidly because more theater owners turned to them for film programming.

Occasionally, Roy would take trips into other Missouri cities and towns, trying to sell projectors, rent films, and help new theater owners with programming. In St. Louis, the brothers rented film to Frank Newman, who owned one of the better theaters. He also operated a theater in Joplin to which the Aitkens furnished films. Newman gave them many leads on new theaters opening in Missouri, and Harry and Roy called on the managers to sell them film programs before their competitors arrived on the scene. Newman became a close friend. He had keen business judgment, fine promotional ideas, and a sense of humor. The brothers settled into a routine with their new business and new friends.

Nevertheless, this streak of good fortune broke on August 3, 1908, when Elvin Aitken died. The boys' father had always provided for them and their sisters and counseled Harry and Roy on their business affairs. Elvin, sixty-one at his death, wore himself out with hard work. Like his own father, he bequeathed a legacy of caring-through-example to his children. After thirty-four years of marriage, Elvin left behind a fifty-eight-year-old grieving widow and five grown children.

He was so well-liked in his community that every living creature in Goerke's Corners, with the exception of woodchucks, seemed to mourn his passing. Neighbors told Harry and Roy that animals grazing in their pastures, especially the horses, seemed to hang their heads a little lower than usual the day Elvin died. No wonder, for of all the farmers in Goerke's Corners, Elvin had taken it upon himself to declare war on woodchucks. He relentlessly tracked these pesky creatures to any woodchuck hole that could break the leg of a horse. At the funeral and thereafter, each of the Aitken children recalled a favorite story about their father's "incompatibility" with woodchucks.

"My father, Elvin Aitken, was a kindly, law abiding citizen, but he certainly disliked woodchucks," wrote Roy in a historical monograph called "War on Woodchucks" in *Landmark*, the quarterly publication of the Waukesha County Historical Society, Waukesha, Wisconsin. "When I was following behind Father on a binder or hay mower, I was startled many times by the sudden call, 'Whoa!' Then Father would be off the machine with a wrench in his hand and after the illusive woodchuck" (vol. 10, no. 4/67, p. 6).

Roy's younger sister Gladys recalled a similar experience while accompanying her mother and father to Lake Mills in a buggy one day. As they were driving along, all of sudden Elvin let out a "Whoa" and handed

Sarah the reins. Gladys didn't know what was happening until she spotted a woodchuck up the road crossing on the other side. Meantime, Elvin looked for a stick or something with which to destroy the animal, but by the time he found a weapon and crawled through the fence, the woodchuck was on its way to its burrow. "Father got there just as it disappeared . . . but too late to give him a whack," said Gladys, not the least bit displeased that no harm had befallen the little critter (*Landmark*, vol. 10, no. 4/67, p. 7). Nonetheless, she reported that her father climbed back into the buggy with a satisfied expression, certain that he had done his duty.

After the services, Roy toured the old homestead. He thought about how his father had bought those wonderful white bicycles home to his two young sons and later engineered the move that brought all of the Aitkens from the farm to a cozy home in Waukesha and the world that lay beyond. But most of all Roy remembered Elvin's wise, honest counsel. From here on, Harry and Roy, thirty and twenty-six, respectively, would have to depend on their own judgment. And judging character was to be one of their greatest challenges in the years following their father's death. Without his guidance, they would have to be extra cautious, for there were plenty of woodchuck holes for them to stumble into along the way.

Twenty-one years earlier, at the age of ten, David Wark Griffith buried his own father in the cemetery near Crestwood, Kentucky. But only after the great director acquired fame and fortune as "the man who invented Hollywood" (in partnership with the Aitken brothers) did he have the means to honor his own father "appropriately." D.W. had Colonel Jacob Wark Griffith's entire Civil War military record carved on the family tomb. Not only would D. W. Griffith use his movies to tell of his perceived injustices in the world, but also he would go to extraordinary lengths to get his viewpoint across.

8

Trustbusters: The Aitkens Produce a Movie

In late 1908, Frank Newman came to the Aitken-owned St. Louis exchange office with a proposition. "I'd like to open a new and better theater in St. Joseph," he said. "If you and your friends will put up $2,500 each, I can complete my financing. I'm so certain of success that I can safely say I'll be able to return your investment and begin to pay dividends within three months."

This was just the type of diversion the brothers needed to get over the loss of their father. Harry began to put the deal together. Investors included T. H. Cochrane, an Aitken friend from Portage, Wisconsin; John Freuler, their partner in Milwaukee; and Harry and Roy. They felt confident in Newman because of his track record as a theater operator.

The assessment proved correct. As predicted by Newman, the new theater began paying dividends almost immediately under his management. Later, Newman built an even more exquisite theater in Kansas City, Missouri, and the Aitken brothers invested in that one as well. So did Freuler and Cochrane.

Newman's theater in Kansas City became the talk of the country. Soon movie operators from many parts of the nation came to view it. Newman was extremely careful in his selection of films and would battle anyone to rent what he wanted. Arguments between the brothers and their new theater partner on what constituted good film programming erupted daily, and Newman often won out.

As a result of the growth of their St. Louis exchange, the Aitken brothers gradually accumulated a large stock of older film. They now owned most of the inventory that had circulated to Wisconsin, Illinois, and Missouri theaters. Although some of the film had deteriorated and had to be scrapped, much of it was still good enough for exhibition. Harry's Scotch-English thrift asserted itself.

"We ought to move that old stock. Perhaps this is the time to open a film exchange in Joplin. I talked with Newman yesterday, and he thought it was a good idea."

Roy stopped the rewind device he used to repair film. "Is that wise, Harry? Why don't we keep operating the St. Louis operation as is until we build a sizable cash reserve? After all, we've been scratching for money ever since we opened the nickelodeons in Chicago. Right now, when we're starting to live better, you want to try to start another exchange. That'll take financing."

Harry paced back and forth as Roy resumed checking film. "The industry is expanding, Roy. If we don't expand, too, we'll be left behind."

"Well," Roy conceded, "you'll have to ask Freuler. He still owns thirty-three and a third percent of our two exchanges. And he's tough to sell."

But Harry did sell Freuler, by letter, and so the brothers went to Joplin to open their third film exchange. Newman did not conceal his delight at the prospect that his Joplin area theater would get exclusive service from the new exchange operation.

Roy had been working long hours, and it was taking its toll on his delicate nervous system, so at Harry's suggestion he took a week's vacation. He journeyed to Biloxi, Mississippi, where he knew friends who had helped him get over his last case of nervousness. While there, Roy went to a dentist Sarah Aitken had recommended on their previous visit some years before.

In the flow of conversation, the dentist inquired about the young man's mother, then asked what type of business had brought Roy to Biloxi. Roy related his hectic work in the film exchange. Then, in an exuberant moment he told the dentist how difficult it had been to get their business on a profitable basis in St. Louis in the first few months but that only a few days ago he had received his first dividend check, $25. He quickly added that previously, of course, he had been getting a regular salary.

The next day Roy returned for a little additional dental work. Upon leaving, he asked how much he owed. The dentist smiled a big toothy grin. "The same amount as that dividend check you told me about—$25," he said.

According to Roy, that painful episode taught him to be cautious about quoting wages or dividends to people from whom he would thereafter seek services.

For their Joplin exchange, the Aitkens hired a manager they considered especially talented to market older film. His name was Jim Carter, and he made friends very easily. Carter's interest in show business veered far afield from the movies. He won his fame as a parachute jumper at state fairs throughout the Southwest.

Carter reminded Roy of Abe Lincoln. He was tall with dark features and a broad smile that filled his entire face below a prominent nose. As Harry and Roy expected, Carter built the Joplin business more on the basis of his reputation as a daredevil than he did on quality of film offered. It took some doing and ingenuity to distribute older film and to hold many accounts with such poor products.

Roy especially enjoyed visiting with Carter, because the colorful manager always had a hair-raising story up his sleeve. Conversation usually got started by Carter asking, "Know any good tales, Roy?" and then when Aitken shook his head, the man launched into a story of his own.

"Which is probably what he wanted to do in the first place," Roy admitted, "but was just being polite to give me the first chance."

Carter chewed tobacco, and this habit made his yarn not exactly a thing of beauty. As his story became more dramatic, he'd get up from his chair and walk back and forth, screwing up his mouth as he talked. But despite this, a fair amount of juice would trickle out of his mouth and dribble onto his jutting chin. When he could hold it no longer, he opened the door to a small room in which a spittoon stood. Finally, he let go with a stream, and only then could he laugh. And his "haw, haws" usually rattled the windows at the exchange.

In Carter's time, balloons and parachutes were prime attractions at state fairs, and crowds gathered to watch ascents. The daredevil used heat from a fire to inflate his balloon, and when it was properly inflated, the balloon was ready to rise. Carter had a number of employees who he pressed into service to hold the balloon ropes to keep it from rising or getting loose while he attached the carriage and parachute.

By the time the balloon ascent was ready, the crowd swelled to witness the event. Carter in his carriage would yell, "Let 'er go!" The rope handlers dropped their lines, and then the balloon lifted, rising with considerable speed to a height of several hundred feet.

"There he goes!" the excited crowd would shout. Many had never seen a balloon ascent, and no movies had been made of the phenomenon.

When the time came for the descent, Carter would open the valve to release the air in the balloon, and then he would parachute to the ground while the crowd gasped. Like the movies, Carter promoted through handbills distributed after his performance; it was all so new and exciting to them.

Meantime, a more pressing problem regarding the inspection and repair of films descended on the Aitken brothers' Milwaukee, St. Louis, and Joplin exchanges. To minimize damage to the celluloid films, the brothers constantly had to train and oversee operations at all three locations to ensure that staff properly handled merchandise that was the exchanges' lifeblood. By far the worst offenders were the theater owners and projectionists whose careless handling of the film in the booth and later while repackaging it into metal containers often caused a great deal of damage.

Film broke when going through a projector or in rewinding it from one reel to another. The projectionists usually rewound the film immediately following the show, and if a break occurred, they tried to repair it on the spot. Too often to suit Roy, the projectionist used a pin to splice the film together. Or he would wet his fingers with spit and paste the edge of the film to hold it together until it got back to the exchange to be properly cemented.

The emulsion on the part of the film carrying the photographic image easily scraped off if dampened. Then cement, often made from ether and banana oil, had to be applied to the dampened film. The next step was to press down on the cemented film to make adhesion firmer.

"If only projectionists would be more careful," Harry wailed when he saw damaged film returning, "then our films would last months longer."

The Aitkens cited this high casualty rate on films as one reason they insisted that exchange personnel get as many runs as possible on a new film each week. Such practice enabled exchanges to get their film cost money back, plus a profit large enough to pay expenses and have a little money left over to split among the partners.

In instances where a film jumped a sprocket going through the projector because of a poor patch or careless projecting, the sharp points of the sprocket made indentations and sometimes holes in the film. These cast weird images on the screen.

The moviemaking trio of Lasky, Goldwyn, and De Mille ran into a sprocket problem of their own just before the release of *The Squaw Man*, touted as the first feature-length film produced in Hollywood. The 1914 six-reel movie had the sprocket holes along the side of the film punched by a British-made machine at the rate of sixty-five holes per foot. De Mille, who had hand-punched the sprockets himself on nonperforated positive stock, and the others failed to realize that American equipment placed film sprockets at a rate of sixty-four holes per foot, one hole less per foot than its British machine counterpart. Since each hole was off the mark by a few microns, the only way to repair it was to paste a strip of film over the edge of the negative and perforate it to American standards. Still sprocket holes showed up like giant beetles on the white sheet used as a screen. But the audience was fascinated, as were two buyers who rushed up to Goldwyn to acquire the rights to run *The Squaw Man* in their theaters. Louis B. Mayer and Adolph Zukor knew it was only a matter of time before the feature-length film would replace the one- and two-reelers that had been a Hollywood staple for years.

As film exchange owners, the Aitkens had to walk a tightrope when it came to damage to their rented product. On one hand, there was the need to keep customers on a regular film-renting schedule; on the other, they had tactfully to try to get theater owners to pay for undue film damage. Occasionally theater men lied and excused themselves from all blame, maintaining that the film was bad when they received it. But a few honest owners paid the Aitkens for legitimate claims.

Now and then, several feet of film would be missing from a returned film. This would cause a tremendous jump in continuity of the story and make the patrons blink in confusion. Such missing scenes in early movies may have added to surrealism in an art form still in its infancy.

Oil from the projector getting on the film was another problem inherent to film exchange operations. The oil would have to be wiped off completely; otherwise it would cast an unwanted shadow on the screen and make the photography appear worse than it actually was.

Early projectors were simply constructed and barely capable of withstanding the steady grind of duty given them in a nickelodeon or a theater when shows ran twelve hours almost continuously. Each machine was equipped with small springs, and unless cleaned frequently, a crust would form and scratch the edges of the film. Sometimes the scratch would split the film.

Billed as "Thomas A. Edison's Latest Marvel," the Vitascope was actually the first projector. It made its public debut at the Koster and Bial Music Hall west of Broadway in New York in April 1896, showing moving scenes of dancers and a surging wave that delighted an audience of sophisticated New Yorkers. The projector had been developed by Thomas Armat and a man named Jenkins, but Armat turned it over to Edison for manufacture because the latter's name was better known. It took a backseat, however, to Edison's interest in the Kinetoscope, a coin-operated, hand-cranked machine that played about fifty feet of film. To accompany the playing of Edison's gramophone, William K. L. Dickson of the Edison laboratory developed a machine that combined sound and pictures, possibly as early as 1889, but the idea was shelved in favor of the more profitable Kinetoscope.

From 1896 to 1900, middle-class audiences saw silent films that supplemented live stage productions in vaudeville houses, but they tired of movement for movement's sake after a while. Hearing the gramophone and peering into Kinetoscopes in noisy penny arcades, however, thrilled workers and immigrants, and soon many of these arcades were turned into picture theaters to increase the size and turnover of audiences and thus reap more profits. Illiterate folk could find escape from bleak lives by watching moving pictures in backroom theaters at an affordable price.

In Chicago, George K. Spoor and G. M. Anderson formed the Essanay Company, which filmed chase scenes, incorporating elements of the Wild

West show. Anderson gained popularity as "Bronco Billy," and another Chicago native, William Selig, hired Tom Mix, who also became a screen idol. Edwin S. Porter's film *The Great Train Robbery* set the pattern for hundreds of other films to follow, and the nickelodeon boom was on. The Aitken brothers and many others answered this silent siren song.

One day at lunch in a St. Louis hotel, the Aitkens met a man named J. C. Graham, an accountant for a lumber firm. Fascinated by the brothers' movie talk, Graham asked Harry and Roy whether he could drop by the exchange someday and see how they operated. He arrived a few days later, and Roy explained operating procedure to him. Graham was so impressed that two weeks after his visit he called Harry and asked for a job in the exchange.

Graham was so intent in going into the movie business that he did not seem to mind when Harry told him they could not pay him what he received at the lumber company. The Aitkens were as delighted as Graham was to add him to the staff. Roy described him as "a quiet fellow with a keen mind." A week after he joined the Aitkens, Graham took Roy aside. "Come, sit down with me," he said. He then fired off a number of questions. "How long will that Springfield, Missouri, film stay there? Where does it go then? To Joplin? I think we could improve our routing of these films, so that we'll save time and the films will work faster for us."

On the spot, Graham worked out an efficient routing system that enabled the Aitkens to get their many films from town to town more smoothly. They shared the new routing system with their partner in Milwaukee. John Freuler implemented it immediately.

J. C. Graham proved very valuable to the Aitken organization. He and his wife became close friends of the Aitkens, and Harry and Roy spent many an enjoyable evening with the Grahams at the theater and other social events.

The business in St. Louis was expanding so rapidly at the time that the brothers hired another young man, Frank Meyer. He proved to be a nephew of an early movie mogul the Aitkens had hardly heard of as yet— Adolph Zukor. Meyer became an asset to the Aitken brothers and remained in their employ for several years before joining the growing Zukor organization that later became Paramount Studios.

Born in Ricse, Hungary, in 1873, Adolph Zukor was one of a half million Jews who fled from Eastern Europe between 1880 and 1910. Although Sam Goldfish (Goldwyn) had met Zukor for the first time after the showing of *The Squaw Man* in 1914, Zukor was an early role model for Goldfish, who stood in awe of the man known as the greatest advocate of feature films.

Roy Aitken was only six years old when Zukor came to America in 1888, where he got a job on the Lower East Side of New York City as an apprentice to a furrier. He later moved to Chicago and established his own fur shop.

With a great deal of money in his pocket, Zukor returned to New York in 1900 looking for investments. He first bought a partnership in a penny arcade in Manhattan. Soon he was operating nickelodeons in Newark, Boston, and Philadelphia. In 1903, Zukor and a fellow furrier named Marcus Loew separately purchased a string of penny arcades with facilities for projecting motion pictures. From these seeds would grow a chain of theaters extending from Atlanta to Boston and from New Orleans up through the Midwest to Hamilton, Ontario. By the beginning of the next decade, Zukor and Loew would be locked in a struggle for supremacy not only in the exhibition of motion pictures but also in their production. But Zukor had an early start, and his empire became enormous after he realized that the public would grow tired of one- to two-reel comedies and cry for something more substantial. He gave it to them in the form of motion pictures specially adapted from stage plays. Soon the audience clamored for these classics.

Of course, to feed this machine, Zukor needed well-known actors and directors. He had the finances. His movie production companies, including Paramount and the Famous Players–Lasky Corporation, were built on attracting Broadway leading ladies, opera stars, and international actors from the legitimate stage. (The latter company had Goldfish as chairman of the board until he was ousted by Zukor and Lasky.) No star performer or director was out of reach for Zukor, and he would later sign four who had been key members of the Aitken constellation: Mary Pickford (aka Gladys Smith), Douglas Fairbanks, David Wark Griffith, and Mack Sennett.

As film exchanges began springing up all over the nation like dandelions in green pastures, the two brothers from Waukesha soon had to combat another evil: price cutting. Most exchanges wanted to get as much volume as they could, even if their percentage of profit was minuscule in some instances.

Harry Aitken saw price cutting as a threat to the financial stability of film exchanges and decided to fight it. By this time, the Aitkens had bought out their major competitor in St. Louis, the Swanson–Crawford Film Exchange, and now they had four exchanges in operation, one in Wisconsin and three in Missouri. So many exchanges in their portfolio made them the second largest buyer and renter of film in the United States at the time. Only Carl Laemmle had more exchanges. Thus, the Aitkens had a great deal to lose if the price-cutting trend continued.

Thus, Harry took an extensive midwestern trip, visiting many film exchanges and also the Chicago movie producers to try to reach an agreement with them for group action that would eliminate or control price cutting. After conferring with many of his associates, Harry originated a plan that gained approval almost immediately. Under the guidelines worked out, each film exchange submitted weekly lists of their customers and prices being paid for films and services. They were also required to share with other exchanges in the system a list of new customers and those who had been dropped.

The agreement specified that no exchange operator could take another operator's theater customers at a lower price on film sales and rentals than that already being paid. However, an exchange owner could take orders for a higher price than was currently being paid by the theater owner to an exchange operator. Specific cases of controversy were to be handled weekly by three Chicago film producers acting as arbitrators: William Selig of Selig Polyscope Company; George Spoor, who with G. E. Anderson (Bronco Billy) made up Essanay Company; and George Kleine of the Kleine Optical Company.

The new agreement, a testimonial to the organizational ability of thirty-one-year-old Harry Aitken, worked so well that in a short time eastern movie producers soon copied it. In the powerful eastern group were Biograph, Vitagraph, Kalem, Lubin, Edison, Pathé, and Mêliês Companies. In 1908, they formed the Motion Picture Patents Company, also known as "the Trust."

The American Mutoscope (off-color pictures) and Biograph Company, under the trademark of a spreading eagle, was the Trust's most powerful yet struggling member. Operating from an old brownstone house at 11 East Fourteenth Street in New York, Biograph (as it was renamed in 1909) produced a number of poor-quality pictures despite having master cameraman Billy Bitzer on its payroll. The problem was twofold: not enough innovative directors and qualified actors and too many independent film companies that copied anything Biograph and the other major producers did as long as it had public appeal.

To solve the first problem, Biograph promoted one of its $5-a-day actors and a part-time playwright to director. It was in the latter capacity that D. W. Griffith later met Lillian and Dorothy Gish and their mother, who had come to Biograph to look up their friend, Gladys Smith. On the movie set, Gladys was Mary Pickford. The natural beauty of the Gish sisters captivated everyone on the set, including Mary, who urged them to follow her lead and talk to Griffith about getting into motion pictures. She made the introductions, and Griffith recorded the scene in the notes for his autobiography:

> One day in the early summer of 1909, I was going through the dingy old hall of the Biograph Studio when suddenly all the gloom seemed to disappear. The change was caused by the presence of two young girls sitting side by side on a hall bench. They were blonde and fair and sitting affectionately

close together. Certainly I had never seen a prettier picture. . . . They were Lillian and Dorothy Gish. Of the two, Lillian shone with an exquisitely fragile, ethereal beauty. Only recently Alexander Woolcott commented in print on Lillian's [stage performance as] Camille. "But in the death bed scene there was around Miss Gish a strange mystic light that was not made by any electrician." And when I first saw her sitting there in that dingy old hall, there seemed around her a luminous glow that did not come from the skylight.

As for Dorothy, she was lovely, too, but in another manner: pert, saucy, the old mischief popping right out of her. Yet she had a certain tender charm. (82–83)

Within a span of four short years, Biograph, now relocated in Hollywood, turned out the best movies in America. And D. W. Griffith, with his eye for star talent and innovation, was on his way to becoming the best director in the business, as was cameraman Billy Bitzer in his field. Biograph's management had solved the quality problem. Now along with their allies in the Trust, they turned their focus to the independents, setting them on a collision course with young Harry Aitken and his plan.

Early in 1909, the Motion Picture Patents Company created a furor in the film exchange field by licensing all studios and theaters using its products. These products included cameras, projection machines, and raw film. The license charge to a theater for using these products was set at $2 per week.

Unlicensed theaters faced formidable opposition from Trust spies who smashed projectors and destroyed film. Finally, many independent movie producers on the East Coast followed William Selig to Los Angeles, where Mexico was close enough to save his cameras, escape darkroom raids, and avoid subpoenas. Moreover, California's climate and variable landscape were very amenable to moviemaking.

This stranglehold on the industry looked formidable and advantageous to the eastern group of producers who still were not satisfied. The Trust then decided to take over all the film exchanges with which it did business and in this manner make a profit on distribution as well as on filmmaking. To accomplish the coups, Trust (Patents Company producer's) stock was offered on a one-for-one trade for film exchange stock. Outwardly, the deal appeared profitable to exchange owners. However, it stripped them of their independence, which Harry and many other exchange owners were quick to see.

Through this bold maneuver, the Trust did take over many film exchanges that were then organized into a distribution corporation called the General Film Company. Of course, Biograph and other members of the Trust controlled General Film Company.

Harry and his colleagues knew that unless these tactics were thwarted, it spelled the end of independent film exchanges. Aitken's Scotch-English blood stirred again, and he called a meeting of independent film exchanges to convene in Indianapolis to discuss the situation. Roy was so worried about the looming battle between the independents and the Trust that his old nervousness returned. But Harry seemed outwardly calm.

"This is the time to fight, Roy," he said. "If we don't, many undecided film exchange owners may sign with General Film Company. Maybe we can put a little starch into some of them, so they'll fight harder."

Persuaded by Harry Aitken, the independents signed a mutual agreement pledging them to protect one another from a possible loss of a right to buy film, now that they had decided not to sell out to General Film. This was a courageous and far-reaching decision for the independents to take, and Roy observed that much of the credit certainly must go to his brother.

Through this action, the independents had now signaled that they did not intend to be swallowed by a giant film trust and would fight for a profitable, independent existence. Anticipating that General Film might decide to cut them off from that company's film service, Harry pushed through a resolution that his group would seek products from independent producers such as Kleine, Spoor, and others.

"Harry worked hard on this resolution," a film exchange man confided to Roy months later. "He convinced us that if we wanted to stay in business, we'd have to enact it. And we did. In addition, all we independent owners got to know one another better."

The motion picture trade journals published long articles on the Indianapolis meeting of film exchange owners, and many predicted that Harry Aitken from Wisconsin would be heard from again in motion picture organizational affairs. Others dismissed the prophecy, but Harry had barely begun to make his mark.

Later in 1909, he and Roy challenged General Film Company again, this time on the conglomerate's doorstep in Atlantic City where a distributor's convention was under way. The Aitkens met many of the exchange owners who had backed Harry's Indianapolis resolution, and the ever engaging Carroll College graduate formed cells on the convention floor to strengthen friendships and talk over trade matters.

"Now we're beginning to know what the industry at large thinks about General Film Company restrictions and the future needs of the motion picture business," Harry told Roy. "It's amazing what ideas fly around when men like these exchange fellows get together."

Not one to rest on past accomplishments, Harry engaged his brother in a follow-up conversation back at the St. Louis exchange after all their employees had gone home. With the western sun pouring through the dust-smeared windows and falling across Harry's shoulders like a mystic mantle, Roy's nervousness subsided a bit as his older brother reminisced about their nickelodeon days in Chicago.

"Roy," Harry said suddenly, "I hear that Carl Laemmle is going to become a producer now. He's making a film called *Hiawatha*, a one-reeler."

"I wish him luck," Roy said somewhat sarcastically, thinking about the former Oshkosh clothes merchant who refused to buy an insurance policy from him and his blind mentor.

Harry frowned. "I wish him luck as well, but what about us? It's time for us to get into movie production, too. We don't have to be left behind. Biograph, Vitagraph, Pathé, Essanay, and Selig have four to six years' start on us. Now Laemmle."

"But production!" Roy protested, the nervousness rising again. "We know nothing about it. Let's stick to our film exchanges, at least for a while yet."

Harry shook his head. "We can't wait. I've thought of a subject, the James Brothers. True, they were robbers, but their exploits thrilled a continent. Let's make a one-reeler and call it the *James Brothers of Missouri*. I think I can round up a competent cameraman and a few actors, and we'll make the picture right here in the hills of Missouri."

Roy knew that his brother's enthusiasm for the project was running so high that it became contagious. Soon afterward, both of them had visions of the *James* picture achieving considerable success in the Midwest and perhaps throughout the country.

A man with stage experience was hired as a director as well as some local men with horses. The ensemble with Harry at the lead journeyed into the hilly Missouri countryside and went to work. They had to rehearse the one-reel picture several times and hire a woman to represent a wife whose husband had been shot by the James brothers in a robbery.

When they screened the film in their St. Louis film exchange office, all members of the production team thought it was quite good, just as parents exclaim over the characteristics of their first and only child and fail to see any blemishes. But, of course, they may have been a bit blinded by their stake in the film.

Proof would come after a showing to the public. Using their combined persuasive skills, Harry and Roy induced a local theater owner to advertise and schedule the *James* picture. The reaction of the theater owner and public was not unlike the victims in the movie. They felt robbed, this time by men masking as movie producers. Naturally, Harry and Roy were disappointed, and to add to the problem, the younger Aitken brother reported another bout of nervous stomach spells.

Roy cataloged the situations leading to his symptoms and decided that the routine of office work, the fighting with theater owners over film programs, Harry's battles with the Trust, and now the movie failure had combined to make him as nervous as a cat on a telegrapher's key. He badly needed a vacation, and as always Harry read his brother's distress signals.

"Why don't you take a print of the *James Brothers* picture and go to Denver for a week?" Harry suggested to his brother. "See Ed Grant. He has rented film from us, and perhaps he'll show the picture at the Elite. The change will do you good."

The Aitkens had dinner together before Roy left by train. Roy took the opportunity to tell his older brother how he felt about the pace he kept. "I've got to get out of that film exchange office. I'm not made for haggling over films, prices, and delivery dates. It wrecks me."

Harry nodded. "I understand. Well, we can turn that work over entirely to J. C. Graham and Frank Meyer. Neither of those fellows shed any tears over customers. They're more coldhearted than you are. They'll do their best to give customers a fine program based on the films we have available, and that'll be it."

On arrival in Denver, Roy got a hearty welcome from Ed Grant, a pudgy, jovial type who agreed to show the *James Brothers* film in his theater that very evening. Roy sat with him in a rear seat and before the reel ended, Grant got up and went into his office.

With foreboding Roy went to see him after the show. "Roy," Grant said, "you and Harry made a mistake. The film has a weak story line, and the photography is terrible. If the film weren't about famous outlaws, I'd never have agreed to show it."

Young Aitken thanked him for his candor and walked dejectedly back to his hotel. He moped around the city for several days until he could get some of his optimism back. Somewhat rested, he returned to St. Louis to find more trouble brewing.

A grim-faced Graham greeted Roy at the door of the exchange. "We're in the General Film Company doghouse. Harry got a letter from them. They heard about our making the *James Brothers* film, and they didn't like such procedure. In fact, they threatened to cut off our supply of film.

"If they do that," Graham continued, "where'll we get film for our four exchanges? There aren't enough independent producers, and they have an inferior product."

Too young, too confident, and perhaps too brash, the Aitkens stood firm and refused General Film Company's ultimatum to cease making pictures on their own. A few days after hearing this, the Trust retaliated.

Frank Meyer, J. C. Graham, and a new stenographer, Edna Thomas, thought the brothers from Wisconsin had lost their minds bucking such a formidable foe. Harry and Roy admitted to their staff that they had not expected General Film to act so quickly. "We thought the cutoff order might come within a month or so, not within a few days," said Roy.

"Well," said Graham, "I repeat, where'll we get film now? We serve three hundred theaters in four states." He looked down at his shoes.

Harry inhaled and let his words roll out slowly with his breath. "Each of our exchanges has been buying one or two new films for the past year and a half. That supply, along with our older films, will carry our exchanges for a while, perhaps two months. In the meantime, Roy and I'll scout around for some new sources of supply."

That task was easier said than done, thought Roy, unaware that Lady Luck was about to intervene. That same evening at the Buckingham Arms, Harry was discussing the critical situation with a man named P. C. Crawford, a vaudeville theater owner the Aitkens had met earlier while operating nickelodeons in Chicago.

Crawford asked, "Why don't you men try to get some films from England and the Continent? There're quite a few movie producers over there, you know. Maybe you can pry them loose from a regular schedule and [they'll] let you in."

Crawford added that he had a brother, Chester, living in England who operated a number of roller skating rinks, and they were prospering. The English had taken to skating like they had the movies, and Crawford was shrewd enough to capitalize on each craze. He was advertising heavily and trying every likely promotion to fan attendance.

"I'll write you a letter of introduction to Chester in case you want to go over," Crawford volunteered. "Maybe he could help you get in somewhere, you know."

Later, when Crawford had gone to his room, Harry said, "What this means, Roy, despite the *James Brothers* flop, is that we definitely have to plan to get into the production of movies. We can't continue to rely on others for a supply of good films."

Roy shook his head in protest. "Just when our exchanges were doing so well, we had to go and make that damn *James* picture."

Harry smiled at the uncharacteristic outburst from his sibling. "Perhaps that flop was just what we needed to force us into another expansion while there's still time, Roy. I'm going to New York to scout around and maybe drum up a film supply or two. If not, we'll go to England. Our film exchanges are in good hands, so don't worry too much about them."

Roy had an old feeling creep into his heart. He was certain Harry would no longer be content to remain in St. Louis and head a growing film exchange venture. Some inner urge had already called him into a larger field—movie production.

In his mind, Roy tallied Harry's previous sales promotion efforts: organizing a family trip to Biloxi, selling life insurance, establishing a string of nickelodeons in Chicago, promoting land deals, organizing four film exchanges, hammering out a trade agreement with other exchange owners, and producing a film on the *James Brothers*. All but the land promotion and *James Brothers* movie proved successful. Roy took this into account as he determined his own course heading. Little did he know at the time that these were all preparations for developments on a far larger and grandeur scale than either Aitken had ever anticipated. New York, London, and an obscure tract of mostly undeveloped land called Hollywood lay on the horizon.

No matter where these ventures led him, Roy knew that he wanted to be at Harry's side, as always. He hoped Harry would invite him to go along. But after his outburst he could not be sure, and this matter caused further worry. Perhaps Harry had really decided to go it alone this time.

9

Off to London to Build an International Market

Since the Denver trip did little to calm him, Roy decided to take a week's vacation at home. Before leaving St. Louis, he traded the electric car for a new Mitchell automobile that he had arranged to take delivery of at the Mitchell factory in Kenosha, Wisconsin, only forty miles southeast of Waukesha.

Sarah Aitken never seemed at ease with her sons' gypsy lifestyle, going to faraway places in the course of conducting a business for which she cared little. She did like to have them home, of course, and since her husband's death, Harry and Roy had helped fill a gap of loneliness that only a widow could know. When Roy told her about their troubles with the eastern film conglomerate, she offered him the kind of advice his father Elvin had imparted to Harry so often.

"You should not have talked so rough with the General Film Company, Roy," she said anxiously. "Everything was going so well for you."

"I know," he said. "But Harry had other ideas. We have to look forward now, not back."

To forget his movie troubles for a while, Roy left for Kenosha to pick up his new Mitchell car. He wasted no time in getting behind the wheel of the shining five-passenger beauty and headed back to Waukesha. About ten miles out of Kenosha, he heard a strange sound in the transmission, and then the car stopped, luckily within walking distance of a garage.

The garage man shook his head. "Nineteen ten's been a bad year for the Mitchell," he said, adding that transmission problems had caused the vehicles to stop for no reason whatever. "But if you crawl under the car and tap the crank case at just the right spot, the car will be ready for continued driving for a while," the mechanic explained. He then slid under the chassis and pointed to where Roy should administer the gentle blow if needed. The repairman tapped the crankcase with his wrench a few times, and sure enough, the car started again.

Since he was in a hurry to get home, Roy passed up the opportunity to drive back to the factory and instead drove on to Waukesha. However, he resolved to take the car back to the Mitchell people at the first opportunity and demand that they correct the transmission trouble.

But with memories flooding his mind of Charles Welch, the boyhood companion who had taught him to drive over these same roads, he piled Sarah and his sisters into the big new car and cruised around the county basking in the admiration of friends and neighbors. The trip to the Mitchell factory could wait until the fun was over, he decided.

The next day, the transmission balked again; luckily the car was still parked in the yard at the Hartwell Avenue house. So, Roy crawled under the Mitchell to tap the crankcase. He had just gotten into position when his sister Mabel rushed over to him. "There's a telegram for you from Harry in New York," she said excitedly. "He wants you to come to the Algonquin Hotel as soon as you can."

"Oh, my," Sarah sighed, as her youngest son entered the house to wash the grease from his hands, "you boys are always chasing somewhere. What will become of you? London, oh, it's so far away."

"Harry leads, and I follow," Roy said gaily. "London ought to be fun, Mother."

That night Roy could not sleep. The crisp autumn air, the moonlit sky and the lonesome wail of the Soo Line drove him outside to the porch. In a neighbor's yard, a dog barked as if the lantern light from the moon was an intruder that turned the grass near his pen from green to silvery flecks of white. Roy looked up and decided then and there that the Wisconsin sky held more glittering stars than anywhere he had been. He took a deep breath and made a similar observation about the quality of air. Hours spent handling volatile film in the small confines of a vault or in the smelly environs of a nickelodeon were forgotten in that moment. Erased, too, were the erratic images associated with his movie work like the spots in front of his eyes put there by damaged film, faulty projectors, or naughty boys hurling BB shot at the screen. In their place in his mind came the natural lights in the sky and the autumn air that had a way of putting a man in his proper perspective in the universe. Roy wondered whether London had anything to match.

Harry was at the Algonquin in New York when Roy arrived. "We're due to sail Friday," he said, "and we've got to have passports and birth certificates by then."

They wired Walter Frame, a Waukesha banker and second cousin, and he hurried to the county courthouse and obtained certification that they were born in the area. Frame's welcome letter reached the steamship ticket office a half-day before their scheduled departure.

Harry and Roy had little pocket money to make the London trip despite their active film exchanges in Milwaukee, St. Louis, and Joplin. They had kept their own salaries low to plow as much of their surplus funds as possible back into the business. Besides operational costs, the money was used to buy a larger stock of new films.

"Freuler agreed to lend us $400 from the Milwaukee exchange profits," Harry confessed to his brother. "The General Film Company cutoff has him sweating for new film, too."

Roy's misgivings about going into debt dissipated in the excitement onboard the *Mauritania* as the passenger vessel sailed from New York. Only once before had he been east to New York, and that was on a side trip following the film distributors convention in nearby Atlantic City during the battles with the Trust. Aware that he was very green in terms of the modern world, he nonetheless intended to keep his social mistakes to a minimum.

"London seems so far away," Roy said while they walked the deck of the big ship as it glided past the Statue of Liberty. "I never dreamed we would ever go there."

"I'm excited, too," Harry confided, "but in a different way, Roy. I feel that profitable business opportunities await us."

The Aitken brothers had a limited wardrobe for the voyage. So they paid particular attention to what the other male passengers were wearing. Fortunately, they found themselves seated at a table with two seasoned travelers from Canada who knew all about shipboard customs. These men shared their knowledge and took Harry and Roy under their tutelage, explaining everything from crossing protocol to conduct on arrival in London—in brief, what might be expected of two unsophisticated American visitors.

Neither brother owned a dinner coat, but each had packed full-dress evening clothes that they had worn in St. Louis at various social functions. This was on the advice of the booking agent who had told them that on the first night aboard ship, one did not dress formally since that was deferred to the second evening. So, on that night at sea, with great care, they donned their full-dress suits, tails and white ties included. Roy noticed immediately upon entering the salon that their two Canadian friends wore dinner jackets with black ties. When the Aitkens sat down to eat, the other patrons scrutinized them from ties to tails, but being gentlemen their dinner partners expressed no concern.

However, as the group moved to the lounge area for coffee, Roy remarked that he and Harry seemed to be the only men wearing evening clothes. This prompted the Canadians to tell them that full dress was dispensed with except at a formal party aboard ship.

"If you don't have dinner coats with you, it isn't necessary to dress so elaborately for dinner. Just wear business suits," one of them advised.

Harry and Roy never forgot the incident and the genteel way the Canadians handled the matter.

In London, the Aitkens stayed at an inexpensive hotel and spent the first day sightseeing. With them they carried two important letters. One was to a film exporter named Frank Brosius. The other was addressed to Chester Crawford and had been written to him by his brother, P.C., the vaudeville theater operator in the United States who had first suggested that the Aitkens try their luck in England.

Brosius proved to be a rather gruff, stocky fellow who eyed the Aitkens as close as the Canadians had on the evening of their faux pas, except the Englishman was cold and aloof until Harry handed him the letter from a film supplier in the United States. "Yes, I can get a limited amount of film for you here, at a price," Brosius stated bluntly. "Most production is pretty well committed, you know."

Back at the hotel Harry suggested an alternative. "While here, Roy, let's survey the European market before we get tied up with Brosius at a high price. Perhaps we can get a greater variety of film and at better prices by inquiring."

So off they went to Paris, Brussels, Berlin, and Copenhagen. At the studios in those countries, they discovered a few people could speak halting English and understand their request for film. Most of them denied, however, that they had any uncommitted film to sell. The brothers suspected that the long-arm of the General Film Company, New York, had reached into these cities securing agreements to use the Trust's products exclusively, although a few smaller independent producers did come forward and offered to sell film to the Aitkens. But when screened, only a few of the films proved fair, while the majority of them were cloudy and unattractive. The Aitkens bought several of the films deemed worthy for showing and agreed to contact their suppliers for more on an as-needed basis.

"Well," said Harry on the bus back to London, "the price wasn't too high. Perhaps we can save money by this arrangement."

Yet, both of them knew that the small amount of film they could secure in Europe would be insufficient to satisfy their film exchange managers back home. They needed more and of better quality. Fast!

"Let's visit Chester Crawford tomorrow," suggested Harry. "P.C. said his brother is quite a promoter. Perhaps we can learn something from him. Besides, I'll want to tell P.C. we saw Chester as he recommended."

En route to Chester Crawford's office, Harry and Roy discussed the matter further. They decided that no matter the outcome of the meeting, Roy should remain in London indefinitely and continue to buy foreign films. Harry expressed apprehension that if the brothers had no personal contact with foreign film producers, even the small independents would sell elsewhere.

Just as P.C. had described him, Chester Crawford was a heavyset man of medium height with black hair slicked back the way the Aitkens had worn their blond tresses the night of the Pink Ball. He was a fashionable dresser, however, and he had a hearty laugh that filled the room.

"P.C. wrote me you were coming over," Crawford chuckled. "I'll take you to lunch, and then you can tell me all about this fascinating movie business in the States. You're way ahead of England in promoting pictures, I hear."

Chester Crawford listened with rapture as Harry and Roy explained the film business and the glamour attached to it. At one point the transplanted American laughed heartily and jumped to his feet. He asked whether they were aware that few American movies were being shown in London. Then before they could answer, he cited the reason. There were no American exchanges in the British Isles to distribute film. "Whatever films we get from America come here direct, and that takes a long time," Crawford complained, although he kept smiling.

His next statement demonstrated that he was also a visionary. "Why don't you chaps open one of those film exchanges over here?" Crawford asked. "If you can't get enough new film—it's short, you say—then bring over some of those older American films you say are on your shelves. Englishmen haven't seen them, and you could rent those until the new film supply gets better."

"Well, said Harry, "that's an idea, all right."

"Fine," grinned Chester, followed by one of his patented laughs. "Need some capital to start such a business?"

Harry nodded. "That's easy," continued Chester. "I'd like to get in on this fascinating venture. This roller skating business may taper off any day now, and I wouldn't mind getting a new business going."

So, at Chester's good-natured urging, the Aitkens agreed to start a three-way partnership, with Crawford putting up most of the money. Harry and Roy soon discovered that their new associate wanted to do things in a big way, for he was a showman just like his brother in the United States. His London skating rinks were widely advertised with weekly prizes for the best skaters.

"Let's rent some elegant offices," Chester said confidently, "in a good section of London. Something real spiffy. Let's put a glamorous front on a glamorous business," he added in between laughs.

Harry and Roy said nothing. Chester was furnishing the immediate capital, and they did not mention that they had originally planned an unpretentious office in London suitable for buying and shipping foreign films to the United States. Chester's proposition changed all that. Now they would operate from an actual film exchange that could not only sell and rent films to exhibitors but also buy them for their own use in the United States.

The next day, Harry delegated Roy to accompany Chester in the search for a new office. Crawford found the place he had in mind on famous Shaftesbury Avenue, just a few doors off Piccadilly Circus.

"It's nice to be financed," Harry told Roy that night. "But try to hold Chester down when you get to operating the exchange. This film business is a long pull, and he had better know it, especially when new film is hard to get."

After two weeks, Harry decided to go back to New York and left Roy in charge of the London operation. He promised to instruct Freuler to send Roy the best of the older films stockpiled in the Milwaukee, St. Louis, and Joplin exchanges.

Meanwhile, improvements in the London quarters progressed as carpenters created counters and shelves and installed a metal vault for film storage. Crawford insisted on a showy reception room in which he placed purchased, not rented, furniture. New lamps and chairs graced the corners, and Roy admitted the office was glamorous but not so pretentious that it would put visitors ill at ease.

Even before the office was officially opened, curious English theater owners came to see the American film exchange. They were accustomed to getting their film direct from the producers or from a few nondescript English exchanges. It was a novelty for them to see what the Yanks were doing and to ponder the fact that they could soon show many American films on their screens.

A week prior to the opening in late 1910, Roy carefully inventoried and checked the films received from Freuler. He was very disappointed in the poor condition of most of them, and those he could not mend or cement were placed in storage.

When he told Crawford about the poor films, the entrepreneur replied, "Well, some of them must be all right, Roy, especially those you checked."

"But I can't guarantee how long they'll last," Roy insisted. "Some could crack again at any time."

However, Crawford pushed to open the exchange and rent film as scheduled. He had advertised quite extensively in English newspapers and some Scottish ones also and thought their best opportunity for getting theater owners interested in the American products lay with first-day sales. Roy swallowed his misgivings and went along with the plan, hoping that those who rented the film would at least get some box-office value from them.

As it turned out, both men were right. Crawford's promotions lured many theater owners to the office on Shaftesbury Avenue, where they selected older American film by title to rent.

However, within a few days, many of the theater owners came back with the film. Their faces were glum. As Roy had feared, the film had cracked and broken in many places because it was so brittle.

"We can't rent any more of this film," he told Crawford. "When the rest of the film comes back, let's store it."

"But then we won't have any film to rent except a couple of new films you got from France this week!" Crawford protested.

Roy nodded vigorously. "That's it. We'd better close," he said. "Without enough film, we'll lose money every day."

So they closed the film exchange, and Crawford wrote off his investment. Later that same year, the ever affable Chester Crawford shut down his roller skating rinks, citing poor attendance. Roy heard that Chester had returned to the United States, where he joined his brother P.C. in the operation of vaudeville theaters.

Despite this setback, Harry and Roy decided that the Aitkens should stay in business in England and try to establish a film exchange on a scaled-down, less expensive basis. They were not going to give up so easily just because one shipment of film was unusable. Besides, they still needed an office to handle the European films they were buying for distribution by their exchanges in the United States.

Roy set out again to explore the British capital, this time with limited finances to rent a suitable office. He found a place on Rupert Court near Shaftesbury Avenue. The two rooms had space for only a few small chairs, plus a counter, a projection machine, and a vault, all of which Roy rented. The office rented for one pound per week, so this left him enough to pay an office girl a pound per week and a young male operator slightly more.

As they had done in Chicago, Milwaukee, St. Louis, and Joplin, the Aitkens worked on a name for the new operation. Since Harry was still in America, they finally decided by mail on the Western Import Company, Ltd. Roy, in particular, liked the rhythmic roll of the words as he read them from their classy yet inexpensive stationery during a briefing for his two employees.

"I want you to treat all customers very courteously," he said. "We won't be able to supply them with all the film they need, because the new American films will be slow in coming. We want those film patrons to come back to Western Import, so you'll have to talk persuasively to get them to give us a second chance."

Harry returned to London before Christmas, and he and Roy spent New Year's at a pleasant resort at Brighton, where they relaxed like Englishmen on holiday. They met some wonderful British subjects who treated the Americans like family. But then Harry got down to business.

"Laemmle and I may get together in a few months and form a nationwide distributing company," Harry said with more enthusiasm than Roy had seen him express throughout their vacation. "As independents, together we own more exchanges than any others, except the General Film Company. While Carl and I don't see eye to eye on many points, this new distributing company may help us both. Besides, this merger gives us access to some of Imp's production of movies."

"We could use them," Roy said, caught up in the enthusiasm. "Then we could win more theater owners as regular patrons."

From a career standpoint, Carl Laemmle, the former Oshkosh clothier and founder of the Independent Motion Picture Company (IMP, forerunner of Universal), had more in common with the Protestant Aitken brothers than he did with his fellow Jews who had fled Europe before the turn of the eighteenth century. Born in Bavaria on January 17, 1867, and ten years older than Harry Aitken, Laemmle, like other German immigrants, settled in parts of Wisconsin where the lakes and forests reminded him of home. From manager in a shop in Oshkosh, he expanded to his own clothing retail business in Chicago. It was there that, like the two men from his adopted home state, Laemmle entered the world of nickelodeons as an exhibitor. By 1906, Laemmle established a film exchange; the same year the Aitkens opened their Milwaukee operation. Then, in 1909, to feed his growing exchange system and thwart the Trust's intention to drive independents from the field, Laemmle, like Harry Aitken, decided to produce films himself under the IMP label.

At various times, throughout his long career, Laemmle was described as a tightwad who often lapsed into boorish behavior. But everyone agreed he was shrewd.

At the time he was battling the Trust and setting up his own motion picture producing company, Laemmle borrowed a formula D. W. Griffith had used to get Biograph moving up the ladder: start with great stories, add great personalities, and keep them stirred with great direction. To accomplish the middle part of the axiom, Laemmle lured actress Florence Lawrence away from Biograph in the spring of 1910. Known as the "Biograph Girl," Lawrence was the forerunner to Mary Pickford and the Gish sisters. Laemmle put out a false press statement suggesting that Florence Lawrence had "died" (later clarified to mean "as the Biograph Girl") only to have her reborn as the new "Imp Girl."

Out of this experience, Laemmle inadvertently ushered in the star system that Adolph Zukor and Harry Aitken later devised into an art form. With audiences flocking to see the resurrected Miss Lawrence, the studios became inundated with "who letters" in which fans requested information about their favorites and what movies they were going to appear in. On the heels of this publicity bonanza, Laemmle again raided Biograph and this time walked away with Mary Pickford and her director-husband Owen Moore. Laemmle knew that with the increased publicity, he would have to pay the actors more, but it was worth it if the public came to see their chosen stars.

"Little Mary is an Imp now," Laemmle boasted in an ad.

Of course, none of this set well with the Trust in its fight against the independents Harry Aitken and Carl Laemmle. The star system forced the conglomerates that made up the Trust to follow suit by naming and publicizing their key players as well, thereby increasing salaries.

In a NANA article by Joe Franklin, which appeared in the *Milwaukee Journal Green Sheet*, November 20, 1961, dateline Hollywood, California, he says the fight between the Trust and the independents increased in intensity between 1909 and 1912:

> Since the Trust controlled the basic patents on both camera and projection equipment, they had the law on their side—and did not hesitate to use it to harass the opposition. But they did not stop there. "Goon squads" were sent out to smash the cameras, and not infrequently the heads of the independents. Prudence, if not self-preservation called for a strategic retreat from the New York area. . . .
>
> That same year (1912), Adolph Zukor, with a nickelodeon on New York's Union square, defied the Trust by importing from France an elaborate, four reel version of "Queen Elizabeth"—with no less a star than the great Sarah Bernhardt. Not only that, he ran it in a legitimate theater on Broadway, at the then extraordinary price of $1 a ticket. Its success prompted Zukor to scour the American stage for stars and properties. "Famous Players in Famous Plays," he called his new film company.
>
> Stage plays and stage stars, often stiff and theatrical, do not necessarily make the best movies; but these and the similar pictures that now began to come from Biograph, Edison and Vitagraph (Trust members), as well as from abroad, performed an important function. They broke down upper class prejudices against the movies. If Sarah Bernhardt, James O'Neill and Mme. Rejane—all reigning stars of the day—were appearing in pictures, then pictures couldn't be all bad. (1, 4)

From his English employees at the Western Import Company, Ltd., Roy learned how to relax over tea and muffins every afternoon at three o'clock. He found the custom soothing to his delicate nervous system and often invited exchange customers to join him and the staff for tea. The

English always seemed warmer after a brisk cup of tea, just as their American cousins did when drinking coffee together, Roy observed. In each case, it was the right ambience for selling or renting film. Sixty-four years later, Roy said he often thought of that tiny London film office in 1911 and the delightful daily tea break with customers and friends.

Though there was money for tea and cakes, the office ran on a tight budget. Roy received $80 per month from Freuler for operational expenses and a weekly check of $25 for his salary, which was to be increased after the film exchange got on a paying basis. Freuler wrote often requesting that Roy ship him new film produced in Europe. But Roy had very little to send him. Much of this film shortage lay at the feet of the European nations that were anticipating a war. Celluloid and high explosives shared the same chemical base, and there was little disagreement that TNT was to become more important than movies until after World War I, when Europe had already fallen behind America's motion picture industry.

After several months, Roy managed to save part of his salary until he had enough to make a trip to the Continent. "Jim," he said to the young man in the office, "I'll be gone for a week or so to try to get additional business. I know you'll take care of things here."

Roy visited Paris, Brussels, Copenhagen, and Berlin, where he saw many of the movie producers he and Harry had called on several months earlier, and they recognized the tall twenty-eight-year-old American who liked British tea. This time he was successful in getting them to part with a few films for his exchange. Some of the smaller producers even invited him to dine with them.

When he told the European entrepreneurs about the Aitken movie exchange operations in the United States, their interest peaked, and Roy was left with the distinct impression that they thought he represented a stable company that might be a prospect for future sales on a much larger scale. Roy spent nearly two weeks buying film and securing promises that more would come on a regular basis. The stock of film he accumulated still wasn't enough to meet all the needs of their American exchanges, but it would help a great deal.

Elated, he went back to London. The success of this trip gave him an idea for future expansion. He would discuss with Harry the profitability of establishing small exchange offices in Berlin, Copenhagen, and other spots to buy European film and also to sell American-made motion pictures. Such offices, he reasoned, would have to be managed by Germans, Frenchmen, or Danes.

More good news was waiting for Roy at his London exchange office. Harry had written that Laemmle and he had formed the Motion Picture Distributing and Sales Company. It was a merger of the exchanges

Harry and Roy controlled and those that Laemmle owned. "Not an outright sale but just a marketing arrangement" was the way Harry characterized the deal.

He added, "We'll also get some IMP motion pictures for distribution in Europe and the United States. This should ease our London film situation. We'll be respectable competition in America for the General Film Company [The Trust]. Last week I purchased the New York Film Exchange from New York Motion Picture Corporation and can now look around and try to formulate plans for establishment of a motion picture producing company of our own. It's time the Aitkens got into that, too."

Roy blinked nervously as he finished Harry's letter. He realized that another big step now lay ahead of them, and Harry thought they were ready to take it, the full-time production of motion pictures. Young Aitken poured a cup of tea and ate a muffin to steady his nerves.

10

The Battle for Mary Pickford

By mid-March 1911, the London film exchange office managed by Roy Aitken had improved a great deal. Not only were the Aitkens getting more new films from Europe to send to the United States, but they were receiving shipments of old and new films, including the IMP brand, from the States.

"I'm going back to New York for a short time," Roy advised his young English assistant. "You're doing very well, and I'm certain you can handle things in my absence. We're now assured of a pretty good flow of films from America and from the Continent. I'll do my best to get more American films on my visit."

At about the time Roy prepared to depart England, London citizens were planning one of their many festivals to commemorate their love–hate relationship with the Tower of London complex. This one dealt with the four hundredth anniversary of the burning of a small chapel in 1512 (located a few gardens beyond the Wardrobe Tower) known as St. Peters. Rebuilt and renamed St. Peter ad Vincula, the chapel was the backdrop for a number of notorious murders and executions. The first of many such atrocities to follow on the site claimed the life of Lord Hastings, who in 1483, enraged future King Richard III. Hastings was dragged out of the Tower to the lawn in front of St. Peter's, where he was beheaded with a poleax wielded by Richard's guards.

John Fisher, the Catholic bishop of Rochester, suffered the same fate as Hastings, only by headman's ax in 1554, as ordered by Henry VIII. Fisher was buried in the Chapel of St. Peter ad Vincula where many a royal victim and victims of royalty came to rest. The marble floors of the chapel are inlaid with the names of other English notables who met similar deaths and became the subject of early English and European stage productions and films.

It was the Aitken brothers' small film exchange in London that would wean the English motion picture public away from such bleak historical introspection. In 1914, Harry and Roy were the first to send a Charlie Chaplin (Keystone) film to England. They were also the first to startle staid British audiences with stirring western cowboy films. As a consequence, the Aitkens moved their London operations from a small side-street office to a three-story building on Wardow Street, closer to Piccadilly Circus. Staff size increased from two to thirty employees between 1916 and 1918, and they shipped movie film to Africa, Australia, Russia, Germany, Norway, Sweden, France, Italy, and other countries.

That spring in 1911, the twenty-eight-year-old film executive stood at the rail of the steamship as it passed Lady Liberty inbound. A jubilant expression made him look even younger. Since September 1910, Roy had been in England without Harry and had grown quite lonesome. But he also felt that he had to survey the city that served as America's business capital to renew contacts with film industry friends living in and around New York. This "touching base," as he called it, would prove helpful when he returned to the London office with the latest trends in movies in hand.

His brother Harry met him at the boat dock. "I'm staying at the Waldorf, Roy," he said. "I suggest we share a double room. We've got lots of things to talk about."

Harry and Roy liked the Waldorf because it attracted many theatrical people, bankers, and other important persons, and it was affordable. They paid $5 a day for a double occupancy in 1911. The two tall former farm boys would make nodding acquaintances with people they met daily in the lobby or dining room or on the elevators.

They took their meals together since it offered a relaxing atmosphere to discuss business. Roy used one such occasion to broach a nettlesome problem that had bothered him since Harry had outlined his expansion plans.

Roy swallowed hard, then asked, "Where are we getting all the capital to operate? When you were in London, you said both you and Freuler were strapped for funds."

Harry smiled. "The film exchanges are doing better now that we've some new films coming in steadily, but the money flow isn't enough for the kind of expansion we want."

"You mean production?" Roy asked skeptically.

"Yes, you and I have talked about that before. We now have five profitable film exchanges and the London office. But we're still dependent on others for our new film supply. If our exchange system grows as I expect, we'll be still more dependent. We need our own supply of films, Roy, and the sooner the better. Otherwise we'll be left behind in this competitive business."

"Forming a film production company requires a lot of money. Where'll we get it?"

Harry let loose a laugh that would have made Chester Crawford proud. "I've got a name picked out for the firm, Majestic Film Corporation. Whenever I meet influential people, I tell them about our prosperous exchanges and that our next step will be production of films."

Roy lifted his eyebrows and waited to hear the rest.

"When the time is ripe," Harry predicted, "I'll approach some of these people and ask them to buy stock in Majestic. In fact, some businessmen and doctors have already told me to let them know when we expect to start. They want to buy shares."

"You always had a liking for promotion," Roy said admiringly, "but it scares me sometimes."

While in New York, Roy kept a close eye on their film exchange operations and maintained contact with the London office through telegrams. But it was Harry who took trips to the Midwest to obtain firsthand information on their operations in Milwaukee, St. Louis, Joplin, and elsewhere. Each place Harry visited, he rolled out his plans for organizing Majestic Film Corporation in an unabashed attempt to enlist his contacts to sign on for a share "in the glorious future of the glamorous movie industry."

Harry never high-pressured anyone, but his enthusiasm and air of confidence combined to persuade many people to believe what he told them. He made one feel that what he was saying would happen. And unlike the hapless land promotion earlier, much of what Harry promised did occur.

After each presentation, a number of people walked up to him and said, "When you're ready to start Majestic, let me know. I'll buy some stock."

John Freuler, the Aitkens partner in the film exchanges, jumped on the Majestic bandwagon right away. The usually stolid German told Harry, "Let's get started. Our competitors are getting into movie production— Zukor, Goldfish, Mayer, Laemmle, and others. I wish you'd go talk to my friend Dr. Wilbert Shallenberger. He's at the Pfister Hotel this week, seeing clients. I had lunch with him the other day and told him about our film exchange business. He's very interested. Maybe he'll buy stock in Majestic. He makes good money fitting trusses. There are an awful lot of hernias around these days."

Harry was delighted to hear that Shallenberger was in Milwaukee. The physician, originally from Iowa, made a name for himself going from city to city in the Midwest, staying at the best hotels, from which he fitted scores of patients with trusses. There was a saying at the time that one could tell when the good doctor had paid a visit last, because the male population of the town seemed to walk a little more upright. In fact, some years earlier on a visit to Waukesha, Shallenberger had fitted Harry and Roy with trusses after they had developed hernias from the heavy farm-work at Goerke's Corners.

The doctor seemed pleased to greet his former patient, and he listened intently as Harry described the proposed movie production company. "It sounds like a profitable idea, Harry," the truss specialist said. "Count me in. I'll buy some shares. And I'll get my brother to buy some, too."

No other movie company was organized in such a manner by obtaining stock-buying promises from ordinary citizens (although Freuler and Shallenberger were the extraordinary exceptions). And that the solicitations for Majestic were carried out over such a wide part of the nation in advance of incorporation remains a remarkable feat. At Waukesha, Harry also visited Charles and William Welch, the Aitken brothers' schoolmates whose father owned the White Rock Springs Company. It was Charles Welch who taught Roy Aitken how to drive the Northern, so that he'd have someone to give him a break when there were girls to cuddle with on the way to Oconomowoc. Charles and his brother Bill now operated a prosperous Packard car agency in nearby Milwaukee.

"Put us down for some shares in Majestic," the Welch boys told Harry. "It sounds like a good investment."

When Harry returned to New York, Roy could see that his older brother was more confident than ever. "It's amazing how many of our friends want stock," Harry said. "They, too, believe the movie industry has a future, and they want to share in it."

In his travels around the film exchanges in New York, Roy also gave his version of the Majestic Film Corporation pitch to people he thought were interested. He and Harry agreed, too, that if they did start a production unit, they should obtain the best actors and directors possible. "People like Mary Pickford and David Wark Griffith," suggested Harry.

Roy laughed. "Mary is Laemmle's new Imp Girl, and Griffith is doing wonders at Biograph. They wouldn't leave."

"Well," Harry grinned, "when the time comes, it won't hurt to ask them. I understand Griffith isn't too happy with Biograph's refusal to let him make longer pictures. And Mary Pickford is said to be fussing about the quality of her pictures under the IMP label."

Evenings after dinner at the Waldorf, Harry and Roy would adjourn to the huge lobby area, which the guests nicknamed Peacock Alley, where a constant flow of well-dressed and interesting people, especially beautiful women, paraded by the gentlemen relaxing in big soft chairs. Seated next to the Aitkens one evening was a tall, fashionably dressed man who remarked, with an eye toward the girls, how stimulating it was to "bear witness to such pulchritude."

In the conversation that followed, the man introduced himself as Crawford Livingston, a Wall Street banker who like the Aitkens lived at the Waldorf. Politely he inquired what kind of business they were in, and Harry and Roy told him. Roy noticed that Livingston's ears perked up when Harry explained that they had plans for a movie production company in the works. The three chatted for another half hour before Livingston excused himself. But as he left, he asked the brothers to drop by his office at Kuhn, Loeb, and Company to continue their discussions on movie production.

The next day in the offices of Ficum, Lewis, and Seligsberg, the Aitkens legal counsel, Harry learned that Livingston was one of the wealthiest and most influential men on Wall Street.

"You're lucky to have met Livingston and to be invited to visit him in his offices," said Walter Seligsberg, who later became the Aitkens' personal lawyer.

Although eager to accept Livingston's gracious offer, Harry and Roy decided that a better strategy was to wait a few days lest they appear too opportunistic.

So, on the fourth day after the chance meeting, they presented themselves to the blond receptionist who ruled the large reception room outside Livingston's office. She greeted them coolly and asked whether they had an appointment. They admitted they did not but quickly added that Mr. Livingston himself had asked them to call on him at their convenience. She still had a distant, hesitating look in her eyes but accepted their cards and went off to check with her boss.

Within a few minutes, Livingston came out of his inner office and greeted the Aitkens as if they were old friends. "Come in," he said cheerfully, and Roy caught a glimpse of the expression on the receptionist's face that seemed to say, "Well, how in the world did you do it? He's such a busy man!"

Crawford Livingston listened attentively as Harry and Roy brought him up-to-date on their activities and plans for the future. They talked about their London exchange and Harry's success in selling Majestic stock throughout the Midwest. The visit lasted about a half hour, and after Livingston invited them back, he added, "I may buy some shares in Majestic myself."

This was the start of a very profitable relationship between the brothers and the first banker-investor who showed interest in their projects. Later, Livingston lent them money to finance some of their early films. He also brought Otto Kahn, another banker, to see them when they were supervising a production unit in New York. But Otto declined to get involved and instead offered a better lead. He said, "Oh, I'm too busy to investigate this movie field, but I have a younger brother Felix who is very interested in the arts. I'll speak to him about it."

Over the next several months, the Aitkens turned to Livingston and Felix, Otto Kahn's brother, who helped them considerably with loans and business management. The two financiers became directors of Majestic Film Corporation after 1911 and also served on the board of the Aitken-controlled national distribution company, Mutual Film Corporation, after 1912.

Nearly fifty years later as Roy looked back on this period, he said, "I can see how many capable and important men came into our personal and business lives through casual meetings at conventions, hotels, dinners, barber shops, and other public places."

A fter he had been in the States for three months in 1911, Roy decided to go back to London to check operations. "I've got some interesting new film to take with me," he told Harry, "but I may be back later in the summer, because I'm anxious to be in on the formation of Majestic."

Harry smiled. "It could be any time, Roy."

Back in London, young Aitken found film-marketing conditions much improved. The brothers' New York offices had been shipping London some IMP pictures and also some from a few other independent producers. Through the Motion Picture Distributing Company, owned by Carl Laemmle and Harry and Roy Aitken, the brothers were able to get more new pictures for American and European use. This bolstered their position in the market, notwithstanding the Trust's efforts to destroy them, and soon the Aitkens began to get film customers from not only Europe but Australia and New Zealand as well.

"We've had a lot of film men in from Europe and other countries while you were gone," the young assistant manager told Roy. "They love to sit around, drink tea, and eat muffins while we screen the latest pictures from America."

Roy realized then and there that they had outgrown their Rupert Court offices. Yet, he hesitated to incur more expenses by renting space in a larger building. He decided to defer action until he could determine whether the current flow of business would continue.

The court leading to the London exchange was only about ten feet wide and projected back from the street about thirty to forty feet. Other small business firms shared the ground floor, one being a barbershop. Roy went there daily because he could get a shave for four pence and a haircut for six pence (eleven cents American) and have enough to tip the barber a penny.

Operated by a German immigrant who had lived in England for many years, the barbershop also employed either young French or German assistants who had arrived only recently. They were, however, artists in their trade. Roy found one, Eric Gruber, so pleasant that he asked for him by name. Like the tea hour, the relaxed time spent in Gruber's chair did wonders for Roy's disposition and nervous condition. It always amused him to watch the other barbers rush through the shaving process, since they made little from tips and salary and instead received a bonus based on the number of customers they could service in a day.

In English barbershops, one did not stretch out and rest comfortably in beautiful chairs such as the practice in America. Roy had to sit upright while Eric spread lather across his face with fast-flying hands and very slow or little conversation.

"The shave was completed lickety-split. Then Gruber handed me a towel, and I was expected to wipe my own face, rubbing off any traces of soap," said Roy. "But Eric dared to take a little bit longer with me because I was an American. That meant, in his mind and the minds of others, that I represented success, money, and prosperity in the land of the free." To sustain the image, Roy tipped Eric Gruber two pence for his services and invited him to come into the exchange now and then to watch an American film. He did this with other people in the little shops in the court, and often they would pack into the little film exchange, four at a time, while Roy rolled the latest feature for them. Through this practice, he got to be well known as the "movie man" in the court area, where he made many friends.

In late August 1911, he received a letter from Harry. "I think the formation of Majestic is near at hand. If you have things in order over there, come back to New York."

This was the news for which Roy had been waiting. He booked passage and arrived in New York in a matter of days where Harry briefed him. In his travels to film exchange conventions, Harry had met Tom Cochrane, a slender, handsome executive working for Carl Laemmle's IMP Company. Cochrane controlled the movie contracts of Mary Pickford and her first husband Owen Moore and in turn had contracted with Laemmle for Pickford's services.

Cochrane, of course, had heard of the Aitkens and their daring innovations—establishing a London office and also welding the independent distributors together at the Indianapolis meeting, thus strengthening their opposition to the General Film Company and sticking a finger in the eye of the Trust.

During lunch one day, Harry informed Cochrane that the Aitkens soon expected to get into the production of motion pictures and that steps had already been taken in that direction. When Harry saw that Cochrane was interested, he asked bluntly, "How would you like to become a stockholder and a director in our new production unit—at a substantial salary, of course?"

Cochrane laughed and seemed surprised. "Oh, I couldn't do that without bringing Mary Pickford, her husband, and their cameraman with me. I'm handling their contracts."

This reply was what Harry had hoped for, and he had his own response ready without revealing the excitement he felt. "All right," he said casually, "how much would it take to hire you, Mary, her husband, and the cameraman?"

Cochrane suddenly became hesitant. "Give me time to think this over, Harry. Mary isn't quite satisfied with the type of pictures she's in at IMP. Laemmle is in Europe taking the baths now, and there are factors involved. It would be a big change for all of us."

When Roy checked in at the Waldorf, Harry had not heard from Cochrane relative to his decision. It shocked the younger Aitken that Harry was seriously trying to lure Mary away from Laemmle's IMP. "Why, that will wreck your partnership in the Motion Picture Distributing and Sales Company, won't it?" Roy asked. "Laemmle will be mighty peeved if you get Mary Pickford and Owen Moore."

"I don't think so, Roy. You see, Cochrane hinted that Laemmle knows Mary's dissatisfied at IMP. If Mary signs with us, Laemmle, as a partner in Motion Picture Distributing and Sales Company, will still get Mary's pictures for distribution."

"Well, that throws a different light on the problem," said Roy. "If Mary bolts, I suppose Laemmle would rather have her jump to the Aitkens than any other producer."

"If we can get Mary, Moore, and Cochrane in one fell swoop," Harry pointed out, "we'll have to launch a drive for additional film exchanges to distribute the big demand in Mary Pickford films I anticipate. And the production company that has its own film exchange organization will have the jump on those who distribute through General Film Company with its rigid policies."

"But we haven't even got Majestic organized," Roy exclaimed, feeling his stomach churn. "Aren't we putting the cart before the horse?"

"Not in this case," Harry replied. "If we get Mary, we can quickly organize Majestic. Everything is set."

"And if we don't get Mary?"

Harry shrugged. "If we don't get her, we'll get someone else with a name that attracts the public."

Such optimism was characteristic of Harry Aitken. He steadfastly believed that obstacles were put in his path to be overcome. This was the one marked difference between the two brothers. Roy was far less confident.

While Harry and Roy waited for Cochrane's reply, they spent the time wisely. They renewed contact with J. V. Ritchey, the Iowa native who had financed their first nickelodeons in Chicago in 1905. When they told him of their progress in forming a production company, Ritchey leaped at the chance to get onboard. "I'll take some stock in Majestic," he said. "What you boys are doing is right in line with what I have in mind. I'm planning to start a business making movie posters for theaters. It's an expanding field. Movies will need advertising with all this competition among producers."

"Good idea," said Harry. "We'll be glad to throw business your way when we start making pictures."

"I like to hear that we can all work together," Ritchey replied.

Shortly after this, Cochrane phoned Harry. "How about lunch tomorrow? I want to discuss a few matters with you," he said.

"Well," chuckled Harry as he hung up the phone, "he didn't say no."

At lunch, Cochrane advised Harry he had discussed the Aitken proposal with Pickford and her husband, Owen Moore. Both had reiterated their feelings toward IMP and saw no possibility of conditions improving there. Therefore, they would agree to a contract with Harry provided that Cochrane and their cameraman were included in the package. They promised that as an intact unit they could make better pictures than they had previously.

On the spot, Harry and Cochrane settled on salaries of $150 each per week for Pickford and Moore. Cochrane and the cameraman were paid slightly less.

Harry later told his brother that his heart was beating so fast during the signing ceremony later attended by all the signatories that he was fearful Pickford and Cochrane heard it thumping. "They're making the contract directly with me," Roy said, "and then I hope to sell it to Majestic when that company is organized."

"How about picture selection?" Roy asked. "Will you have any control over that?"

"I agreed to give Mary and Tom a free hand in what pictures they want to make," Harry confided. "I had to, in order to get them. After all, they've had much experience at Biograph and at IMP. Now, since they're their own bosses, so to speak, they'll have full rein to exercise their talents."

The next step for the Aitkens was to organize Majestic Film Corporation. Letters, telephone calls, and wires soon brought checks from stockholders who had promised to buy shares. Thus, on September 11, 1911, two years before U.S. film producers Cecil B. De Mille, Jesse Lasky, and Samuel Goldwyn selected Hollywood for making *The Squaw Man*, Majestic Film Corporation came into existence. As the parent for a string of film companies, Majestic owed its rapid organization to the woman with the golden tresses, Mary Pickford, now under the Aitken banner. Among the first officers of Majestic were Harry Aitken, Tom Cochrane, and Frank Meyer, nephew of Adolph Zukor. Within a week, the newly formed corporation bought from Harry the contract he had made with Pickford and her associates.

As soon as the Pickford-Cochrane contract was finalized, Harry called J. V. Ritchey and told him the good news. "We've got to get a studio now," Harry said. "Do you have any suggestions?"

"Yes, I've been looking for a headquarters for my movie poster business," Ritchey replied, "and I came across the old New York Transportation car barn on West Twenty-third Street near the Hudson River. It's for rent, and I figure it's a good place for me to start, but I'm not quite ready, so perhaps you could use half of it for a studio."

Ritchey and the senior Aitken went to look at the place. It was huge, lonely, and drafty and had a dumpy office at one end. Harry was dubious but arranged for Tom Cochrane to look at the car barn, too. "Well, it's not much to look at," complained Cochrane, "but neither is the studio we've been operating out of. So let's take it and get started."

Carpenters and painters were called in to renovate the office space, and within two days Mary Pickford and company stood in the abandoned car barn discussing her first picture to be made for the Aitkens. Luckily, Indian summer was in full swing at the time, so the car barn did derive some warmth from sunrays filtering in from the rafters during daylight hours. Pickford dressed warmly and would often come into the renovated office to sit with Roy in front of the round-bellied coal stove he tended there.

Roy sensed that Pickford was growing apprehensive about the wisdom of her change in contract after being subjected to such primitive conditions while making her first Aitken picture. But she did not complain at the outset. Perhaps she felt, as did her mentor Cochrane, that the Aitkens could be trusted to allow her group to make distinctive pictures, which is why they left Carl Laemmle. What's more, Roy realized that Moore and Pickford were still honeymooning and, like other grooms and brides, had learned to shut out the outside world.

Harry and Roy refused to go near the makeshift studio on the first day Pickford and company worked on a picture. They had promised freedom of opportunity and were determined to stick to that policy. But this did not mean the brothers took the contract-signing coups lightly. "Just think, Harry!" Roy exclaimed one day as they sat in their New York Film Exchange office. "At last the Aitkens are in the movie production business!"

"Yes, but we have a long way to go to catch up with some of the others," Harry pointed out, and Roy noticed that for once Harry was the cautious one.

Pickford, Moore, and their cameraman made slow progress. After all, Moore was not an experienced director. Before long, the winds of late fall began to blow and the old car barn admitted them all; drafty or bone chilling, it made no difference. Pickford asked the Aitken brothers for a different studio, a warmer one, but they failed to locate a suitable place immediately. The temperamental star also fussed about the poor lighting, which, as she knew, was under control of Mother Nature. Roy noted that the cameraman did not complain about either the lighting or the weather. Nonetheless, they had to do something.

A few weeks passed with Pickford getting unhappier by the moment before the Aitkens hit upon a solution to the climate control problem. They decided to send the star and her entourage to make pictures for them at the studios of the newly organized North American Film Company in Chicago, the firm founded by John Freuler, their Milwaukee exchange partner, and his friend, Samuel Hutchinson. Freuler had also sold stock in the Chicago operation to Harry and Roy. The two associates were glad to rent their Chicago studios to the Aitkens on a temporary basis, especially since America's sweetheart was involved in the project.

"That ought to solve the situation and please Mary Pickford," Cochrane told Harry happily. "I'll go out there and see that everything runs right."

Harry and Roy also did their part to make their lovely star's stay at North American Film Company studios as pleasant as possible. They hired a chauffeur, Matt Hosely, a family friend from Waukesha, to drive Roy's big Mitchell car to Chicago to use as a limousine for transporting Pickford and the film crew back and forth to the studio.

Aside from the transportation arrangements, things did not go well for Pickford and her group. In fact, the celebrated star made seven one-reel pictures for the Aitkens, four in New York and three in Chicago, and only one of them was released, and that one for limited use.

"What went wrong?" Roy often asked himself when he already knew part of the answer. First, poor photography stemmed from low-quality film stock used. This made the developing process more critical, and unfortunately careless or inexperienced employees handled it. The solutions left silver-like spots on the film, which could be seen on a movie screen and distracted from the picture. Some of Pickford's films were simply overexposed, others overdeveloped. The upshot was that the Aitkens had to write off practically all the films Pickford made for them.

In reviewing his Majestic Film Corporation records of the period, Roy discovered how disastrous the Pickford fiasco had been. Nearly half of her films shot for the Aitkens bore the notation *n.g.* for "no good." So, instead of enthralling audiences around the world, they gathered dust on the corporation's stock shelves. Roy never learned what became of the original negatives.

But the fact remains that the Aitkens lost about $25,000 in production costs for the Mary Pickford films. Both producer and star expressed deep disappointment. In later years, Roy often speculated how the fortunes of the Aitkens might have changed if these films had been suitable for exhibit and if, being satisfied, Pickford had remained in their employ.

In mid-January 1912, an infuriated Carl Laemmle, just back from Europe, tried to reinstate Mary Pickford, but instead she contracted with Biograph, where David W. Griffith was now the top director. Henceforth, one legend took charge of productions in which another legend would star, and this pleased her.

As for Harry and Roy, they tabulated their losses and cataloged the seven lost films that Pickford had made for them:

1. *Dan's Reward* (negative static)
2. *Kleptomaniac* (n.g.; doubtful)
3. *Red Riding Hood* (negative static)
4. *Rose of Yesterday* (n.g.)
5. *Fudge* (negative static)
6. *Magic Vase* (n.g.)
7. *Courting of Mary* (released and shown once in New York, then sent to London office)

"Now what?" Roy asked his brother one evening over dinner at the Waldorf. His voice betrayed the gloom he felt. Harry did not answer, so Roy went on to fill the silence. "Our *James Brothers* moving picture was a flop, and now all the pictures Mary made can't be exhibited. Our Majestic Company did not get off to the flying start we had expected. I've even heard some grumbling by a few stockholders."

Harry nodded but still did not say a word about the matter that night.

11

Westerns, Keystone Kops, and Rescue Movies

It became quite clear to Harry and Roy at this time, as it had to Carl Laemmle and others in the infant motion picture industry, that theirs was a highly unstable business. The reason was simple. Most of the pioneers in film had too little experience in producing motion pictures. They operated on a trial-and-error basis. This often resulted in poorly constructed stories, below-par photography, and uncertain distribution.

Roy chalked up the Mary Pickford defection to his and Harry's lack of experience in making movies. They allowed themselves a few days to get over the shock of losing such a celebrated talent, an experience unfortunately to be repeated at various junctures in their blazing movie careers. They got over their dismay by planning the production of other pictures through Majestic.

Within a few weeks of Pickford's departure to Biograph, the Aitkens had one-reelers such as *The Birthmark* and *The Better Influence* ready for the film exchanges. Under the rubric of the Aitken-Laemmle Motion Picture Distributing and Sales Company, they were able to get Reliance Film Corporation releases for their exchanges as well. Charles Bauman and Adam Kessel owned Reliance, through which they produced the famous Bison pictures. The New York Motion Picture Corporation, also owned by Bauman and Kessel, was the holding company for Reliance. Production facilities for Reliance and Bison were located at Fort Lee, New Jersey, where the holding company operated a small studio. Fort Lee was also the home of Carlton Motion Picture Laboratory, which the Aitken brothers later acquired. Early Reliance pictures distributed through Aitken exchanges in 1912 included *The Better Man*, starring Gertrude Robinson and William Walthall; *Bedelia's*

Busy Morning; Bedelia at Home; and others. Later Harry and Roy distributed *Rip Van Winkle,* starring Gertrude Robinson as Rip's wife.

Roy was in New York when Reliance began shooting *Rip Van Winkle,* and so he went with the small troupe on location near the Hudson River. James Kirkwood, the director, had some stage experience, which is why he had been selected to produce the picture. Greatly impressed, Roy congratulated Kirkwood and his crew on the good job they had done with the filming.

Later, as the rushes were shown at Fort Lee, Roy was also present. He joined in the moans and groans that greeted one scene of a disheveled and bearded Rip Van Winkle standing in the sunlight, blinking his sleepy eyes while several telephone poles seemed to grow out of his head. Those shots had to be retaken, of course. Later directors and cameramen learned to scrutinize the background more carefully to avoid a serious scene turning into an unintended comical episode.

About this time, John R. Freuler, the Aitken's Wisconsin exchange partner, also awakened from a slumber of sorts. He had met Edwin and Gertrude Thanhouser, a husband-and-wife team celebrated in the Milwaukee area as exceptionally gifted theatrical producers and actors. Freuler mentioned to the Thanhousers that his associates Harry and Roy Aitken had gone into the production of films in New York by organizing the Majestic Film Corporation.

Freuler further suggested that the couple look into this new type of business. He said the Thanhousers' background and ability in the theater might transition smoothly to film production, which they may find quite attractive and lucrative.

"I don't think I'm too interested in the movies right now," Thanhouser said. "However, my wife and I occasionally go to New York looking for new stage plays we can use in Milwaukee. If you'll give me a letter of introduction to the Aitkens, I'll look them up on our next trip."

Harry had heard of the Thanhousers and welcomed the couple when they presented themselves in his office. He had already decided to expand picture production, and he hoped to persuade them to enter the field. To sweeten the deal, he offered to help finance their company and regroup his investment by distributing their film products through the Motion Picture Distributing and Sales Company.

The couple acted on Harry's offer immediately and shortly after the meeting rented a studio at New Rochelle, New York. Within a few months, Thanhouser was producing motion pictures of very high quality. Because of their stage experience, they insisted on dramatic story ideas.

Thanhouser films usually carried a run-to-the-rescue theme, an idea that David W. Griffith was already exploiting at Biograph. One Thanhouser picture with this dramatic sequence stood out in Roy's mind.

It centered on a little girl whom the villain had tied to a big log fastened to a carriage at a sawmill. The carriage slowly carried the log and the girl toward a huge blade cutting logs into planks. Had the log reached the saw, the girl surely would have been cut to pieces.

Matters got more tense. The girl's father was the mill operator, but he was no help. The villain had tied him up. The child's mother, missing her daughter, searched in vain for the child throughout most of the movie. Then, suspecting that the girl might have wandered down to the sawmill to visit her father, the mother went there.

"The suspense in the film was gripping," said Roy, "all the way up to the part where the mother and some friendly men reach the mill in time to stop the carriage, rescue the child, and capture the villain."

In the London exchange, the film was so popular it sold out in England and on the Continent. Perhaps, the British moviegoing public, in some convoluted way, connected the innocent little girl's peril with the villainous acts committed on and by royal persons near the little chapel of St. Peter ad Vincula.

After launching a number of "cliff-hangers," as they came to be called later, Edwin and Gertrude Thanhouser became enthusiastic about the new medium. For several years, they turned out a steady stream of pictures that pleased the public. But they had neither the efficient management skills nor the physical stamina to meet the increasing demands of production. So, in 1913, the Thanhousers hired energetic Charles J. Hite of Iowa as their business manager and company president.

Harry, too, was impressed with Hite, who had been a film exchange owner in Chicago and a member of the Aitkens' new distributing arm, Mutual Film Corporation. Earlier Hite had operated lunch counters in Ohio and had a proven business sense. The senior Aitken took the energetic and intelligent Hite under his wing as a protégé. And when the Thanhousers decided to sell their holdings because of ill health, Harry helped Hite finance the purchase. Naturally, Mutual continued to distribute Thanhouser films, now produced by the young man from Iowa.

Through James Cruze, one of Hite's directors, the new head of Thanhouser pictures met Cruze's first wife, Marguerite Snow, and another leading lady who introduced herself as Florence La Badie. Hite's good looks, charming personality, and great success as a motion picture producer made him a welcomed guest in any parlor, especially those of unattached women. Soon he invaded upper-crust society and engaged in their activities such as flying and racing.

Returning to New York City with Florence Labadie one night, Hite's speeding automobile careened off the road, flipped over the Harlem River Bridge, and plunged into the murky waters below. Both Hite and La Badie were killed.

Harry took the death of his protégé extremely hard. He had regarded the young man as someone on whom he could place greater responsibilities, perhaps as a chief of staff for the growing Aitken empire. He also respected Hite's excellent business judgment. Hite's death forced Harry and his brother to take over active management of Thanhouser Film Corporation in addition to supervising Mutual, Majestic, and Reliance plus the Western Import Company, London, which Roy managed pretty much on his own. To add to the stress, the Aitkens retained distribution rights to all the output of New York Motion Picture Corporation, which required them to supply huge sums of money to Bauman and Kessel. Instead of a blessing, the acquisition of Thanhouser added to Harry and Roy's financial burden.

To unwind from business problems, Roy frequented the neighborhood theaters, where he relaxed to the show tunes accompanying the feature film presentation. The music reminded him of his mother's sing-a-longs as all the Aitkens, except Elvin, gathered around her piano.

In 1912, practically all movie theaters, large and small, had an organ or a piano to furnish music for the patrons. The pianist was usually a well-dressed woman with coiffure to match the style in vogue. She was actually a very important part of the show, setting the proper atmosphere and monitoring behavior. The light above the piano, with the rest of the theater in darkness, signaled that the audiences direct their attention on her.

Instinctively, the pianist helped increase the audience appreciation of the motion picture by using selected music to intensify the emotional scenes as they flashed on the screen. In sad scenes, with the piano music soft, one could often see many white handkerchiefs dabbing at eyes and cheeks. No one was ashamed to weep in public if the picture had stirred his or her emotions.

Edna Hunt, whom Roy met when she was in her midseventies and living in retirement, once played piano at the Old Atlas Theater in Milwaukee and at theaters in Michigan. At the time of her meeting with Aitken, Hunt said she still accepted an occasional invitation to play for the silent movie showing of special art groups and golden age clubs. When interviewed by Roy Aitkin and Al Nelson, she described her work in movie houses showing silent film in the 1900s:

> The Atlas Theater was chilly on winter nights, and I often had to drape my coat over my shoulders to keep warm. My fingers were cold as ice, but if I pounded real hard on the keys, they got warm. We had rowdy kids in the theater in those days, too. In spring and summer they would bring peanuts to the show and throw them at me. If I wore a low back dress, the peanuts would fall down my back.

I couldn't stop playing in the midst of a scene with a cowboy chasing a robber, or a man making love to Lillian Gish, so it might be twenty minutes or more before I could rush backstage to get those scratchy peanuts out of my dress.

I played on Saturdays for matinees and evening shows. Sometimes I saw a show so often I knew every scene and development before they were flashed on the screen. Often I would put a box of bonbons on the piano, and between bars I would snatch one, put it in my mouth, and go right on playing.

Finally, I got so I could read a book in my lap, snatch a bonbon and eat it, and go right on playing a love song or a march without missing a beat.

I used no sheet music in playing the piano in theaters. I merely listed the titles of the songs on ruled cardboard. . . . A glance at the board enabled me to select the song appropriate for emotional and other scenes. Sometimes I would sing the words of the song in a low voice especially in the love scenes, and the audience liked it.

Coming out of a New York theater one evening before setting sail for England, Roy whistled a catchy tune he had heard played by the pianist and took stock of his young life. He and Harry had faced up to a number of challenges, and, whether they won triumphantly or went down gallantly, they retained their sense of boldness for the next attempt. He realized that he was developing into an optimist after all, thanks to his brother's leadership.

Yet, he was aware, too, that people like Laemmle and Freuler, paradoxically their business partners and competitors, considered the Aitken brothers mere farm boys with acres of ambition but little experience in forging lasting relations within the fast-paced movie industry. Roy decided that these critics would be silenced once they learned that the Aitken boldness stemmed from an awareness of the right and wrong choices in a particular course of action. The Aitkens were taught these values first in a little place called Goerke's Corners; in Harry's case, at Carroll College; and throughout their formative years, in a small town where especially good spring water flowed. This revelation came to Roy Aitken in the nick of time. The turbulence ahead would often have him whistling a different tune.

12

A Turbulent Year for Aitken Enterprises

The year 1912 marked the greatest scramble to form effective film distribution systems that anyone had ever witnessed. For example, Motion Picture Distributing and Sales Company (MPSCO, owned by Carl Laemmle and Harry and Roy Aitken) was a loose organization of eighteen independent exchanges used to distribute independent products from a host of filmmakers. Producers supplying film for distribution by MPSCO included the New York Motion Picture Corporation, Bison and Reliance, the Aitken-owned Majestic Corporation, Thanhouser films, and the Aitken's foreign films imported from London and Paris through the Western Import Company, Ltd. Laemmle furnished MPSCO his Nestor, Champion, Republic, and Gem film labels for distribution.

These independents had banned together under the Aitkens' MPSCO unit, because it was the only way they could survive in a field dominated by the rich General Film Company, whose moneybags overflowed but were controlled by the hard-fisted policies of its stern parent, the Motion Picture Patents Company (the Trust).

"Sometimes Laemmle's very difficult to deal with," Harry complained at breakfast one morning. "He wants fast service to his exchanges from Majestic and Western Import, but he makes it difficult for members to get his pictures without considerable delays. If we were a bit stronger, Roy, we could perhaps do better on our own at this point."

It did not take Harry long to put his words into action. Week after week, he and Laemmle disagreed about policies. Then one day Laemmle complained to Harry, "You move too fast for me. I'm not ready to act like that."

"Well, I am," Harry retorted.

In March 1912, Harry severed connections with Laemmle in the Motion Picture Distributing and Sales Company, and then he set out to form another group to replace MPSCO—Film Supply Company of America.

Roy worried about the split because he knew unsettled differences between partners meant that each would try to take with him as many assets as he could for himself. The sunny side of the equation was that Harry and Roy knew many film exchange owners who expressed a desire to follow them into the new distribution company.

Two months after Mary Pickford left the Aitkens to return to Biograph, the Film Supply Company of America began shipping and collecting for film. Ledgers from Majestic, the Aitkens' parent company for all their holdings, show that Harry had lined up about twenty film exchanges to take service from the brothers. About half were exchanges formerly associated with MPSCO and Laemmle. The rest were new independents whom Harry persuaded to join his new venture. Thus, the Film Supply Company of America supplied film to the following exchanges in March 1912:

Western Film Exchange, New York
Consolidated Film Exchange, Atlanta
Independent Western Film Exchange, Portland, Oregon
J. H. Swanson Film Exchange, Denver
H & H Film Exchange, Chicago
Majestic Film Exchange, Chicago
Western Film Exchange, Kansas City
Western Film Exchange, Milwaukee
Swanson-Crawford Film Exchange, St. Louis
Continental Film Exchange, Boston
Western Film Exchange, St. Louis
Progressive Film Exchange, Omaha
Independent Film Exchange, Philadelphia
Lake Shore Film Exchange, Cleveland
Pittsburgh Photoplay Company, Pittsburgh
Michigan Film and Supply, Detroit
Canadian Film Exchange, Calgary, Alberta Canada
Superior Film Company, Toledo
Exhibitors Film Exchange, Wilkes-Barre, Pennsylvania
Great Eastern Film Exchange, New York

At his post in London, Roy missed most of the reorganization problems that dogged his brother Harry. But in early April 1912, he decided to return to the States for a month or two to visit friends and business associates in New York. Roy also wanted to see firsthand the new movies the brothers' Majestic and Reliance companies were filming on the East Coast. He further resolved to take a side trip to visit his mother and sisters, whom he had not seen for a year and a half. So, with these plans firmly in mind, Roy booked passage on a new luxury liner scheduled to make its maiden voyage from Liverpool to New York on April 14.

Englishmen were quite excited about the huge steamship and with good reason. At that time, the *Titanic* was the largest ship afloat and considered unsinkable. It was 892 feet long, the beam was 92.5 feet, and the ship's depth was 73.3 feet. And it was fast, expected to reach speeds of twenty-one knots (twenty-four miles per hour) for its maiden voyage. Roy was proud to be among the 2,223 passengers, many of them notables from several nations, scheduled to make the first crossing in the state-of-the-art vessel. "I looked forward to a very pleasurable voyage on this glamorous ship," he said.

The day before the liner was to sail, however, a theater manager from Paris sent word that he and six associated regional film buyers needed an urgent meeting with Aitken. The Frenchmen wanted to come to London in two days to consult with Roy on films to rent or buy for runs of three months or more. They refused to discuss the matter with anyone but Aitken.

Disappointed, Roy canceled his *Titanic* passage. Two days later, while in conference with the Frenchmen, he heard the shocking news that the ship at full speed had collided with a huge iceberg at 2:20 A.M., April 15, about 1,600 miles northeast of New York. It had sunk with a loss of 1,517 passengers.

Roy was stunned. He certainly would have been on that doomed ship had not the unscheduled business appointment intervened with his plans and kept him in England. "Is there such a thing as fate?" he wondered aloud and then answered his question in the affirmative as he pondered grim news releases about the unprecedented sea disaster.

The following month, he arranged passage to New York and upon arrival went straight to his brother's offices. Roy was amazed to see how fast the Aitkens' Majestic-Reliance film operations had grown in the New York area under Harry's firm hand. Attendance at numerous theaters and nickelodeons was up nationwide, and Harry was riding an investment spree as businessmen, doctors, lawyers, dentists, and others placed their money in new movie theaters that sprang up in cities everywhere. "You would have thought we were selling pure, delicious, spring-fed Waukesha water," Roy quipped. "These wise investors saw a great future in the movies, and they wanted to put their spare cash to work in that field at a profit."

On Sunday morning in June 1912, as they dressed for church, Harry began whistling cheerfully. "What's up?" Roy asked.

His older brother gave his patented chuckle. "I understand that Charlie Bauman and Adam Kessel are having disagreements with Laemmle in his newly formed Universal organization. In fact, I had lunch with them the other day and expressed the wish that we could get their New York Motion Picture products for our Film Supply Company distributing setup."

Harry let the matter rest there until they stepped into the church amid the sound of an organist playing soft religious music. Reminded of his mother's quiet manner in handling people, Harry whispered, "At least I hope I stated our case well."

After a month in New York, Roy became acutely aware of the trouble among Laemmle, Kessel, and Bauman. Each was a shrewd operator who knew how to look out for his interests. During the split-up of Motion Picture Distributing and Sales Company, Kessel and Bauman had first remained with Laemmle at Universal instead of joining the Aitkens in the Film Supply Company. But the two New Yorkers found that Laemmle, now rid of Harry, was a stern taskmaster who gave no quarter whether it rubbed against one's grain or not.

Like their feuding partner, Laemmle, Bauman and Kessel both had come from poor German families. But the similarity ends there. Carl Laemmle, a round-faced, bespectacled immigrant, saved his money as a clothing store manager in Oshkosh for twelve years until he had enough to open his own store in Chicago and concurrently a nickelodeon theater in competition with the Aitkens in 1905. Beyond Laemmle's ready smile lay the mind of a promotional genius that kept pace or exceeded his fellow movie pioneers from Wisconsin, John Freuler and the Aitken brothers, in taking an infant and struggling industry and turning it into a great entertainment and educational empire. Many Hollywood associates referred to Laemmle as "Uncle Carl" after he moved his Independent Motion Picture Company (IMP) west in 1912. Indeed, he had so many relatives from the old country on his payroll that by the time he reorganized IMP into Universal Studios, it was hard for an outsider to know when an employee was using the real title or the honorary one.

On his yearly sojourn to enjoy the German baths, Laemmle inevitably found a nephew or cousin whom he invited to America to work in one of his companies. There was a catch, however, for as the people who spoke his mother tongue phrased it, Laemmle *"hat die Faust in der Tasche."* The translation, "has his fist in his pocket," indicates that Laemmle was stingy. Uncle Carl got this reputation from the way he treated relatives brought from the old country and placed on his payroll. Laemmle's cousin William Wyler, the great director of *The Best Years of Our Lives* (produced by Sam Goldwyn), explained how the Laemmle patronage system worked. After arrival in America, the immigrant got the job Uncle Carl had promised at a low wage. From this meager sum, he was docked $5 a week until his boat fare had been repaid.

As his business grew, so did the size of Laemmle's family, and limerick master Ogden Nash had some fun with the unusual pronunciation that Carl used. The poet quipped

Uncle Carl Laemmle
has a very large faemmle.

Uncle Carl also had a very large spread near Hollywood. By 1915, he opened Universal City on a 275-acre ranch at Cahuenga Pass, five miles north of Hollywood. Meanwhile, in that same year, the Aitkens produced the *Birth of a Nation*, directed by the talented David Wark Griffith. This epic movie was the first twelve-reel picture ever made. *Birth's* costs were phenomenal by 1915 standards. The Aitkens had to raise $40,000 for this blockbuster picture. What's more, they had to do it at a time when a great amount of their capital was tied up buying and (after the dispute with Laemmle) distributing the pictures turned out by the New York Motion Picture Corporation, owned by Bauman and Kessel.

From humble origins, Charles Bauman and Adam Kessel first joined together to publish a weekly sporting paper for racetrack fans in the New York area. They decided that publishing was more of a hit-or-miss affair than racetrack gambling, so they suspended their newspaper and concentrated on making wise wagers as bookmakers. However, here, too, the gaming profits were more often lean than lush.

When New York outlawed bookies, Kessel, a thin, dark-complexioned man, left his chunky partner and set out to collect debts owed to him. One of his debtors operated a small film exchange in downtown New York. The man had no cash, but he did have a few old reels of film that he rented to such theaters as would pay for them.

Kessel knew nothing about the movie business, yet the glamour of the new field seized him. He agreed to finance the little exchange and put his desk in the office. Thus, he could learn the business. He was an effective salesman, and soon the film exchange began to prosper.

When Kessel decided to open another small film exchange, his former racetrack-publishing partner joined him. After Charles Bauman signed on, so did Adam's younger brother Charlie Kessel.

The trio did very well, renting and selling film to New York and New Jersey area theater owners. Some jealous, unsuccessful competitors felt they did too well and set out to slow down the supply of film to Bauman and Kessel exchanges.

Adam Kessel was no fool. He immediately saw that a film exchange was too dependent upon its source of film. Therefore, he and Bauman hired enterprising Fred Balshofer, who owned an Edison camera, to produce a number of short pictures for them. Most of the films were pictorial views of New York. Others were one-reelers with rather weak story lines yet full of action.

Despite these defects, the films sold surprisingly well to a movie-hungry public, and Kessel was delighted. He began to look toward the future and within a short time organized Bison Film Company and hired Thomas Ince, a promising young director.

In October 1910, when the Aitken exchanges were already thriving, Bauman and Kessel organized a second production company called Reliance Film Corporation. Thus, with Bison and Reliance, they became major players in the industry. When Harry Aitken had tried to negotiate with Laemmle in 1910 to contract for IMP pictures for the Aitken exchanges, Uncle Carl turned him down. But in the process he had become acquainted with Bauman and Kessel and other film production, exchange, and distribution magnates in the New York area. These friendships paid dividends later, especially during the period 1912–1916, when Bauman and Kessel became closely associated with the Aitken brothers.

While Bauman and Kessel feuded with Laemmle, the Aitkens concentrated on steadily building Film Supply Company of America, a distributing subsidiary. Here and there, they picked up a film exchange or two. Aitken-owned Majestic production cranked out more films to meet the increased demand, and the brothers added to the pool by acquiring a few good films from European producers through their London, Berlin, and Paris offices.

During the turbulent months of March through June 1912, Harry often had lunch with Crawford Livingston, the Wall Street Banker, whom he and Roy had met while girl watching at Peacock Alley in the Waldorf lobby. One night in that same area of the hotel, Roy sat telling a few friends about London, its theater district, the beautiful women, and the trends in English fashions. His brother, who beckoned him to come over to the elevator where he stood, interrupted Roy.

"Let's go up to our room. I've got news," said Harry.

Upstairs, Harry closed the transom and the half-open window. Either spies were tracking him down, or Livingston must have been impressed with Harry's careful planning and organizational ability, thought Roy as he watched his brother's eyes shine with repressed excitement.

"Crawford Livingston will finance a new film exchange system for us," said Harry.

Even though he suspected Harry's demeanor had something to do with his luncheons on Wall Street, Roy could not understand why Livingston or, for that matter, Harry wanted to tamper with success.

"What's wrong with Film Supply of America?" he asked. "It's moving."

"Yes, it is," replied Harry, "but our new company, Mutual Film Corporation, will be much better financed. It will also include John Freuler, Sam Hutchinson, Charlie Bauman, and Adam Kessel."

"Bauman and Kessel!"

Harry nodded. "Yes, they'll join Mutual and give us their production, but we have to buy their two film exchanges in the deal, so they can concentrate on making movies. We are also buying from Bauman and Kessel control of Carlton Motion Picture Laboratories, placing Reliance Film Corporation under our banner. This new combine will make us much stronger, Roy. Along with your Western Import Company, Ltd., in London, we'll have an impressive setup."

Roy shook his head and massaged his queasy stomach. "I think I'll never get used to this fast-stepping movie business, Harry. We just get settled in one spot, and then we move into something different, bigger, and with more risk. Doesn't this bother you, too?"

Harry took a chair, sat down, and crossed his legs. "No, Roy. I love this movie development. It has so many possibilities. We're going places, maybe way to the top. I feel it, but we have to act when the time is right, and I think that means now."

"Laemmle will be surprised, losing Bauman and Kessel."

Harry chuckled. "Oh, Carl will do all right. He'll get there in his own way and at his own pace. He was never meant to be in partnership with anyone. He likes to run things his own way."

The film exchanges serviced by the now defunct Film Supply Company of America were happy to get into the new Mutual Film Corporation arrangement—as well they should be. Now exhibitors had access, through one company, to Majestic and Reliance motion pictures, Thanhouser, and New York Motion Picture Corporation's Bronco, Kay Bee, and Domino brands. Thomas Ince was producing excellent western pictures, and these were in strong demand. One pleased film exchange operator summed it up in two sentences: "Mutual certainly has a diversified program to offer, especially with Ince's pictures included. Mutual needs only one more thing: some good comedy."

The comedy pictures were around the bend. And the intrepid Bauman and Kessel, now able to concentrate solely on production of pictures, were in hot pursuit.

They arranged to meet Mack Sennett, who, like so many others, resented the manner in which Biograph was trying to force him into making the type of comedy that noncreative, front-office people had dreamed up. Sennett balked. He had other ideas and poured them out along with his complaints to sympathetic Bauman and Kessel.

After a dogged uphill struggle, Sennett had become a bit actor in 1909, graduated to better roles in 1910, and finally began directing in 1911. He produced interesting and profitable comedies into 1912, but his pay was reported to be very low, $50 to $75 per week. Thus, when Bauman and Kessel offered him $100 per week, plus a reported one-third interest in a new production company they would form named Keystone Film Company, Mack Sennett envisioned a golden future. He signed, and Keystone was incorporated in 1912.

Sennett, still in his early thirties, became part owner in a new production company, but, more important, he had free creative rein as "production czar." Naturally, he liked the title and the responsibility that went with it.

The one factor that made the Bauman and Kessel offer so sweet was the one-third interest in Keystone Film Company. A creative genius like Sennett could hardly turn down the opportunity to share in the profits of his own labor. An ever-watchful Harry Aitken observed the financial negotiations conducted by Bauman and Kessel with Sennett. A year later he would use the same free stock idea to persuade another famous director to join the Aitkens.

So, within seven months, from January to August 1, 1912, the Aitkens severed their partnership with Laemmle in the Motion Picture Distributing and Sales Company (MPSCO), formed Film Supply of America to replace MPSCO, and established Mutual (Film Supply's better-financed successor). Mutual included the purchase of Carlton Motion Picture Laboratories and Reliance Film Corporation. Any part of this deal guaranteed the Aitkens movie mogul status, but the link to Keystone Film Company became cream in the coffee for Harry and the tea and muffins for Roy.

Both brothers were as jubilant as the day Elvin Aitken presented his sons with the shiny bicycles back on the farm at Goerke's Corners. Harry had more reason to be pleased. He had counteracted the actions of both Laemmle and the Trust.

"Now we have enough good film to satisfy the best exchanges," he said. "Ince and Sennett are top directors. They're young men with creative ideas. It was a lucky break for us that we pried Bauman and Kessel away from Laemmle. We'll also be able to make things rough for the General Film Company [the Trust]. We'll have as good, if not better, film programs than they do most of the time."

"It'll help our London, Berlin, and Paris offices, too," Roy chimed in, caught up in Harry's elation. "How about sending Mother a wire and telling her the good news?"

"Why not?" Harry replied. "Let's send it right now and then go out to eat at the best place we can find."

With purchase of the Reliance Film Corporation and its Twentieth Street studio, the Aitkens acquired the services of Stan E. Taylor and his wife, Marion Leonard, a producing and acting pair. Others who joined the Aitken fold included James Kirkwood, Henry Walthall (who later starred in *Birth of a Nation*), Dorothy Davenport (who later married Wally Reid),

Gertrude Robinson, and Arthur Johnson. Johnson later joined Sigmund "Pop" Lubin, a man of small stature who created giants in the movie industry. Lubin had immigrated from Germany to Philadelphia, where in 1896 he became one of the earliest pioneers in the film business. He made Johnson world famous.

Hal Reid, another celebrated actor-director-dramatist, took Kirkwood's place at Reliance and enlisted his son, Wallace Reid, to serve as his assistant in camera work and acting. The younger Reid eventually joined the cast of *Birth of a Nation* and gained considerable recognition in the role of the blacksmith.

With so much going for it, Reliance was destined to become one of the Aitkens' best-producing companies, turning out many pictures that pleased the public and brought high grosses. Unresolved matters between the Aitken brothers and their longtime partner back in Milwaukee needed attention, however.

13

Policy Rift Shatters Exchange Coalition

The one blatant weakness in the Aitkens' Majestic Film Corporation in 1912 was the inability to attract well-known directors. Harry and Roy employed some promising young men such as James Cruze, John Emerson, Raoul Walsh, and Victor Fleming, who would have their day in the sun, but in 1912 they were still considered apprentices when compared to big-name directors such as Griffith, Ince, and Sennett. The Aitkens needed someone whose reputation they could turn into box-office magic.

Aitken associates Bauman and Kessel, on the other hand, had Thomas Ince and Mack Sennett on their New York Motion Picture and Keystone payrolls. Ince's reputation as a film producer and director was steadily enlarging with every stirring western bearing his imprint from California. Harry and Roy luckily had a tenuous connection to Ince through the Miller Brothers' Wild West Show at Venice, California. In 1911, the Aitkens had contracted with Miller Brothers for use of their cowboys, cowgirls, Indians, horses, and equipment to use during the winter months when shooting in New York was out of the question. This gave Ince a vast resource to tap, and the innovative director worked a large part of this conglomerate cast into practically all his westerns. His horse-galloping chase scenes (using Miller Brothers' extras) caught on, as evinced by growing box-office appeal, while real war clouds loomed in Europe and North Africa.

Meanwhile, Sennett, too, added a diversion from politics and strife as he tickled the funny bones of many American and European silent film fans with his Keystone comedies, billed as a cure for the "glooms." As a result, film exchange owners, theater operators, and movie patrons around the world soon knew and respected Ince and Sennett.

But Majestic Film Corporation, the company the Aitkens had formed to handle Mary Pickford's disastrous pictures in 1911, was still unknown to the public. The one bright spot was the brothers' stable of young directors who were making inroads by turning out good pictures for Majestic. Both Harry and Roy realized that Majestic needed a top-flight director to make the step up to big-time movie production on a par with Ince and Sennett. But their search for such an individual had to be postponed because of rumblings in Milwaukee involving Mutual, the Aitken company held in partnership with John Freuler.

Over the years, Freuler had increased his stock holdings in Mutual and apparently decided to review his own situation vis-à-vis the fast-moving Aitken brothers from his home state. The crafty old German saw that while he owned stock in three midwestern exchanges with the Aitkens, as well as stock in the Majestic Film Corporation, his partners had left him behind in the movie world. He wanted to close the gap. Evidently a separate, part ownership in the North American Film Company in Chicago, where portions of the Mary Pickford filming fiasco had taken place, was insufficient to assuage Freuler's concern. So, he arranged to visit New York often enough to become a very helpful and steadying influence in Mutual. Bankers Livingston and Kahn especially liked the congenial German because he was cautious and analytical and hardly ever took risks.

With Freuler in New York checking on the Aitken partnership, operations of the North American Film Company were left in the hands of his partner in that venture, Samuel Hutchinson. Hutchinson, a former druggist, was a dashing risk taker like the Aitkens. The direct opposite of Freuler, Hutchinson established North American Film's second studio in Santa Barbara, California, and the Aitken-Freuler-owned Mutual had a contract to distribute all films produced by North American.

"Hutchinson's inclined to make pictures which some families might not wish shown to their children," Harry said to Roy one day. "I'm worried. We'll have to do something about such films."

Since Harry had made public statements insisting that Mutual would purge its distribution program of unsavory motion pictures, Hutchinson knew that he was on a collision course with the Aitkens, his partner's (i.e., Freuler's) partners. He apparently chose to sidestep this fact. Shortly afterward, in the absence of Freuler, Hutchinson produced *The Quest*. When Harry viewed it, he put it on the shelf.

"It's risqué," he said. "Our policy is clean pictures for clean people. I've written Hutchinson that if he doesn't clean up his pictures, we'll refuse to distribute them through Mutual," Harry confided to Roy. "And I've also warned Freuler."

As expected when called on the carpet by a contemporary, both Hutchinson and Freuler reacted coolly toward the Aitken brothers. One month after Harry had stated that Mutual would not distribute *The Quest*, Hutchinson took the matter further in an escalation of bruised egos. Roy received a cable from his London office stating that Hutchinson had raided the place and enticed manager George Manivering to leave the Aitkens and establish a separate exchange for the North American Film Company. Hutchinson had been to Paris as well. There, he sowed poison among the Aitken employees in much the same manner.

When advised of the developments, Harry was quite grim. "You'd better get back to London, Roy, and see if you can do something about this. I never did trust that Hutchinson."

Onboard the ship to England, Roy's traveling companion was a Wall Street friend who worked for the American Express Travel Company. Roy told him about losing the manager for his London office and asked if he would recommend someone for the position. He agreed to try to help. After the ship docked, the friends shook hands and parted.

Several days later, the American Express executive sent a pleasant, middle-aged man to the London exchange office bearing a letter of introduction. Roy liked Tom Davies and hired him on the spot. He eventually became a very loyal and valuable asset to the Aitkens' firm.

Upon querying his secretary, Roy learned that Hutchinson had spread rumors among the staff and led them to believe that Harry and he were about to go belly-up in the United States and that undoubtedly the Aitkens would be unable to carry on their many overseas distribution ventures as well.

Unanswered at this time was Freuler's role in Hutchinson's personnel raid. Did he sanction the actions of one partner against the Aitkens, with whom he also shared a partnership? Whatever the answer, Roy noted that the rift between the Aitken brothers and Freuler had deepened. Two years later when Harry and Roy produced *Birth of a Nation*, they refused to grant Mutual Film Corporation, then headed by Freuler, an opportunity to distribute it.

As evidence that the Freuler-Aitken relationship had grown colder than the waters of Lake Michigan in February, Harry complained that at the time *Birth* needed financial support, "Freuler's making it hard for us in every way he can. One would think he was sole owner of Mutual, instead of just a sizable stockholder."

The dispute between Freuler and Hutchinson and Aitken led to later critics on one side or the other distorting the record. Some use the censorship incident (refusal to distribute a risqué movie) and the banning of *Birth* for distribution by Mutual as evidence of Harry's "vindictive nature" or as proof that Harry engaged in "floating ethics." The later term implies that Harry considered his own "good" as the only end that justified the means. Both observations are off the mark, if Roy's account is credible as an eyewitness.

Roy defends his brother on the ground that the rift started over Freuler's partner, Hutchinson, who worked to distribute risqué pictures to a public that included children. Instead of praising this first recorded attempt at self-censorship by movie producers, the Aitkens are castigated in some accounts for destroying a partnership that may have been doomed by other philosophical differences, such as how fast to grow the business and what risks are acceptable.

As for John Freuler, he seems to have emerged in some quarters as a victim of the Aitkens' unfair practices and in others as the guiding genius who, on his own in the manner of a Carl Laemmle, created a movie empire without any input from his partners. By this account, Hutchinson and the Aitkens were bit players who don't even merit a footnote to Freuler's achievements. Remarkably, in chapter 2 of a book called *Milwaukee Movie Palaces*, published by the Milwaukee County Historical Society, authors Larry Widen and Judi Anderson fail to mention the Aitkens (of adjacent Waukesha County) even once in their account of John Freuler's career spanning the nickelodeon years (1905–1911). Consider this excerpt from the cited work:

> After running the theater [Comique] for a short time, Freuler realized that he could make a great deal of money by supplying films to other theater owners as well as showing them himself. He reasoned correctly that if a film distributorship were located in town, exhibitors would be more apt to rent more films and change their programs more often.
>
> On July 1, 1906, the Western Film Exchange was created in Freuler's real estate office. Soon the company was renting films to beer gardens, summer parks, and legitimate houses such as the Bijou, Alhambra, Crystal, and Star, as well as to the storefront picture theaters that were beginning to appear on the city's busiest streets.
>
> Freuler later went on to organize two motion picture studios, the North American Film Company in 1910 and the Mutual Film Corporation in 1912. Freuler was the president of Mutual until 1918 and operated 68 subsidiary companies out of his Chicago office, which supplied 7,000 theaters across the United States with films each week.
>
> But in Milwaukee, he began by encouraging the owners of the new storefront picture theaters to change their film programs three, four, and even five times each week. (22)

Later, after Freuler had supplanted Harry as president of Mutual, each side went its separate way in the movie industry, and it seemed they would never reconcile. However, many years later when both Freuler and the Aitkens were out of the movie business, Roy met Freuler in Chicago, and over coffee they had a chat.

"If only we boys could've stayed together," Freuler said ruefully. "What a combination we'd have been! With you and Harry raising the money and with me handling distribution, nobody could have topped us."

Under Harry's leadership, Mutual, with about thirty-five leading film exchanges tied to it in 1912–1913, quickly became known as a progressive film distribution company with alert, creative management and a variety of film products.

Harry also served as president of Majestic Film Corporation of America. Majestic had part ownership in most of the film exchanges, organized under the Aitken-owned Film Supply Company of America, which Mutual, of course, had now supplanted. Actually, Majestic did not sell its part ownership in these exchanges until April 5, 1914, when it accepted 1,434 shares of Mutual's preferred stock. This is the way things were done in the infant film industry—interlocking stock holdings in associated companies ensured a fallback position in times of crisis. While this trend is widely practiced today by many large industrial firms, back then it backfired on Harry before the decade ended.

Roy could not always keep informed on the developments of the brothers' vast movie empire because he spent so much time at the London office. Harry, so efficient in so many areas, disliked letter writing more than he did dancing. In brief, little correspondence existed between the two brothers. However, on his frequent trips to the United States, Roy usually managed to get Harry to bring him up-to-date on what had occurred since his last visit.

One spring day in early 1913, Roy interrupted his brother's report and announced that he had never been to the West Coast to see their operations there. "I've been dying to look them over. I especially want to see Mack Sennett and Tom Ince in action producing pictures," he said.

Harry thought for a moment. "Well, why don't we start for the coast next week, you and I? We'll make a tour of our studios."

Roy clapped his hands. He liked comedy pictures and had not seen a live cowboy in action since that day his father took him to Chicago to see the Buffalo Bill show on the lakefront. He couldn't believe more than nineteen years had passed since he had come home from that experience, saddled the mare, and tried to pick up every handkerchief in sight or rope everything that came across his path, including fence posts. From then on, no one was safe around the Aitken farm at Goerke's Corners, because cows, chickens, and even Roy's three sisters were in danger of having a noose dropped over their heads.

So naturally the thirty-one-year-old was excited when he and Harry started on their western tour. They stopped first at Mack Sennett's studio in Edendale and spent two days watching the big Irishman direct stars such as Mabel Normand and Teddy Sampson. In fact, they joined Sennett and the two women at lunch during a break in production. The Aitken brothers exchanged proud looks at each other, knowing they had raised the money every week to finance Sennett and his comedy actors and actresses whose antics delighted American and European audiences alike.

Next, they visited the Ince studios in Santa Monica. To get there, they borrowed an automobile from Sennett's studio. Roy's first view of Ince's headquarters came from the driver's side of an open car. He spotted a few straggling wooden buildings right along the ocean shore. Then, as he looked up to the nearby hills, an entire western town with streets and many saloons came into view.

After dismounting the vehicle to take a closer look, the brothers saw a sheriff's office, livery stable, several country stores, and a church on the set. Ince had all these buildings and props for his pictures plus a large dining room in which to feed the regulars as well as the extras who were working in a particular picture. The two farm boys from Wisconsin sat down to a morning snack with Ince and the cowboys, who were in make-believe roles of many different characters. For Roy, this was a show in itself. He had to rub his eyes in an effort to bring him back to the reality that all these people depended on him and Harry for their livelihoods and in exchange produced pictures that might or might not make a profit for the Aitkens. Even stranger was the feeling that thousands of his and Harry's hard-earned dollars poured into such a fascinating make-believe world every week. However, Roy was too thrilled to think about the money, especially when Ince slapped him on the back and invited him out to the stables.

"Take off those English clothes, Roy, and I'll let you ride one of those broncos," said Ince.

Roy replied that he wanted to do it, but not on a bucking horse. However, Harry squelched the deal since they were due back at the Sennett studio in a few hours. So, as a substitute for the wild horse, Roy got to watch Bill Hart rehearse a western picture. He was especially pleased to hear that the cowboy star would be breaking for lunch and had been invited to join the Aitkens.

Hart sat next to the younger Aitken, and the two got into a lively conversation about making western pictures. Roy noticed that Hart had deep-set and distant eyes, more like a philosopher lost in thought than those of a cowboy actor. Hart spoke in a slow, deep voice, much like the way Roy imagined Socrates must have sounded on the streets of ancient Athens.

After lunch, the Aitkens momentarily forgot their search for a top director as they watched America's top cowboy perform. Hart treated them to a typical trademark scene in which he leaped off his horse, walked unflinching through two swinging doors of a saloon, drew both guns, and got the drop on two bad hombres seated at a poker table.

Incredible, Roy thought. He had been selling the finished product for years in the Aitkens' London exchanges. Now as an executive, he had witnessed the real thing, legendary William S. Hart in action!

14

D. W. Griffith and the Gish Sisters Sign On

On the train ride back to New York, Harry Aitken turned to his brother and said suddenly, "Roy, now is the time we must try to get a top-notch director for Majestic. We've delayed long enough. We need someone like Edwin Porter or David W. Griffith."

"Porter? Griffith? Why, Harry, you can't lure men like that away from Vitagraph and Biograph. We're not that rich. Mutual has just started paying handsome dividends. Let's leave it at that for a while."

"Money isn't everything, Roy. Mary Pickford was willing to leave Laemmle because she wasn't satisfied with assigned pictures and working conditions. I've heard, for example, that Griffith is unhappy at Biograph. He wants to make longer pictures, and Biograph officials won't let him. They're a pretty conservative bunch."

Roy objected, "But Griffith or Porter will want more money than we can pay them. Sure, we've got a little capital now, but we also have a lot of obligations. Look what Mary Pickford cost us. It took us months to recover."

Harry smiled. "If we can sign either Porter or Griffith, we could easily find the money to pay them because directors like that attract capital!"

Once again, Roy realized that his brother was a very daring and ambitious man. The old caution returned as he felt his own stomach go through its usual contortions prior to a nervous spell. Roy decided he was neither equipped nor willing to shoulder the risks Harry was taking. Yet, he knew that once Harry started a new enterprise, he could not abandon a brother who had always stuck by him. In the end, nervous condition and all, he worked as hard as Harry did to make it succeed.

Roy looked at his position in Majestic Film Corporation in baseball terms. Between trips to London, he stepped in as a pinch hitter or a relief pitcher substituting for Harry. In many instances, he acted as liaison between Harry and Majestic's workforce. Roy cultivated the corporation's directors, actors, and actresses and won their confidence so that they often talked to him about problems they dared not raise with Harry, whom they assumed too far up the corporate ladder.

"Tell Harry this, will you, Roy?" a disgruntled actor sometimes asked.

And so, awaiting his opportunity, Roy would approach Harry with the information or complaint, get his reaction, and then take a message back to the actor.

He also dined and danced with some of the actresses, the most pleasurable aspect of his duties. In this capacity, he heard considerably more movie gossip and information than Harry did. The latter was too busy with his executive position, although information relayed by Roy often helped his older brother make important decisions.

One night in August 1913, Harry came to the hotel about ten o'clock. Roy as usual was engaged in conversation with a businessman in the lobby. As he had done following his meeting with Crawford Livingston two years earlier, Harry motioned for Roy to accompany him upstairs. He seemed very relaxed and cheerful.

"Tony O'Sullivan has arranged to have me meet Griffith at dinner tomorrow night at the Algonquin," Harry said with a note of elation in his voice.

He then broke into a laugh as he saw the surprise on Roy's face. O'Sullivan had been a former director under Griffith at Biograph before switching to the same position at Reliance.

"Griffith will want too much," Roy cautioned.

"We'll see," Harry chuckled.

The next evening Griffith and Harry spent two hours at dinner. When Harry returned to the Waldorf, he found Roy sitting alone in the corner of the big lobby.

"It was just as I suspected," Harry said. "Griffith is discouraged at Biograph. He feels hamstrung. His *Judith of Bethuliah* is on Biograph's shelf. They won't release it at the moment. They say it's too long. This hurt Griffith deeply. He said he enjoyed making that picture."

Harry paused. "Griffith told me he was impressed by the product Mutual was distributing. And he thinks our trade paper advertising about our companies and pictures is outstanding. He asked me several times how much supervision we give directors at Majestic. That's where we stand at the moment."

"What's the next step?"

"He and I are having dinner again Friday," Harry said. "I think he's considering our offer, although no definite salary has been mentioned. I told him we're looking for a top-ranking director and that we'll permit him to produce the kind of pictures he likes so long as he turns out enough standard pictures for us to earn a steady income. I also learned that Adolph Zukor is after Griffith's services."

In the days that followed, Harry had several more meetings with Griffith, but no deal was closed. The Aitkens discovered that Zukor had offered Griffith $1,000 per week, which, as one of Roy's confidants reported, was "a terrific salary." This was more than double what Griffith was earning at Biograph, and upon hearing this offer, Roy became quite discouraged.

"That eliminates us, doesn't it?" he asked Harry one evening over dinner just two days before Roy was scheduled to go back to London.

"I don't think so," Harry said confidently. "I have a plan. Don't worry."

Roy later learned the details of his brother's plan to snare the great director. It had two parts. The first involved paying Griffith a cash salary of $300 a week, considerably below the Zukor offer. Roy thought the second part of Harry's plan contained the clincher. As a bonus for signing a first-year contract with the Aitkens, Griffith stood to receive four hundred shares of Majestic stock valued at $100 per share, worth a neat $40,000. This stock, together with the $300 per week cash salary, amounted to $55,000 per year, compared to Zukor's offer of $52,000.

Harry no doubt remembered how Bauman and Kessel had attracted Mack Sennett from Biograph with a promise of one-third of the stock of Keystone Film Company. Furthermore, Harry had promised D. W. Griffith, so he told Roy, the opportunity, in partnership with Harry, to make at least two of his special feature pictures per year. Because of Griffith's well-known independent streak, this may have been the most important factor of all, Roy thought.

Harry confirmed that Griffith liked the idea of owning Majestic stock and being a part owner. Aitken also pointed out that no other executives, with the exception of Bauman and Kessel, had permitted stars or directors to buy in, or receive stock, as a bonus. The brothers and Griffith had set a trend with this package, and both sides were pleased.

"Griffith also knew when he signed with the Aitkens that careful Adolph Zukor was probably better financed than Majestic or Mutual, but since he was young, he probably decided to go with Harry, someone closer to his age," said Roy.

In her book *D. W. Griffith: American Film Master*, the late Iris Barry quotes Billy Bitzer, Griffith's famous cameraman at Biograph:

> When Mr. Griffith decided to leave Biograph, I refused to join him, although he offered to treble my salary. I didn't think the independent outfit he was

going with [the Aitkens] could possibly stand the gaff of Mr. Griffith's spending of both film and money.

Among the inducements Mr. Griffith pictured to me was one in which he said, "We will bury ourselves in hard work out at the coast . . . for five years, and make the greatest motion pictures ever made, make a million dollars, and retire, and then you can have all the time you want to fool around with your camera gadgets, etc., and I shall settle down to write."

Now I thought how can he be sure of that when even now in the pictures we had . . . we never did know whether we had a best-seller until it went out? (20)

Barry also notes, "But Griffith was persuasive and so was Mr. Harry Aitken, with whom he had now joined forces under the banner of Mutual films, and Bitzer went along."

Bitzer and others had stamped Griffith as extravagant in filmmaking, but while Harry respected their opinions, he paid scant attention to the implied warning. He was too excited about signing the talented Griffith, who gave Majestic Film Corporation America's finest movie director.

In later years, Roy set the record straight on just which Aitken holding company Griffith had contracted with in 1913. "Many movie historians mention that Griffith signed with Mutual Film Corporation, our film distribution company. This is not true. Griffith's contract was with Majestic Film Corporation, our film-producing firm," he said.

In any event, Harry and Roy had occasion to remember Billy Bitzer's warning, but for the moment they were overjoyed at obtaining Griffith for their company. To the Aitkens, the deal seemed even sweeter at the thought that Biograph, leading member of the Trust, and Zukor, one of their main competitors, had been outsmarted by a couple of farm boys from Wisconsin.

"Now Majestic can become the top production unit in the nation," Harry said. "We've got Griffith, Ince, and Sennett, the best in the industry. Griffith is eager to get started. I like his attitude. He feels he can work with us on better terms than at Biograph. But we'll have to get him a studio."

A recent purchase came to Roy's mind. "How about our Clara Norris studio at Yonkers?" he asked.

"Griffith has looked at it. He doesn't think it'll be adequate. It's too far from New York City. But I have my eye on a Broadway loft that was a former rug factory. The Angelus Film Company used the space until four months ago. Then the company folded."

"And Griffith will work in a place like that? Why, he's been operating in California in the sunshine during the winter."

"I told you he was cooperative," Harry said coolly. "I put it on the line to him. I said we wanted him to make four or five four-reel pictures for us as revenue makers quickly, and he has consented. But I also promised him I would get him to California as soon as possible."

Later, Roy went down to take a look at the Broadway loft. It certainly was unpretentious, and the windows were dusty. But Griffith was working enthusiastically with his players, and young Aitken had the feeling this man meant business and would help the brothers' enterprises grow.

With the signing of the master filmmaker of his time came some valuable fringe benefits. Griffith brought to the Aitken studios many capable assistants, actors, and actresses. Behind the cameras, these included cameraman Billy Bitzer, Joseph Aller of the Biograph Laboratory, and director Christy Cabanne. Out front were actors Bobby Harron and Edward Dillon, along with Mae Marsh and Dorothy and Lillian Gish. As one of these stars wrote in her 1969 autobiography, *Lillian Gish: The Movies, Mr. Griffith, and Me*, the movie world buzzed with excitement relative to the Aitken-Griffith pact. (Although, as Roy noted, the facts relative to contracts and salary were inaccurately reported. Corrections are in italics.) Wrote Gish:

> Even before the rumors began, we all had an unhappy feeling that Mr. Griffith would eventually be forced to break with Biograph. The front office was putting altogether too much pressure on him. None of us felt that we were working for Biograph. Our ties were with Mr. Griffith. As I remember, none of us had a contract with him; we simply worked for him. He would say to a player, "I'll give you . . ." and name a sum; he always kept his word. In those days, we were continually being offered jobs by other companies, but Biograph was the top—thanks to Mr. Griffith—and one didn't descend from the peak just for money. . . .
>
> Having made a fortune as distributors, the Aitkens were eager to produce films as well. Mr. Griffith wanted an alliance with a producing company that would allow him to exercise his talents. In October 1913 they joined forces. He became head of production for the Mutual Film Corporation *(Majestic)*, the distributing agency for the producing companies of Majestic and Reliance, also owned by the Aitken brothers, at the salary of $1,000 *($300)* a week. He was also promised the right to make two films of his own a year.
>
> "The new director of the Reliance and Majestic studios, Mr. Griffith joins the Mutual companies at one of the largest salaries ever paid to a Motion Picture Director," wrote *Reel Life*.
>
> Mr. Griffith took many of the Biograph directors with him. Though Dorothy and I had been offered contracts to remain with Biograph without Mr. Griffith, we never even considered the offers. Nor did others of his company, even though this loyalty meant going without work. Everyone wanted to stay with him—everyone except Billy Bitzer, who, incredibly, at first refused to go with Mr. Griffith. (113–15)

This was probably the first large-scale personnel raid in the history of motion pictures. Yet, so great was Griffith's hold on his directors and players that even those who were dubious about making the switch from an established company to one that had so recently expanded joined the Aitkens. For some, it took persuasive arguments by Griffith and Harry to get them onboard, but eventually they swallowed their fears about independent movie firms and started work for the Aitkens, regarded by many as interlopers whose futures were uncertain. The public, too, looked askance at independents until they saw the Aitken-Griffith team produce four- and five-reel-length movies at the huge cost of $5,000 per picture.

The Great Leap, in which famed stuntman Rodman Law together with Mae Marsh and Bobby Harron enthralled audiences, was among the first pictures Griffith made for Majestic in 1913. Next was E. Philip Oppenheim's *The Floor Above*, which was directed by James Kirkwood, then Paul Amstrong's *The Escape*, made from his famous play with Mae Marsh and Blanche Sweet. Other pictures turned out that year were *Home Sweet Home* and *Battle of the Sexes*.

At Biograph, Griffith had filmed many short stories, novels, plays, and poems by celebrated authors such as Alfred Tennyson, Charles Dickens, Jack London, Shakespeare, Robert Stevenson, and Leo Tolstoy. He liked to work with stories and plays by famous writers. Perhaps one reason for this was that Griffith himself was a frustrated author, and he admired people who could do what he could not.

Some sections of *The Escape* were made in the Broadway loft, but it was finished in California. *The Avenging Conscience*, also in the Griffith schedule, took its plot from Edgar Allen Poe's *Annabel Lee* and *The Tell Tale Heart*.

In fact, some movie sources claim that Griffith also began working out scenes for *Birth of a Nation* while at the Broadway loft. But neither Roy nor Harry ever mentioned it at the time. However, Roy did say later that if Griffith was thinking about producing *Birth* while programming four other pictures for the Aitkens, "It indicates the energy and determination of the man and the fiery eagerness with which he worked."

One thing is certain: Griffith and the cast of professionals he brought with him to Majestic would have no regrets about the career move to the independent movie firm. Nearly all of them became celebrities or stars while working for the Aitkens.

15

D.W. and Roy
Become Friends

D. W. Griffith made motion pictures for Majestic in the Broadway loft from October 25, 1913, to January 15, 1914. When in New York, Roy shadowed the courtly, southern-born director as he produced pictures. He was fascinated by moviemaking and liked to see the master at work even if it meant going straight from the dock to the studio, still in his London clothes.

Young Aitken and Griffith got along extremely well. The director always seemed to have time to comment on Roy's fashionable attire and expressed a desire to meet his English tailor someday. Roy obliged by furnishing Griffith the tailor's address, and after the director became affluent from *Birth of a Nation* profits, he did indeed have clothes made for him by Roy's English tailor.

D.W., as his closest friends called him, left the impression that he was haughty and humorless, which he sometimes was with strangers. But Roy found that once one engaged Griffith in talk about the movies, then he would unbend considerably.

He looked right at Roy as they conversed, and Roy could see why Griffith had been credited with a hypnotic gaze. He spoke in a quiet yet sonorous, deep voice that, like Bill Hart's, added emphasis to the philosophical importance of his words.

Roy wondered why Griffith had singled him out as the Aitken to befriend. Harry with his organizational genius appeared a better match, he thought. Then it came to Roy's mind that Griffith sensed that unlike Harry, whose work equaled fun, the younger Aitken liked to relieve the tedium of daily routine when given the opportunity. And perhaps at this

SCHROEDER, 359 Third Street, MILWAUKEE.

(Left to right) Roy E. Aitken, age six, and Harry E. Aitken, ten, when they lived on a farm at Goerke's Corners on the outskirts of Waukesha, Wisconsin, in the 1890s. Unspoiled as youngsters, they followed the song of a silent siren that called to them throughout their lives.

Harry Aitken, the older brother. He was the guiding genius and entrepreneur behind the Aitken movie empire. He described their rise to movie mogul status as, "That career of ours—that delirious decade—I still can't believe it. The nickelodeons, the exchanges and studios, the huge salaries, the fabulous stars, the millions of dollars that passed in and out—things moved fast, so crazily—sometimes the whole experience seems to be a huge kaleidoscopic fantasy—grotesque, incredible."

Roy E. Aitken, Harry's younger brother and chief confidant. Roy was outgoing and a good mixer and had the soul of a poet. He outlined to a friend the Aitkens' biggest shortcoming in their long, hard-fought battles against rivals MGM, Universal, and Paramount: "We did not know how to protect our companies like Goldwyn, Laemmle, and Zukor did."

Mary Pickford, "America's Sweetheart," made several pictures for the Aitkens' Majestic Film Corporation in 1911. Her first husband, director Owen Moore, also appeared in the pictures that were filmed in New York. But lighting was so poor, none of the pictures were released nationally. The Aitken brothers lost $25,000 in the deal. Photo from Waukesha County, Wis., Museum Collections.

Roy Aitken relaxing at the beach with silent film stars Teddy Sampson and Mabel Normand. Roy often attended parties with D. W. Griffith, noted director, actor Douglas Fairbanks Sr., and numerous film lovelies.

Charles Hite (left), shown conferring with Harry Aitken, managed Thanhouser Film Corp. for the brothers. After Hite was killed in an automobile accident in New York, Harry took over the reins of Thanhouser, but Hite's death was a terrible blow to the Aitkens' growing movie empire. Harry was grooming him to become "chief of staff."

Tall, well-dressed Roy Aitken at his desk in 1914. Roy traveled Wisconsin, Illinois, and the South selling film and helping new theater owners with their film programs. Often he taught them to run film projectors as well. Later he worked at Aitken film exchanges in Milwaukee, St. Louis, New York City, and London. Movie production followed for the Aitken brothers.

One of the Aitken brothers' early triumphs on their march to establish America's first movie empire was to sign David Wark Griffith. This great director revolutionized Hollywood under the Aitken banner. Griffith was a man of many moods, and as his fame increased, so did his imperious air.

Thomas Ince was a careful and talented director. Ince scripts were much more detailed than those that either of his counterparts, Griffith and Sennett, produced for the Aitkens. Ince had no peers when it came to westerns starring cowboy actor Bill Hart.

Mack Sennett, the third star director in the Aitken Hollywood constellation, cranked out two Keystone comedies a week for the brothers. His Keystone Kop antics and other comedies brought laughter to a world on the brink of war. Griffith, Ince, and Sennett became famous under the brothers, directing some of the best of the 2,500 silent films produced by the Aitkens.

The Aitkens were able to sign numerous, beautiful movie stars during the height of their production companies. Many like Norma Talmadge, with dark hair and brown eyes, got their start as extras at age fourteen.

Brooklyn-born Constance Talmadge, like her sister Norma, started out in bits and small parts. But after she starred in the Aitken-Griffith blockbuster Intolerance, *she skyrocketed to fame. Constance's golden hair and brown eyes distinguished her from her sister.*

Lillian Gish, made famous through her role in the Aitken-produced, Griffith-directed Birth of a Nation, *corresponded with Harry and Roy Aitken during all the years of their retirement in Waukesha. Lillian was born in Springfield, Ohio. Photo from Waukesha County, Wis., Museum Collections.*

Dorothy Gish, winsome younger sister of Lillian, was born in Dayton, Ohio. She played many humorous parts in Aitken movies, usually wearing a dark wig to set her apart from Lillian, who was also a natural blue-eyed blonde. Here she appears in Victorine. *Photo from Waukesha County, Wis., Museum Collections.*

In a scene from the Aitken-produced movie He Did and He Didn't, *Roscoe "Fatty" Arbuckle grabs fellow Keystone star Mabel Normand just in time to keep her from sliding down the stairs. Photo from Waukesha County, Wis., Museum Collections.*

William S. (Bill) Hart, born in Newburgh, New York, learned to ride with great skill, growing to manhood on the Idaho plains. Under Thomas Ince's direction at the Aitken western studio, Hart was the first to introduce the "two-gun" cowboy image, although in this scene a knife seems to be the weapon of choice for the heroine.

Battle scene from the Aitken-Griffith movie Birth of a Nation starring Henry B. Walthall as commander of the Confederate forces at Petersburg. Born in Shelby County, Alabama, Walthall received lasting fame for his role as the "little colonel." The film grossed over $60 million from 1915 through 1925.

This lovesick Union soldier, played by William Freeman, concentrated his gaze on beautiful Lillian Gish, who became famous for her role as Elsie Stoneman in the Aitken-Griffith superpicture Birth of a Nation.

Anita Loos, author of Gentlemen Prefer Blondes, *became a famous scriptwriter for the Aitkens. She was married to Aitken director John Emerson at the time. In a letter to Roy after their careers were over, Anita expressed dismay that the Aitken brothers had gone unheralded for their achievements in Hollywood.*

Scene from Intolerance, *the Griffith-directed extravaganza that cost the Aitkens $200,000 to produce, more than twice as much as* Birth of a Nation, *which it followed.*

Gloria Swanson, the superstar from Chicago, spent her early acting days in the Aitken fold. Inscription on photo to Roy Aitken asks, "How painful can fishing be!"

Lovely Edna Purviance played in many Keystone comedy pictures.

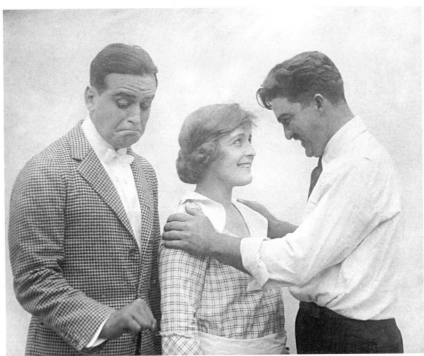

Douglas Fairbanks Sr. does not appear too happy as Aitken director Christy Cabanne congratulates actress Jane Grey for meaningful acting. Fairbanks was lured away from the theater to star in Aitken movie productions when the Aitkens took him to the Liberty Theater in New York to see Birth of a Nation.

Mischievous Mabel Normand, an Aitken actress who had a tempestuous affair with director Mack Sennett. Hollywood mogul Sam Goldwyn was also attracted to the fun-loving Normand.

Scene from Triangle picture **Hoodoo Ann** *starring Mae Marsh and Robert Harron. Triangle was the name for the Aitken company producing pictures directed by Griffith, Ince, and Sennett.*

Louise Fazenda (left), native of Lafayette, Indiana, and Charles Murray (center) merge their humorous talents in Her Fame and Shame.

Ford Sterling (center) in Maiden's Trust. *Sterling led the Keystone actors in 1912 when the Aitken brothers controlled Mutual, the marketing arm of Keystone. Later, Sterling was applauded as an actor and director of many Triangle-released films.*

Cameramen at work filming Dorothy Dalton as she stood in a pond rehearsing a love scene for a Triangle movie. The Ince star was born in Chicago and educated in the Sacred Heart Academy of that city. The director holding the light reflector is Reginald Barker.

Bobbie Vernon and Gloria Swanson share the stage with dog actor Teddy, in the title Teddy at the Throttle, *an Aitken-Keystone release.*

Bathing scene from The Dark Room Secret, *a Triangle film.*

Harry Aitken (second left, center row) with stars during a filming break at one of his studios. They are, from left to right and seated in the front row, Douglas Fairbanks, Bessie Love, Constance Talmadge, Constance Collier, Lillian Gish, Fay Tincher, De Wolf Hopper. Center row: Robert Harron, Harry Aitken, Sir Herbert Beerbohm Tree, Owen Moore, Wilfred Lucas. Top row: Dorothy Gish, Seena Owen, Norma Talmadge.

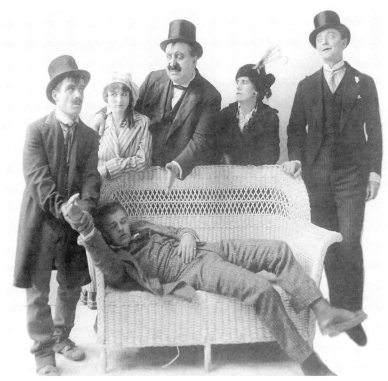

A scene from His Auto-Ruination, *starring Mack Swain, Harry Gribbon, Julia Faye, May Wells, and Harry McCoy.*

A scene from His Bitter Pill, *an Aitken production.*

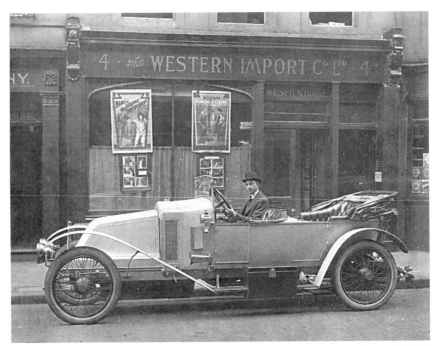

Roy Aitken in his Renault Car in front of his London office in 1911. He also established film exchanges in Copenhagen, Berlin, Paris, Rome, and other European cities.

*Mack Sennett's timeless **Keystone Kops** are enormously popular with all audiences for their comical stunts, spoof of authority, and crazy antics. Photo from Waukesha County, Wis., Museum Collections.*

Pretty Norma Phillips played the part of the Mutual Girl in a weekly newsreel the Aitkens used to generate interest in movies. With her entourage, Phillips visited fashionable stores, art galleries, and other spots to interview personalities.

Charlie Chaplin in Dough and Dynamite, *also directed by Chaplin for Mack Sennett. Chaplin appeared in thirty-nine films for the Aitken brothers in the year he worked for them. Photo from Waukesha County, Wis., Museum Collections.*

The Aitkens built this splendid Culver City studio. After the brothers encountered financial difficulties, they were forced to sell the film production facilities to Sam Goldwyn in 1918. In 1924, they became Metro-Goldwyn-Mayer studios, now a familiar landmark.

Adolph Zukor (center), the Aitken brothers' movie mogul nemesis, with actor Adolphe Menjou (left) and famous violinist Rubinoff. Photo from Waukesha County, Wis., Museum Collections.

When Harry and Roy Aitken left active movie production, they returned to Waukesha, Wisconsin, and promoted various film products in conjunction with local photographer Warren O'Brien, shown here between Roy (left) and Harry.

Mike Kornick, now deceased, and part of his vast collection of movie data including those from the Aitken era. Kornick was one of hundreds of thousands of movie buffs in the United States and Canada with extensive collections.

In 1974, the Waukesha County Historical Society erected a marker at the new Holiday Inn built on farmland once marking the site of the Aitken family home. Roy Aitken (far right), in his nineties, attended the marker presentation. Left to right are history professor Charles Calkins, the late Al P. Nelson, Aitken's collaborator on a book about the Birth of a Nation *picture, and Libbie Nolan, editor of the Historical Society's* Landmark *magazine.*

The late HENRY B. WALTHALL as "THE LITTLE COLONEL" and LILLIAN GISH as ELSIE STONEMAN in a scene from D. W. GRIFFITH'S **"THE BIRTH OF A NATION"**

"'THE BIRTH OF A NATION' is without doubt the most important film of all time. D. W. Griffith brought the movies to maturity with this one great classic."
—New York Herald-Tribune

"'THE BIRTH OF A NATION' is among other things, the most important single film ever made and a landmark in motion picture history."
—Museum of Modern Art Film Library

Exclusive Showing in New York !

Birth of a Nation *playbill, a threefold.*

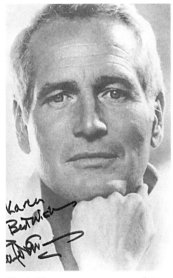

Paul Newman was one of Roy Aitken's favorite movie stars and the last Hollywood celebrity with whom he had official contact. Roy presented Newman with a copy of his book, co-authored with Al P. Nelson, during a Newman campaign swing through Wisconsin in behalf of presidential candidate Eugene McCarthy.

Harry Aitken (left), D. W. Griffith (center), and Roy Aitken (right) shown together in 1930 when a soundtrack was added to Birth of a Nation.

THE BIRTH OF A NATION

The Cast

Col. Ben Cameron	Henry B. Walthall
Margaret Cameron	Mae Marsh
Mrs. Cameron	Josephine Crowell
Dr. Cameron	Spottiswoode Aiken
Wade Cameron	J. A. Beringer
Duke Cameron	Maxfield Stanley
Mammy	Jennie Lee
Hon. Austin Stoneman	Ralph Lewis
Elsie	Lillian Gish
Phil Stoneman	Elmer Clifton
Tod	Robert Harron
Jeff	Wallace Reed
Lydia Brown	Mary Alden
Silas Lynch	George Seigman
Gus	Walter Long
Abraham Lincoln	Joseph Henabery
John Wilkes Booth	Raoul Walsh
Gen. U. S. Grant	Donald Crisp
Gen. Robert E. Lee	Howard Gayle
Nelse	Willard DeVaull
Jake	William Freeman
Stoneman's Servant	Thomas Wilson

Written and Produced by D. W. Griffith

Photography by G. W. Bitzer

Music by Joseph C. Briel

Locale — Southern United States

The Time — 1860 to 1870

The Original Musical Score Now Recorded on Sound Film

A Few Facts About The Picture

"THE BIRTH OF A NATION" was produced in 1914. Mr. Griffith worked eight months on the production before releasing it for exhibition in 1915.

"THE BIRTH OF A NATION" was the first film to run twelve reels, the first to be shown at a $2 admission price. The film ran forty-seven weeks at the Liberty Theatre in New York.

D. W. Griffith achieved fame as the greatest director in the world. For three years the pi re toured the key cities of the Unites States, of Europe, and South Africa and Australia.

The picture's longevity is still unequaled. After its premiere showings, the film has been rereleased periodically during the past thirty-two years.

Today, the picture is recognized as a museum film and acclaimed the greatest piece of movie making in the history of the motion picture.

D. W. Griffith's masterpiece set the standard for one of the world's finest arts.

Birth of a Nation *playbill, a threefold (continued).*

First Triangle Night
Wins New York

This morning New York is in possession of a new standard of Play Presentation.

DOUGLAS FAIRBANKS,
RAYMOND HITCHCOCK,
DUSTIN FARNUM

have made good in their new theatric environment. "The Lamb," "My Valet" and "The Iron Strain" have all proved worthy vehicles for these well-known players.

The Triangle Plan of presenting dramatic stars of the first magnitude in plays of the highest quality has proved a huge success.

If you were not at the Knickerbocker Theatre last night, you surely will be to-night—to-morrow —or next week.

It was said that New York would not pay as high as Two Dollars for this form of entertainment. That question has now been definitely settled.

New York will render value for value received. It will pay Two Dollars for an entertainment of the Two Dollar Calibre.

If you tried to get into the Knickerbocker Theatre last night—and failed—you probably realized that somebody else's Two or Three Dollars preceded yours through the Box Office window.

The present bill — Fairbanks — Hitchcock -- Farnum—will continue all next week, afternoon and evening, until Saturday night.

Then will come a new series.

TRIANGLE FILM CORPORATION.

New York Times ad placed by the Aitken brothers.

Laemmle Trustbusting Cartoon—Carl Laemmle, the Aitken brothers' former partner and founder of Universal Studios, got credit for breaking the "Movietrust" because of his lawsuit, but it was Harry Aitken who defeated the monopoly in the court of public opinion.

stage in his career, Griffith felt that he needed some diversion from his de-
votion to movie production. Thus, now and then, the great director
yielded to Roy's invitation to go out and dine and dance. Of course, their
common backgrounds buttressed the friendship between them. Both were
farm boys, and both had quit school early to make their way in life. Each
expressed a deep respect for their parents, especially their mothers, and
this was a trait the two Methodists unknowingly shared with Jewish immigrants such as Louis B. Mayer.

After his success with *Birth of a Nation*, one of the first things Griffith
did with his money was to buy his widowed mother, Mary
Oglesby Griffith, a comfortable house in La Grange, six miles from the
family home and twenty miles from Louisville. Upon hearing that she
was ill, he went there to visit. She praised his theater work but then expressed her old sentiment that she wished that he had chosen to be a
Methodist minister instead. This led to a lively conversation, with the
director defending his pictures as trying to show what is right and what
is wrong in the world. Mary Griffith countered by pointing out that
words spoken from a pulpit carried with them God's meaning, and no
uttering in a theater could match that. In the end, he conceded the point
and tried to turn the discussion to her state of health. She thanked him
again for buying the house for her and said it was comfortable enough
but that she was partial to the homestead at Crestwood, where she
wanted to be buried in the nearby peaceful cemetery next to his father
and sister. "I'm willing to stay here until God calls me," she said.

"That'll be a long time yet, Ma." He choked.

But it wasn't. It was the last time Griffith saw her alive. She died December 11, 1915, at age eighty-six. He returned for the funeral and
stood at the grave in the cemetery, head bowed, with a prayer in his
heart that Mary Oglesby Griffith had found the peace she had sought
and deserved.

At about the same time Griffith and Roy were forging their friendship,
Louis B. Mayer was emerging as a leading distributor thanks to the
deal he had cut with Goldfish, Lasky, and De Mille on *The Squaw Man* feature film. But, as pointed out by biographer Gary Carey in *All the Stars in
Heaven*, Mayer suffered a severe setback in his own personal life:

> In the early fall of 1913, he received word that his mother was seriously ill.
> He rushed to Saint John where he had learned that Sarah had undergone a
> routine operation after which serious complications had set in. Two weeks
> later, she was dead. Her death was a great blow to Mayer. He had adored his
> mother and was to cherish her memory in many ways. Nothing, nobody was
> ever able to shake his belief in the sanctity of motherhood; anyone taking the

name of Mother in vain was sure to feel the full force of his wrath. As production chief at M-G-M, Mayer kept careful check over the studio's output to see that motherliness was honored as being next to godliness, and that the sanctity of the family, another of Sarah's ideals, was similarly respected. (25–26)

Often Griffith was a guest at the Aitkens' apartment on West Fifty-seventh Street. He would spend the evening dining, chatting and listening to the brothers' player piano. Once a group of English models visiting the United States stopped in when Griffith was present. He had a fine time dancing with the English girls, whom Roy had met on a previous boat trip from Europe.

After this, Roy became a regular Anglophile and began to wear gloves and carry a cane in the manner of English gentry. This really caught Griffith's eye. He chided young Aitken about it, but Roy could see that he was impressed.

"Roy, I'll just have to put you in one of our pictures," Griffith joked. "When New York sees you with the cane and gloves in a picture, there's sure to be a rush to the haberdasheries."

The fact that Griffith was working in a studio on Broadway for Majestic Film Corporation created quite a stir in New York, especially at the Algonquin Hotel, owned by Frank Case. Griffith and Roy often dined there together and visited with all the stage and film notables who dropped in after the theater for something to eat. They would run into John Barrymore, Douglas Fairbanks, John Drew, and other celebrities who stayed to sip hot chocolate or cognac as they talked about the theater.

Often, when the other guests had departed, Griffith would unwind and talk to Roy about his personal goals. He was extremely frank with Roy about the $300 a week salary he received from Majestic (plus his four hundred shares of stock in the corporation). He had never received pay like that at Biograph, he confided to Roy.

Griffith also showed a sense of humor that most people never knew existed. One evening after dinner, he said to Roy, "You and Harry must not expect too much from me on this kind of salary." Both of them laughed. In Roy's case, the laughter was prompted by his surprise that he and Harry could raise that much money for one man per week. As for Griffith, Roy supposed that he got a kick out of going to the bank and depositing such a large salary of cash and stock in a city where he was once down on his luck.

Sometimes the conversation drifted into Roy's involvement in the foreign distribution of film. This subject intrigued Griffith, who questioned Aitken endlessly about the sale of film abroad and asked what particularly appealed to the British and European taste. Roy told him that they most often followed the American pattern and were interested in the trends being set in the United States.

Roy also told him about Harry and his early entrance into the film business in 1905. Griffith observed that the Aitken brothers had predated him in the field by three years. This led to further discussions on the very first film exchanges the Aitkens opened and how Roy's job had been to make up programs for the theater owner clients. He explained that he and Harry would buy as many Biograph films as they could because they possessed a quality and strong story line missing in many other brands of film.

Griffith brightened when told that theater exhibitors asked for his films from 1908 on and that often Roy could appease a disappointed client by suggesting a rerun of some Griffith films, although the exhibitor had often shown them a month or two earlier. "These films," said Roy, "stood out from all the others because they had the Griffith touch. The story was easier to follow and had high entertainment value. The photography was better because you had a top cameraman in Billy Bitzer."

Roy continued, "I consider myself a competent judge of good pictures, because I've had experience in operating theaters and also making up hundreds of film programs for which we had to review available films."

As Griffith listened, Roy could see his eyes gleam. These words of praise no doubt pleased him coming from someone who had worked his way up through every stage of the business except acting and who had seen the reactions of audiences in America and Europe. Roy related how the Aitkens split with General Film Company (the Trust) in 1909 over the aborted *James Brothers of Missouri* film, and Griffith laughed. He laughed again as Roy shared the story of the Denver theater owner who had advised young Aitken not to try to sell that awful *James* film to other exhibitors. "So that's why you and Harry became financiers," Griffith chuckled. "I often wondered."

In these informal sessions, each man gave something to the other. Griffith learned that Roy and his brother were more than financiers, exhibitors, exchange operators, or even film producers; they had vital knowledge and movie information that he had not yet acquired. Later, when the great director went to Europe to make a war picture, he used the information from these discussions and credited Roy as his first tutor.

As for the Aitkens, these conversations reinforced the decision to go after a director of Griffith's stature no matter the cost. Roy reported to Harry how much Griffith seemed to value his association with the Aitkens. The team was exactly what each member wanted. Harry was a dreamer with an eye toward the future, and he was easy to deal with most of the time. He was quick to grasp a new idea and enjoy the thrill of seeing it on the screen months later. Griffith, like Harry, was an idea man.

In the Aitkens, Roy believed, Griffith saw a spirit of daring and adventure that almost matched his own. This is what he both wanted and needed, and only with the Aitkens could he have secured this relationship. Harry and Roy were fully aware of the groundbreaking pace they set in the early days of silent film. Like them, Griffith crossed into territory none of their competitors were bold enough to charter.

It wasn't long before Harry and Griffith realized as well the publicity value of making movies in downtown New York in a Broadway loft. Harry constantly brought to the loft studio (on appointment, of course) a selected group of bankers and other men in moneyed positions. These men, such as Crawford Livingston and Felix Kahn, liked to watch the magnetic Griffith direct *The Escape* and other pictures. Even in that loft emerged the aura of excitement and glamour that always accompanies the making of a movie.

The bankers enjoyed a close-up view of the Aitken-Griffith team's lovely actresses, such as the Gish sisters, Mae Marsh, and others. Roy often heard some spectator gasp for air or sigh as a handsome actor clasped a beautiful actress in a movie love scene and kissed her long and passionately. Perhaps the Wall Street types were reliving their youth, Roy thought.

By inviting such influential men to visit the loft, Harry laid the groundwork for investments and loans in the Aitkens' movie companies. *The Escape*, like so many Aitken movies, was a syndicate production. Investors put a specified sum of money into a syndicate picture, as if buying stock in a special company. The advantage to the producing company was that a syndicate picture required less cash up front, since the investors carried a portion of the load for a particular picture. This freed assets for filmmakers to produce many profitable pictures for the market with ensuing profits to many investors.

Harry was a master at persuading many businessmen and others that the silent movies had a profitable future for them.

While Griffith appeared to like young Roy and enjoy his company, he probably also appreciated to some extent the opportunity that Harry had offered to him in motion pictures. Yet, there was a side of Griffith that Roy found very egotistical and self-serving.

For example, despite the special agreements and free stock Harry had made available to Griffith and the generous royalty arrangements, the eccentric director could still send a telegram filled with petty carping. Written in 1914, one was addressed to Griffith's New York lawyer, Alfred H. T. Banzhaf:

HAVE WIRED M—TO GET AS MUCH GRIFFITH ON POSTERS AS POSSIBLE. DON'T THINK MUTUAL OR ANY OTHER COMPANY SHOULD BE USED AT ALL. *ESCAPE* JUMPED HERE FROM ABOUT A THOUSAND ON SECOND WEEK. IF THEY HAD SPENT ONE HALF HERE AS THEY DID ON *RUNAWAY* WE WOULD HAVE CLEARED FOUR OR FIVE THOUSAND PER WEEK FOR TEN OR FIFTEEN WEEKS. SO SAID THE MAN AT THE THEATER. LET AITKEN THINK EVERYONE KNOWS I HAD A BAD DEAL ON FEATURES. NO ATTENTION PAID TO THEM AT ALL. ALL SERIALS SEEM DEAD. *ESCAPE* NOW TRANSFERRED TO JOINT ON STATE STREET.

                                                    D. W. GRIFFITH

Dissatisfaction with the way that the Aitkens had promoted his features was not the only thing on Griffith's mind as the winter of 1913–1914 approached. As snow covered New York rooftops, he continued to press Harry for a California studio. One day he made his same pitch to Roy.

"You know, New York is no place to produce pictures. Give me California. There's plenty of sunshine there, and we can work outside most of the time. Work faster, too. New York Motion Picture Company has studios out there for Tom Ince and Mack Sennett. Why doesn't Harry show some speed in sending me out?"

Griffith even enlisted Billy Bitzer in his campaign. The ace cameraman corralled Roy whenever he caught him at the studio and extolled the virtues of California. Sunshine would help him and Griffith produce better pictures with greater box-office totals, Bitzer told Roy.

"D.W.'s pressured me, too," Harry said after Roy relayed the news. "I'd hoped Griffith would stay here to finish some of these specials so we could get quick revenue. But perhaps he's right. A California studio might be in order now."

In late December, Harry sent Joe Allers, Majestic's laboratory man, and Christy Cabanne, a promising director, to California. Their mission was to try to find a suitable studio site for Griffith and his entourage.

They found an old house and some other buildings on a corner of Hollywood and Sunset Boulevards in Los Angeles. Majestic Film Corporation remodeled the house slightly to provide a laboratory for developing films and showing them. A couple of offices were fashioned out of the large downstairs rooms. Measured against later studios, the Aitkens' Fine Arts California facility was, even after remodeling, a poor excuse for a movie production headquarters. "But it probably was no worse or more crude than studios operated by some of the other movie companies of the day," Roy admitted.

For a happy Griffith and his troupe, it might as well have been the Taj Mahal. They left for the West Coast early in 1914, and to Roy especially, New York seemed a little lonely without them. Nobody at the time, neither Griffith nor the Aitkens, realized that the Fine Arts studio, crude though it was, would shortly achieve fame for Griffith and the Majestic Film Corporation. And from its success would come a tremendous expansion of the Aitken enterprises that competitive forces could only view as obnoxious good luck since it had not happened to them.

Harry remained in New York, at the main offices of Majestic, Reliance, and also the Aitkens' distribution company, Mutual Film Corporation. The head office of New York Motion Picture Corporation, whose pictures the brothers distributed, was also located in New York, even though its studios were in California.

Through their large stock holdings in Majestic, Reliance, Thanhouser, North American Film Company, and Mutual, Harry and Roy actually had control over all the pictures made by these companies and also those of the New York Motion Picture Corporation. Since the Aitkens handled distribution, they decided which types of pictures were to be produced. They also determined what directors, actors, and actresses the various companies hired.

In a later comment to Roy, Lillian Gish and Anita Loos summed up the prevailing view of the Aitken brothers: "You and Harry were the bankers, and we actors were afraid of you. We peeked out at you when you visited Hollywood from our safe positions behind sets. Everyone thought both of you were very rich."

As Griffith swung into movie production in California, finishing the four syndicate pictures he had started in New York, he seemed to become more aloof, especially under the stress of a highly productive program. When news of this character change reached New York, Roy refused to believe it.

But when he met Griffith in New York City later, he noticed the change, too. It was even more evident a few years later when Harry and Roy made a trip to California to see their top director. By 1915, he was no longer the man they hired in 1913. When the Aitkens suggested that Griffith join them and some of the staff one night at Nate Goodwin's pier-side restaurant, he replied quite brusquely, "I wish I could go with you, but I'm just too busy to take any time off. So why don't you take some of the actresses and go to dinner?"

At that time, Roy thought back sadly to the New York days two years earlier when at the Broadway loft, Griffith would gladly have accepted such an invitation. Now, apparently, he had no time for such things. The director loved only his career, and he began to look and act like a man on a treadmill trying desperately to keep up.

Ironically, later critics would level the same charge at the Aitkens, who remained married to their careers so that the only progeny they produced appeared on movie screens. However, in 1919 during his New York City sojourn, Harry, like Griffith, was secretly and briefly married. "Harry considered his wife a spitfire," said attorney Willard S. Griswold, who handled the divorce for his brother-in-law. "None of the Aitkens, including my wife Mabel, ever mentioned the matter again," Griswold added.

Like Griffith, Harry had also undergone some changes. For the first time, Roy noticed that his brother moved more cautiously and conservatively albeit for a brief period of time. At first, Roy welcomed the new Harry, but as events unfolded, he became concerned that Harry passed up a golden opportunity to forge new business relationships. As the "honeymoon" phase of the Aitken-Griffith partnership faded, the trust factor in others and the old self-confidence seemed to have temporarily gone out of Harry Aitken.

16

The First Full-Scale
Movie Publicity Program

For many years, the Aitkens considered Carl Laemmle their fiercest competitor. But the man who entered their lives so casually in 1904 as the clothing store manager from Oshkosh, Wisconsin, had faded into the background following his policy split with Harry over the Motion Picture Distributing and Sales Company partnership.

By 1912, another nemesis had replaced Laemmle, and soon Adolph Zukor became the Aitkens' most ruthless competitor. Zukor and Marcus Loew, his partner, had parlayed a string of penny arcades into a motion picture empire that included the idea of using a special production company to film well-known Broadway plays.

No doubt prompted by his Uncle Adolph, Frank Meyer approached the Aitkens, his employers at the Mutual film exchange in New York, on the possibility of joining Zukor and William A. Brady, who was to head up the new stage-to-film venture.

The papers outlining the partnership for the special production company were drawn and presented to Harry. But at the last minute, Harry felt he had to withdraw because he and his brother had so many other activities to finance and keep operating. This was one time when Roy saw his brother show a conservative inclination instead of grasping every promising opportunity shoved in front of him.

At the time Roy applauded Harry's action. He, too, felt that they had enough to handle and should concentrate their efforts on promoting adequately their own film distribution and motion picture companies. Later, however, when Laemmle (Universal) and Zukor (Paramount) created their great studio dynasties, Roy regretted that Harry and Zukor had not combined their outstanding talents in 1912. With hindsight, Roy believes the motion picture company resulting from an Aitken-Zukor merger would have had the artistic and financial clout to produce the best work Hollywood had to offer in both quality and quantity of product. But it was not to be then, or later, when Zukor had another opportunity to join the Aitkens.

After Harry's rebuff, Zukor went ahead with his plan and enlisted the help of Daniel Frohman and Ed Porter. They secured the services of Mary Pickford, Pauline Frederick, Marguerite Clark, and other prominent performers. Within a short time, Zukor's production of filmed stage plays began to secure so much attention and favor from the larger theaters that Harry felt something had to be done to offset it.

The excellent financial condition of Mutual Film Corporation at this period made it possible for Harry to spend considerable money on a publicity campaign. His initial promotion included the creation of a famous Mutual trademark, a clock where moving hands on a dial in theaters called attention to the fact that "Mutual Movies Make Time Fly." This idea was handled by a Chicago advertising agency, and it became a hit.

Next, Harry secured the services of Ingalls Kimball, an outstanding advertising expert. Kimball wrote striking full-page advertisements that appeared in the *Saturday Evening Post*, the *Ladies Home Journal*, and other national magazines. All ads featured Mutual Master Pictures, their stars, and directors. No other publicity campaign had the depth or magnitude of this one undertaken for the exploitation of motion pictures. It was another first for the Aitkens. These advertisements created a tremendous impression on the public and on the movie industry as well. The latter followed the Aitkens' lead.

Since the brothers' ads highlighted the names and accomplishments of their top directors—Griffith, Ince, and Sennett—they helped boost patronage for Mutual pictures throughout the nation. It also made the public more eager to see Griffith, Ince, and Sennett films than those of other directors.

As an offshoot of the ad campaign, the three directors derived an enhanced self-image. Overnight, they became successful, famous figures in the entertainment world. Each bathed in this new aura of instant, nationwide celebrity status.

"I hope our three big directors won't have to order larger hats after all this publicity," Roy quipped to Harry one day. "I notice each has changed considerably. They feel very important now."

"I noticed it, too," Harry replied. "Well, we have to take risks with every new idea we try. I know our directors will be asking for more money soon, but if we produce better pictures that the public flocks to see, then we can afford it."

So successful was Harry's publicity campaign that lucrative offers to buy his companies rolled into the New York headquarters. But the senior Aitken brother was on a crusade. He firmly believed that the motion picture was the greatest educational force of the day and that it was to play as important a part in the lives of people as the printing press. Harry refused to sell his interests since he did not trust anyone to carry on this legacy.

He confided to Roy that in motion pictures they had been given a mission: an opportunity to show people how to get more out of life. It was clear to Harry that if the Aitkens were to accomplish this, they must not only make interesting pictures but also find ways of properly exploiting them. In addition, they had to organize their distribution of films to get maximum showings at reasonable prices.

No two men in the fledgling industry were better prepared for such a challenge. The Aitken brothers had paid their dues at every step—nickelodeon operators, film salesmen, projectionists, exchange owners, financiers, and movie producers—and then they became the first to combine or consolidate these many pathways to moviemaking prosperity under one banner. Only acting in front of a camera had escaped their résumé, yet they had the good looks and intelligence to do this if called on to do so. Although it was a flop, they had directed the *James Brothers* film, so they at least knew what *not* to do from behind the camera.

"Movies enrich life for many people and through the subtitles promote literacy, Roy," Harry said at dinner one night, as the talk invariably turned to things connected with films, "and we are important factors in this great development."

Working from such a blueprint, Harry earnestly began to hire the best writers, actors, and directors he could find. He paid Montgomery Flagg $1,000 for the first theater poster before the artist became famous for his Uncle Sam "I Want You" recruiting effort. Harry enlisted Flagg in his drive for more artistic presentation in motion pictures. The older Aitken brother did some recruiting of his own in and around Wall Street where he signed up executives from such banking institutions as the Corn Exchange Bank and the Central Union and Trust Company. Men like Frank Vanderlip joined Harry by helping coordinate the Aitken company operations. Price, Waterhouse and Company and other leading accounting houses furnished new auditing systems that made the governing of the brothers' fast-growing business easier.

Eight short years after Harry and Roy Aitken opened their first nickelodeons in Chicago, they were on top of the movie industry. And by 1912–1913 Harry was hailed as the man who had lifted the motion picture "game" into a more stabilized position by bringing big-business methods into its operations.

Mutual Film Corporation, with Harry as president, began to cash in on yet another promotion designed to counter the Biograph and IMP campaigns. He began a weekly newsreel featuring Norma Phillips as the "Mutual Girl."

Harry had met Miss Phillips while with his sister Gladys on a trip to Europe in 1912. Harry and Gladys immediately liked the statuesque model and were captivated by her dark brown eyes, thick brown hair, and graceful figure.

In 1914, when Harry decided to create a Mutual Girl who might publicize Mutual Master Pictures, he remembered Norma. He contracted her for this role, and shortly afterward Mutual began weekly fashion reels that gained popularity throughout the country.

To write the script for the Mutual Girl, the Aitkens hired Daniel Goodman, an author whom they had met during their St. Louis film exchange days. He was talented and welcomed the opportunity the Aitkens offered.

Norma Phillips, dressed in fashionable clothes furnished by Macy's, Bonwit Teller, and other stores, impressed many women the country over. A number of films were shot in the New York style shops, and the proprietors, of course, loved this. When it was known that Phillips would appear at certain hours, women flocked to see her.

The next step in the promotion of the Mutual Girl program was to have Phillips meet famous movie and other personalities and screen these events. Among those who appeared on her program were Inez Mulholland, Blanche Ring, Douglas Fairbanks Sr., James Montgomery Flagg, William Faversham, and George Barr McCutcheon. If the Aitkens got word that a celebrity was arriving in New York by ship, they saw to it that Phillips and her troupe got down to the dock to meet them and photograph the scene. In this respect, the Mutual Girl program also emerged as a newsreel.

The program now became a topic of conversation at tea parties as well. Harry and Roy were delighted, of course, for this kind of reception kept Mutual Master Pictures before the attention of millions of Americans. The Mutual Girl gave them just one more ploy to draw women into their theaters to see the latest fashions and national celebrities.

Roy credits the program with getting Douglas Fairbanks Sr. interested in movies. Fairbanks, then a stage star, appeared on a program with Phillips. "Until he saw the rushes of the film with our Mutual Girl, I don't think he had ever seen how he looked on celluloid," said Roy.

Beautiful and stylish as Phillips was, she failed to impress D. W. Griffith. When he and young Aitken met at the brothers' New York office one day and then went out to dinner, Griffith volunteered, "I don't think the Mutual Girl is so great, do you, Roy?"

"She impresses many people," Roy replied. He let the matter drop there, not wanting to contradict Griffith on something he thought insignificant at the moment.

The Mutual Girl served her purpose for one year. She was one of the many factors that helped make the moviegoing public aware that Mutual Master Pictures turned out wholesome pictures and that Mutual had many of the best stars on its payroll.

Socially, too, Harry and Roy began to extend their sphere of influence through their acquaintance with many prominent people. They invited bankers, actors, writers, and others to come to their ten-room West Fifty-seventh Street apartment on special days to view the new films that shortly would be distributed through Mutual.

The guest list read like several pages from *Who's Who.* There were the ever present Montgomery Flagg and George Randolph Chester and their wives, also Mrs. Randolph Hearst, Conde Nast, Barrett Andrews, Messmore Kendall (who later built the Capitol Theater), May Wilson Preston and her husband, George Barr McCutcheon, Charles Hanson Town, and others. The conversation that followed as these people gathered for drinks and snacks, before and after film showings, was fascinating grist for the gossip mills. But the distinguished visitors helped give Harry and Roy a better perspective of New York life and the progress being made in art, music, and literature.

At this time, too, the brothers began paying more for worthy scenarios. Earlier, they had obtained screenplays for $75 to $200 for their Reliance and Majestic film companies. In 1911, when they bought the movie rights to *Phillip Steel* (James Oliver Curwood's first full novel), they paid only $100 for it. But in 1913, a scant two years later, the Aitkens paid George Randolph Chester $15,000 for a scenario for their Majestic Film Corporation. "That's how rapidly opportunities and costs accelerated in those days," Roy observed.

But he and Harry were too excited about their growing movie empire to worry too much about rising costs, for out on the West Coast Mack Sennett and his Keystone comedy crews were producing pictures that sold well in the United States and all over the world. Charles Chaplin, who had signed with the New York Motion Picture Corporation, whose pictures the Aitkens distributed, had caught the imagination of the American people, and the entire nation seemed to be laughing at and enjoying his screen antics.

Roy felt that he deserved part of the credit for getting Charles Chaplin into the film business. He saw the baggy-pants comedian in the London music halls in 1912 and 1913 and thought his brand of humor would catch on. Along with staid British patrons, Roy laughed at Chaplin's stage routine. When he got back to New York, he mentioned Chaplin to Harry who passed on the information to Adam Kessel.

Less than a year later, Chaplin was signed by the Keystone Film Company. Some dispute persists as to the first person to discover Chaplin, for later Roy picked up a book in which Mack Sennett said he was responsible for bringing the actor to America. John Freuler, the Aitkens' former partner in Milwaukee, also laid claim to the famous comedian when, after the rift with Harry in 1915, he paid Chaplin $650,000 to join Mutual Film the following year.

The facts on Chaplin's brother Sydney are clearer, however.

After Charlie Chaplin began to work at the Keystone lot in 1913, he asked Roy to look up his brother Sydney on his next trip to England. Charlie also wrote to Sydney to expect Roy.

So eventually the two got together over lunch in London. Roy could easily see many of Charlie's physical characteristics in Sydney, and in answer to his question, advised Charlie's brother that there might be a place for him in American films.

Within six months, Charlie phoned Roy in New York and said that Sydney was coming to America and would arrive on the *Mauritania* within the week. He asked Roy to go down to Ellis Island and meet him, since he was in California working hard on a picture.

Roy went to the "gateway to America" and met Sydney, who was very happy to see him. After all, Charlie and Roy were the only people in the United States he knew. To get off Ellis Island quickly, he needed an American sponsor, and so Roy performed that duty.

Sydney had talent, but his famous brother overshadowed him. Nevertheless, he played important roles in pictures. Shortly after his arrival in the United States, he was cast in a picture called *The Submarine Pirate* and received favorable reviews. Years later, a relative of the Aitkens who was a commander in the navy at the time told Roy that his ship was one of those used in the filming of Sydney Chaplin's picture.

In mid-1914, Harry and Roy took a trip to California to tour the three studios—Ince at Santa Monica, Mack Sennett at Edendale, and Griffith at the Fine Arts studios in Los Angeles. On the way west, they stopped off at Waukesha to see their mother and sisters. This new movie business was such a strange thing to Sarah Aitken. She listened as they told her about many things they were doing, trips to London and Paris, and the new companies they had formed. She confessed, however that she wished they were in a business closer to home, perhaps as drugstore clerks or working in their uncle's bank. But she never tired of hearing about the pretty movie actresses her bachelor sons mingled with—Mary Pickford, Lillian and Dorothy Gish, Mabel Normand, Mae Marsh, and others. Sarah loved to go to the movies, as did her three daughters Jessie, Mabel, and Gladys.

Always when her two sons departed, Sarah's eyes would fill with tears as she kissed them good-bye. "Be good boys," she would call after them. "And don't fail to go to church on Sunday."

Griffith had wired Harry that he was so busy at the studio that he could not meet the Aitkens at the Los Angeles railroad station. However, he would have a studio car and driver awaiting them. The chauffeur had been instructed to take the film company executives first to the studio, then to the Alexandria Hotel, where Griffith had arranged rooms for them.

The car was there, and they got into the plush back seat. Roy whispered to Harry, "This is a Pierce-Arrow. Pretty darn good-looking job for a studio car. This is where some of our hard-earned money is going."

Harry smiled. "Remember what Billy Bitzer said. Griffith has expensive tastes."

The drive along the palm-lined streets was exhilarating as the bright sunshine beat down on their backs. Finally, after a short ride, they drove up in front of a large, rambling frame house that looked as if it had been built before Grandpa Aitken's move from Illinois to Wisconsin.

"This doesn't look like a studio," Roy said.

"Well, let's not worry about that now," Harry replied. "Remember, we're getting some very good program pictures out of this place, no matter what it looks like from the outside."

The Aitkens were ushered into the office first. It was nothing but a small room with a couple of pigeonhole desks and two or three chairs. Griffith had heard that the Aitkens had arrived, so he came in from an outside stage where he had been helping John Emerson direct a picture.

Griffith began introducing Harry and Roy to his staff. The first to greet them was Frank Woods, head of the scenario department. Next came petite Anita Loos, who had been hired to write scripts when Griffith first opened the studio. Later, she would marry John Emerson and write *Gentlemen Prefer Blondes*.

Roy had heard a great deal about Loos and told her so. He had sold some of the pictures made from her stories to London, Paris, and Berlin theaters. She seemed very pleased that foreign movie audiences liked them.

After a short visit in the office, the talk about production matters bored Roy, and he began to get restless. He was anxious to get out on the nearby stage and see what was going on, so business matters could wait as far as he was concerned. As always, Harry picked up his brother's nervous signals. "Roy, why don't you take a look around? I know you want to see some production in action."

In a few minutes, Roy stood on an uncovered stage next to John Emerson, who was directing a picture. Aitken was astonished at the simplicity of it all as one woman assistant listed the scenes, descriptions of clothes, entrances, exits, and so forth, on the set for the director.

Unlike the elaborate preparations for later movie productions that cost millions of dollars, the set that Roy stepped onto that day at his Fine Arts studio required only a few days to get ready and a few more days to actually shoot the scenes. If this represented the ridiculously low-cost side of moviemaking, he was soon to witness the sublime effort.

17

The First Superpicture:
Birth of a Nation

Because he traveled back and forth between New York and the London, Paris, and Berlin offices several times a year, Roy Aitken was never able to attend board of directors meetings of Majestic Film Corporation. He left these matters to Harry, who was often too busy to bring Roy up to date on developments by letter. So there were huge gaps in Roy's knowledge of company activities.

Whenever he did come back to the States for several weeks or a month, however, he and Harry would spend hours over pleasant dinners while Roy listened to his older brother explain many of the financial and expansion moves he had made in Roy's absence.

For example, he told Roy that Griffith had formed the D. W. Griffith Corporation to handle his special pictures made in partnership with Harry. Griffith cited financial arrangements as the basis for such a corporation. He also organized Wark Film Corporation a year or so later. Wark's purpose was to raise money for expanding *The Mother and the Law*, a Majestic picture, into the expensive *Intolerance*, which Griffith earmarked for release in 1916. Actually, Roy found it quite confusing that the Aitkens and Griffith needed all these corporations to conduct their business, but Harry being on the scene felt them necessary, and Roy left that part of the business to him.

It is worth noting, however, that in January 1914 at the height of this reorganization, the Aitkens' Majestic Film Corporation records show that Harry owned 556 shares of stock and Roy owned 95, which gave the brothers control. Griffith owned 40 shares. Thus, the Aitkens and Griffith owned 1,051 out of 1,200 shares of Majestic stock. Men who were the

Aitkens' close friends held the remainder of the stock. They came from various businesses and professions.

In their special contract, Harry and Griffith also had varying arrangements concerning the profits made from pictures under its terms. *The Escape* is one of those in which the senior Aitken and Griffith had a very complicated arrangement.

Majestic Film Corporation, the brothers' parent company, lent its facilities and sometimes its money to finance the Griffith-Aitken specials. Facility rental accounted for about 10 to 15 percent of the total cost of the picture. If not enough funds were available from Majestic to finance the specials, then Harry and Roy would form syndicates, at generous interest rates, raising money here and there.

On April 16, 1914, the Majestic Film Corporation records show that Harry advised the directors that *The Escape*, starring Blanche Sweet, cost $28,000 to produce. He said he had promised Griffith 15 percent of the net profits of this picture in excess of $50,000 gross. Harry offered to purchase the picture from Majestic for $30,000. He then paid author Paul Armstrong a third of the net profits. After this deduction, Griffith was to receive his 15 percent of the remaining profit.

Many of the big four-reel pictures that Majestic made in the early days needed extra financing. "Majestic just hasn't the money to finance some of these pictures," Harry once told Roy, "so we have to seek outside money and pay a stiff price."

Regardless of its budgetary twists and turns, *The Escape* had a wonderful run in a theater located on Broadway, and this success made Griffith happy for a while. But later, he complained that the Aitkens did not promote the picture strongly enough to bring still greater returns to him.

Despite Griffith's grumbling, *The Escape* continued to play successfully in theaters throughout the nation and earned a splendid gross until it was sold to other interests to raise cash. Later in 1919, hearing that the picture was offered at a sheriff's sale, Harry and Roy bought it from the successful bidder. They had a sentimental attachment to *The Escape* since it had launched them into a major competitive position in the motion picture industry. Then, in 1922, when they needed money badly, the Aitkens sold the picture at a profit. "How we hated to see that film pass out of our hands," said Roy.

Battle of the Sexes was another picture that changed ownership several times in the course of its history. Made by Griffith for the Aitkens the first year he joined Majestic Film Corporation, it was a Griffith-Aitken special. But a few years after production, Griffith sold his interest in *Battle* to Harry.

Another three years passed, and Harry sold the *Battle of the Sexes* to Roy, who in turn sold it to Triumph Pictures Corporation. Subsequently, the picture ended up at another sheriff's sale, where Harry Clay Littick bought it. Then remarkably it came full circle and was purchased by Aitken, Inc.

"From this," said Roy, "one gets an idea how films were sold time and time again to investors who thought they could see additional release profit advantages for pictures they believed in."

The first six months of 1914 revealed further growth of the movie enterprises headed by the Aitkens. These included Majestic Film Corporation, Thanhouser Film Corporation, Reliance Film Corporation, Mutual Film Corporation, and Western Import Company, Ltd. In addition, the brothers had contracted for the film production of New York Motion Picture Corporation and North American Film Company in Chicago.

All the film companies under Aitken control through majority stock holdings or film contracts made two-to four-reel pictures popular with theater owners. Competitors envied Aitken film production companies and their bold promotions in the industry.

Even John Freuler and Samuel Hutchinson, disgruntled as they were with Harry's critical appraisal of pictures they had produced at North American Film Company studios, seemed pleased at Mutual's steady growth. Both owned stocks in that distribution company. If Freuler and Hutchinson had any objections to Harry's iron-handed control of censorship on Mutual pictures, they hid them temporarily behind a wall of reserved politeness whenever they met the Aitkens at Mutual board meetings.

The London, Paris, Copenhagen, and Berlin offices were doing well, too. The brothers even had to open film distribution offices in Rome and Vienna to supply the demand for motion pictures under their control. In fact, New Zealand and Australian film buyers, hearing about the box-office power of Griffith, Ince, and Sennett pictures, came to London to view them and buy prints.

Despite the increased interest in his products, Roy was often quite restless with office life in London. On many occasions, he would take some Ince prints and a few Keystone comedies and travel through England and Scotland visiting unfamiliar theaters and opening new accounts by this method.

He also enjoyed traveling by train over the beautiful countryside and stopping in Birmingham, Edinburgh, Glasgow, and other cities. He grew especially fond of the colorful inns and the people who passed through their doors with a grace and charm that earned the English and Scottish people a deserved reputation as "most hospitable." Roy hoped some of their civility had rubbed off on him.

One spring day in 1914, as he stood on a New York pier to supervise the unloading of his fancy Leon Bollee car purchased in Paris, Roy was surprised to see Harry striding toward him. After admiring the car, Harry said, "You arrived just in time for an important conference. Griffith and Thomas Dixon, author of *The Clansman* and *Leopard's Spots*, are having dinner with me at the apartment tonight. They've got a plan to propose to us about a superpicture."

"Superpicture! What's wrong with the four-reelers Mutual is turning out now? They're selling well in England and on the Continent. And over here, too, I hear."

Griffith did have a story to tell that evening. He wanted to produce a long motion picture to be made from several of Thomas Dixon's books, and he thought such a picture would sell well. His eyes shining, the usually taciturn Griffith told the Aitkens his *Clansman* picture would be filled with love, battles, and historical Civil War scenes. Nothing like it had ever been done. It would be a movie first. It would further enhance the reputations of Majestic and Reliance, its directors, and stars.

"The real story of the Reconstruction era has never been filmed," said Griffith. "Tom is a southerner. He knows how deeply the South was hurt and how long it took her to regain her strength. My father was a Confederate officer. I know the hardships the southerners endured in defeat."

Listening to the director's passionate appeal and Dixon's enthusiastic approval, Roy could feel the personal magnetism of the two men. He watched Harry closely, too, and he could see that his brother was also impressed. All the Aitkens knew about this period of American history had come from the lips of the southerners who visited Waukesha each summer, and none of them spoke of the postwar era in such revengeful terms. Yet, the Aitken brothers were raised in a northern liberal tradition in a community where the Prairie Home Cemetery, burial ground of a brother who died in infancy, was also renowned as the last resting place of Lyman Goodnow, conductor of the famed Underground Railroad that had spirited slaves to freedom. With this background in mind, Harry and Roy set historical accuracy aside and viewed the proposed Griffith-Dixon version as little more than the Reconstruction era as many southerners believed it to be.

"How much will this picture cost?" Harry asked cautiously.

"About $40,000," Griffith replied. "But the appeal will be so great that the production cost will be insignificant."

"Forty thousand!" Harry repeated, looking at Roy. The brothers were in shock. No other picture any of their companies produced had cost that much.

After much discussion, Griffith and Dixon persuaded Harry, and he promised to try to get the $40,000 from Mutual or Majestic. Griffith's superpicture was to be a special Aitken-Griffith production, with Majestic merely financing it.

But Harry failed to persuade the boards of either company to back such an expensive picture. They considered a twelve-reel picture, such as Griffith proposed, too much of a gamble. Therefore, Harry and Roy had to try to raise the money on their own. They did just that in what Roy called "the hardest-working campaign I've ever engaged in." He and Harry contacted practically every wealthy person they knew and asked for money. They even invested some of their own savings in the picture and like cavalrymen on a long march went on restricted rations to do it. But they raised the $40,000, and Griffith was elated.

As an organized company, Majestic was used to channel the money to Griffith as needed. Thus, on July 4, 1914, at the Fine Arts lot in California, Griffith joyously began filming *The Clansman,* later reentitled *Birth of a Nation.* He tentatively began producing the picture bit by bit, simultaneously continuing to turn out standard four-reel pictures on contract for Majestic.

It is important to note that in 1914 as the superpicture *Birth of a Nation* went into production, many actors, actresses, and directors, who later became stars, got their start with the Aitken companies. The Gish sisters, Dorothy and Lillian, Mae Marsh, Henry Walthall, Charles Ray, Blanche Sweet, Billie Burke, and many others were being assigned better roles in better pictures and received more advertising as players. During this period, too, men such as John Emerson, Raoul Walsh, James Cruze, and Victor Fleming (*Gone with the Wind*'s director) learned directing techniques from Griffith, Ince, and Sennett. The Aitken companies were schools of a sort from which important actresses, directors, cameramen, and other personnel graduated. Emerson later directed many of Douglas Fairbanks's pictures, and Cruze produced the *Covered Wagon.*

A quarter century after it was produced, *Birth of Nation* became a model for the promotion of another epic Civil War picture. *Gone with the Wind* producer David O. Selznick riddled his famous memos with references to the groundbreaking techniques that the Aitken-Griffith team employed. Some excerpted examples from *Memo from David O. Selznick* (edited by Rudy Behlmer) demonstrate the scope of *Birth*'s influence on later movie promotion:

Mr. Howard Dietz
Metro-Goldwyn-Mayer Executive
May 2, 1939
You do whatever you see fit on this, but I should like most respectfully to suggest that it might be preferable if *Gone With the Wind* were omitted from these announcements for a couple of reasons; to begin with, Al Lichtman shares my hopes that the picture is turning out so brilliantly that its handling will have to be on a scale and of a scope never before tried in the picture business. The only close approach to it would be *The [sic] Birth of a Nation.* (211)

Mr. Al Lichtman
MGM Vice President
October 20, 1939
I think it is wrong not to road show *Gone With the Wind* as it would have
been not to road show *The Birth of a Nation*. In fact, I think it is infinitely
more wrong. It is not for me to say that *Gone With the Wind* is as outstanding a picture for its day as *The Birth of a Nation* was when it was made; however, your own people have said this, and much more. But what I do claim
is that *Gone With the Wind* actually has an infinitely greater audience waiting for it than *The Birth of a Nation* had in advance of its release. And I call
to your attention that the public paid road-show prices to see *The Birth of a
Nation* to an amount, I understand of between $10,000,000 to $15,000,000, at
a time when motion-picture theaters were charging five to fifteen cents per
ticket. (231)

Miss Katharine Brown
Selznick's Eastern Representative
October 7, 1939
As to the advertising, I still think that to use the names of four stars in anything more than fifty per cent of the height, width, and heaviness of type that
is used for *Gone With the Wind* would be the equivalent of having done the
same thing with Henry Walthall and Lillian Gish and Bobby Harron on *The
Birth of a Nation*. What was sold was *The Birth of a Nation*, and what should be
sold is *Gone With the Wind*. (233)

Miss Brown
October 7, 1941
As for remake rights of GWTW, I don't think this should be a consideration,
because Jeffrey and Danny [Selznick's sons] will have to worry about this,
and hopefully they will want to venture into new fields. I think it will be
many, many years, if ever, before anybody wants to think about remaking
GWTW. Imagine, for instance, somebody remaking *The Birth of a Nation*. Although, on second thought, this isn't a bad idea! (256)

All the early pioneers, whether executives, promotional people, directors, cameramen, or stars, were as inexperienced in their fields as the
Aitkens in operating burgeoning movie companies. "There weren't any
experience charts to follow in the movie business when *Birth* burst onto
the scene. That's what made it all the more exciting," said Roy.

Before the filming of *Birth* was completed, an extravagant Griffith had
spent the $40,000 Harry and Roy had raised. The director blamed high
costuming, property, and other costs. Grumbling, Harry and Roy went
out and raised another $10,000. Later, they raised an additional $9,000 for
a total investment of $59,000.

But Griffith still clamored for money, and now the Aitkens began to realize how on the mark was Billy Bitzer's prediction that "the Aitkens might

not stand the gaff of Griffith's extravagant methods." There was nothing to do but confront Griffith, so the brothers told him he'd receive no more funds from them for finishing *The Clansman* (*Birth*) movie. Harry and Roy urged him to complete the picture with available funds. If this were impossible, Griffith would have to go out and raise additional money himself.

Stung and angry, Griffith did just that! Despite the money troubles he was encountering, Griffith let some potential investors view his filming of the *Birth* scenes so that word quickly spread that he had a masterpiece under way. This was encouraging news to the Aitkens, but they still felt that the picture might not be profitable, for its costs now were approaching $80,000. Of this sum, the Aitkens' $59,000 investment was clearly a majority interest.

"I hope that when Griffith finishes the twelve-reel *Clansman*, he'll be ready to go back to four-reel pictures for a while," Harry said. "Perhaps we've been too easy with him on these special picture deals."

The additional financing of the *Birth* picture by D. W. Griffith through sales to outside investors was both daring and productive. The director proved he could sell effectively when the need arose.

Griffith never did go back to the production of shorter pictures of the 1913–1914 type. The success of the *Birth of Nation* catapulted him into a league by himself. It also changed the opinion of many people concerning the future of the motion picture industry. But the most astonishing aspect was the public acceptance of *Birth*.

Roy's notes from the official opening of the colossal film at the Liberty Theater in New York City carry this entry: "The place was sold out in advance, and hundreds of people clamored to get in. We put chairs in the aisles when the theater became filled, and I even helped find seats for famous socialites, bankers, and movie stars. Never before had a motion picture attracted so much attention."

By any measure, *Birth* was a rousing success. Griffith, Dixon, and the Aitkens could hardly believe it. The picture ran for forty-eight weeks at the Liberty. A short time thereafter, they booked eighteen road shows, complete with separate orchestras and publicity men touring the major cities. One *Birth* road company even toured Australia. The admission to the Liberty Theater and at all the road show theaters was set at $2 per person, a new high for motion pictures.

At least three patrons had free admission as guests of the Aitkens, according to their brother-in-law Willard S. Griswold, a practicing lawyer in Milwaukee when Roy and Harry opened *Birth of a Nation* in New York. "Mabel and I and their mother Sarah Hadfield Aitken went to New York to see it," said Griswold. "We stayed several days at their apartment across from Trinity Church and only two blocks from Central Park. Harry and Roy introduced us to many of the actors and to D. W. Griffith, their director."

Harry also invited the same family members to Chicago to see the opening of *Birth* in the Loop. "It was a stupendous thing!" Willard said. "Harry was a prince and the brains of the Aitkens. He was a genius with a lot of ability. Roy liked fancy clothes and cars and they both liked to put on the dog. They sent out eight- and ten-piece orchestras around the country to introduce *Birth of a Nation*."

From all over America, feedback poured into the Aitken offices. "What a thrilling, dramatic story of the South," people said almost with one voice. And many critics, executives, and others were saying, as the huge gross receipts rolled in, "The superpicture is here! Everything will be changed now. Let's get on the bandwagon."

One man who leaped aboard very rapidly was a shrewd theater owner and exchange operator, like the Aitkens: Louis B. Mayer of Boston. According to Gary Carey's biography of Mayer (*All the Stars in Heaven*), the future MGM head grabbed at any opportunity in 1915 to earn the money to feed his own ambitions as a movie mogul.

> His [Mayer's] chance came when D. W. Griffith's *The Birth of a Nation* [*sic*] was placed on the states-rights market after playing advance-price "special engagements" in Los Angeles, New York, Boston and Chicago. Mayer immediately got in touch with Harry Aitken of Mutual, the company that had financed Griffith, and inquired how much was being asked for the New England franchise. The price quoted by Aitken was staggering for that period— $50,000 plus 10 percent of the net profits—but Mayer accepted the deal without hesitation.
>
> He had put aside a few thousand dollars for investment, and Fanny Mittenhal, who knew a good thing when she saw it, offered a thousand from her savings. The bulk of the money came from some of Mayer's friends who became partners in a new corporation, Master Photoplays, of which Mayer was president and major shareholder—he owned 25 percent of it. The company had been established to separate *Birth of a Nation* from Mayer's other distribution interests, and to underline this autonomy, Master Photoplays maintained offices separate from those of the Louis B. Mayer Film Company.
>
> *The Birth of a Nation* opened its general-release New England run at the Colonial Theatre in Haverhill on September 3, 1915. Two years later Mayer boasted that his company had made over $1 million from the film, but probably he was exaggerating—the records of the Mutual Company suggest that Master Photoplays made no more than $665,000. Minus the advance and the producer's percentage, this means Master Photoplays cleared about $600,000, of which Mayer's share would have been $150,000, a very tidy sum for a time when income tax was low. (28)

To the Aitkens, who longed to build their own cash reserves, these stories of how *Birth* helped their competitors earn capital for independent ventures provoked a mixed reaction. "Mayer soon became the first motion picture executive in the nation to receive a salary of $1 million annually while we still had tremendous obligations to our exchanges and movie companies," said Roy.

Aitken did note, however, that *Birth* receipts had helped the brothers' treasury somewhat. But Griffith took account of this as well and persuaded Harry to invest $200,000 in *Intolerance*, his second special picture under the Aitkens' contract. Expanded from his picture *The Mother and the Law, Intolerance* carried a higher price tag than *Birth of a Nation*, and Griffith considered it a better picture than its predecessor also made under the Aitken banner. Oddly enough, the critics agreed. *Intolerance* was an artistic success but a financial failure.

For the Aitken brothers, this experience showed how fast things moved in the movie industry and only served to spur them on to consolidate their holdings in Epoch Producing Company. Organized solely for the distribution of *Birth of a Nation*, Epoch broke new ground since no single picture had been so honored. Roy thought that the "sudden and wise organization of Epoch again showed that Harry was back in old form as a careful yet bold planner."

18

Bolting Ahead of Competitors

Two developments led the Aitkens to form a separate corporation for distributing *Birth of a Nation*. The first involved their new associate D. W. Griffith and the second their longtime Milwaukee partner, John R. Freuler.

Originally Griffith had applied for a copyright of *Birth* in the name of D. W. Griffith Corporation, ostensibly because the picture needed protection immediately. At any rate, in the rush of movie company development, Harry and Roy did not protest Griffith's move, but later they inquired why the director had not consulted them before this action. Since no satisfactory answer came forth from Griffith, the brothers searched for ways to protect their huge investment.

Griffith took another action that later raised suspicion in the brothers' minds. Only the Griffith Corporation's name and logo appeared on the filmed introduction to *Birth of a Nation*, which posed no problem except Griffith thereby implied that he had majority control of Epoch, the Aitken company established to distribute the film. As the actual majority shareholders, Harry and Roy deplored this attitude on the part of Griffith. So did author Thomas Dixon. He resented Griffith's claim to ownership of *Birth of a Nation*, which was adapted from his books.

Meantime, relations between Harry and John Freuler had soured, especially after the censorship episode involving Freuler's partner, Sam Hutchinson, and his allegedly risqué movie, *The Quest*. But underlying the Aitken-Freuler relationship was a more philosophical question: "Where are we heading and how much time should we allow to get there?" Freuler was slow and cautious, but the older Aitken brother was full of ideas and anxious to get them into operation. Most inside observers, like Roy, believed that someday the two men would part, even though together they had weathered many financial crises from 1906 to 1915.

In June 1915, Freuler's steady courtship of New York bankers Crawford Livingston and Felix Kahn, whom Harry had first persuaded to invest in Mutual Film Corporation, began to pay dividends. Freuler succeeded in ousting Harry as president of Mutual, which at the time was the largest film distribution firm in the world. Freuler convinced a majority of Mutual stockholders that Harry, because of his constant expansionist policies, was undependable. Harry remained with Mutual for a few months after Freuler became president. And in an incredible show of naiveté, Freuler fully expected that when the much-trumpeted *Birth* was marketed, Mutual would be chosen to distribute it. It was not to be so.

Freuler and the Mutual board were shocked when Harry, Griffith, and other stockholders formed the Epoch Producing Corporation. Griffith assigned the D. W. Griffith Corporation copyright of *Birth* to Epoch and took in return $5,000 stock in a $110,000 corporation plus a royalty arrangement, as did writer Thomas Dixon.

Of course, the establishment of Epoch Producing Corporation severed completely any remnants of a relationship between Harry and Freuler, and no attempt at reconciliation was made until many years later. By that time it was too late to have an influence on either of their movie careers.

As president of Epoch, Harry inherited some new personnel problems. He was forced to handle two very temperamental men, Griffith and Dixon.

Dixon's unique contract called for a 25 percent royalty on the net profits. After this was subtracted, Griffith received a 37.5 percent royalty of the remaining profits. The remainder went to Epoch Producing Corporation stockholders. Harry and Roy held a 51 percent majority in the corporation, so they received a commensurate share of the profits.

About three months after the launching of *Birth*, Harry had lunch with Roy just before the younger Aitken set sail for London. "Griffith has some odd ideas about *Birth* profits," Harry said. "He thinks you and I are making too much from our Epoch stock. He wants to swap part of his royalty in Epoch for a slice of the profit our stock receives. It's a crazy idea."

"What shall we do about it?" asked Roy.

Harry laughed. "I suppose we can try it for a while and see how it works out. I've tried to run the numbers, and it comes out about the same either way. Let's keep Griffith happy. He certainly wants every dollar he can get."

Later, to silence his brother's critics who wrote scathing pieces about Harry's alleged stubbornness in dealing with movie executives and associates, Roy cited this conversation to demonstrate that Harry did not always insist on having things his way. "People writing about their business relationships with Harry should consider that he often yielded to many odd requests from Griffith, Ince, and Sennett whenever it did not adversely affect the development of our movie companies. All this in the name of harmony," said Roy.

Harry's greatest weakness was his love for promotion. He seemed compelled to grasp and exploit opportunities when they appeared. He did not like to see them go unheeded and felt he was the best man to implement and follow an idea through to the end. It was as if Harry followed Plato's advice that to decline to lead is to be led by someone inferior to yourself. He viewed this trait of always being out in front of the pack as an asset that kept the competition off guard. Harry saw little value in looking back even to consolidate his gains.

"Competition forces one to look ahead, Roy," he once told his brother. "We must constantly look ahead to try to see what's coming next year or five years from now."

Within two months of its organization, Epoch Producing Corporation began issuing dividends to its stockholders from *Birth of a Nation* profits. By October 1, 1915, Epoch's ninth dividend had the movie industry buzzing. The Aitken corporation stock returns reached a spectacular rate on the original investment at 25 percent.

Epoch stockholders and the shares they owned were as follows: Harry E. Aitken, 385; Roy E. Aitken, 197; W. H. Clune (Los Angeles theater operator), 150; Goldstein Company, 62; L. Hampton, 50; Mae B. Ranger, 50; R. J. Huntington, 10; Majestic Motion Picture Company, 24; D. W. Griffith, 60; E. Banzhaf, 50; A. H. Banzhaf, 3; J. R. Barry, 7; and W. Seligsberg, 2.

In the first year, Epoch issued forty-one dividends, most of them quite large. The size and frequency of these dividends continued to astonish the movie and business world. Investors tried to buy stock in Epoch, but no stockholder wanted to sell.

As expected, *Birth of a Nation* receipts set a torrid pace in the first sixteen months of Epoch's operation. Road show appearances from March 3, 1915, to July 1, 1916, accounted for receipts of nearly $3 million, while the net profit was $1,449,624.89, plus $237,000 for the sale of state rights to distributors like Louis B. Mayer.

Dixon, with a 25 percent royalty contract, siphoned off $438,137 for his share. With slightly less than 38 percent royalty, Griffith received $485,182, while Epoch stockholders shared $526,205 or put it into operating capital.

No other motion picture to date had achieved such a financial record. And *Birth of a Nation* was just getting started. A number of sources report that the film was seen by one hundred million Americans who forked over $30 to $40 million before *Birth* faded ten years after it was first filmed. Roy greeted such statistics with a dose of healthy skepticism. "Final figures are difficult to determine," he said years later, "because so many agencies and distributors handled the film and total records are scanty. Also, theaters took much of the gross for their expenses and profit. The profits that reached Epoch, of course, were considerably reduced in many instances."

He added, "But it was a profitable motion picture, and all of us associated with Epoch were 'in clover,' so to speak, for a little while."

Beneficiaries from *Birth's* success ran the gamut in movie and business circles as the motion picture brought fame and financial security to the Aitken companies, directors, stockholders, actors, and actresses. To some extent, they all shared in the steady stream of box-office receipts from road companies and individual theaters that were showing the picture. Most of all, the picture brought recognition to the Aitken brothers, who were atop the popularity polls in 1915. Competitors such as Carl Laemmle, Adolph Zukor, Sam Goldwyn, Jesse Lasky, William Fox, Cecil B. De Mille, and others, although progressing well in their own film production programs, envied the Aitkens who had bolted far out in front of the pack. The brothers had the top talent in stars and directors and the most outstanding pictures on the market. And Harry knew how to promote them. He ran eye-catching publicity articles and advertised on a large scale in the *Saturday Evening Post* and other mass media publications. From the time they entered movie production in 1909, the Aitkens had leaped over other pioneers who once had a three- to five-year start on them.

Perhaps even more remarkable, in ten short years, Harry and Roy had gone from nickelodeon operators in Chicago (1905) to producing the popular *Birth of a Nation* in 1915. They had progressed from small-time, money-short opportunists to the highest stature in the public entertainment field. To be at the top was a rather giddy but nonetheless exhilarating experience for Harry, thirty-eight, and Roy, thirty-three.

Then, in mid-1915, new problems surfaced, and the ominous warnings that should have been seen went unnoticed at first by the two young movie moguls from Wisconsin. One matter related to Griffith's director-colleagues and the other to *Birth's* perceived unfairness in depicting black people during the Reconstruction period. Each would have far-reaching consequences for the Aitkens.

"Thomas Ince and Mack Sennett are becoming a little jealous of the fame Griffith is getting," Harry briefed Roy one day in their New York office. "Ince wants to make a superpicture, *Civilization*, and Mack Sennett is also casting around for a proper script for a super. They want some financial backing for these specials and a share in the profits."

"Well?"

Harry shrugged. "I suppose we'll have to allow them support. We've lent it to Griffith to help him make *Intolerance*. Ince and Sennett won't be happy if we don't help them, too."

"That's the trouble with having three top directors with big ambitions," Roy grumbled. "Each wants exactly what the other gets, or more if he can arrange it."

Shortly after the New York opening of *Birth of a Nation*, Oswald Garrison Villard, editor of the *Nation*, and the self-styled champion for the advancement of blacks in the United States, printed a diatribe against the motion picture as unfair to the southern Negroes.

This attack came as a surprise to board members of Epoch Producing Corporation, and the Aitkens issued a statement that Griffith had handled his subject masterfully and justly. Harry pointed out that no such protests had occurred in California or Washington when the picture was shown there. Villard went further and laid the matter before the mayor of New York City, John J. Mitchell.

Suddenly the Boston papers headlined race riots in that city as well after the picture was shown there. However brief, the news of the riots was in the minds of millions of Americans. In fact, newspaper accounts actually sparked interest, and the lines of people wishing to see what the controversy was all about boosted attendance.

Censorship battles also erupted in Chicago and Ohio. The attempt to ban the picture in Chicago resulted in numerous jury trials, and when they were over, the Aitken forces prevailed.

Griffith and Dixon were deeply upset by the censorship troubles. Dixon further inflamed the situation with fiery retorts to the press and in speeches from his pulpit. The minister defended his script by pointing out that the attacks on *Birth* were without foundation, since the depiction of the white carpetbagger's reign of terror over the South was based detail for detail on the *Congressional Record* of the period prepared by a Joint Select Committee of Congress. Dixon challenged his critics to review this vast work, labeled "An Investigation into the Condition of the Late Insurrectionary States," and other documents and published records of the Reconstruction era on which he had based his writings.

In the meantime, a bewildered Griffith, hurt at the flood of criticism directed at his superpicture, tried at first to ride out the storm. But his own southern honor required that he defend himself.

Privately Griffith expressed disgust that a vocal minority saw *Birth* not as a movie classic but as an elaborate excuse for racial hatred. The director appeared caught off guard by the protests against portraying blacks as buffoons in southern state legislatures or rapists pursuing white maidens to the edge of cliffs where they had to choose between honor and death. Yet, Griffith could not deny that while his superpicture depicted widespread black debauchery in several reels, it closed with the Klan in "heroic" revolt against oppression by blacks and northern carpetbaggers. As an excuse for his portrayal of the Klan in such terms, Griffith offered a comment that he attributed to Woodrow Wilson. Griffith asserted in his autobiograpy that President Wilson viewed *Birth* in its true light when he referred to the book on which the movie was based as "a run to the rescue scene of the downtrodden South after the Civil War" (88).

The continued attacks on *Birth* led Griffith to mount a public counteroffensive. A careful reading of the facts, as preserved by Roy's recollections, indicate that Harry refused to join Griffith in the public debate. Harry's drive and emotion centered on his organizational skills, and he preferred to concentrate on the legal aspects of censorship. Among the Aitken papers is a copy of a speech delivered from the stage by Griffith at the Tremont Theater in Boston at the height of the controversy. It is hard to imagine that D.W. would entrust such a personal document to his partners unless he sought their help in toning down the rhetoric.

Griffith began his speech by tracing for his large audience the legal steps that he and the producers took to ensure that *Birth* was not offensive to any group as claimed. In this connection, the director cited action by a committee of the National Board of Censorship that voted fifteen to eight to certify the movie for its "excellent technical aspects and good moral effect."

To demonstrate that he had local statutes on his side as well, Griffith next presented a lengthy case-by-case summary of failed attempts to ban the movie in New York, Chicago, and other cities. He concluded by addressing the measures taken by him to edit out the morally offensive parts of the film and asserting that revised as such it had passed through every channel required by law and custom in the motion picture field. "I think this shows our good intent and effort to be fair and open minded," he said.

Then in a light jab at the excessive tactics he thought the protestors were getting away with, he added, "Upholding the dignity of the law and the keeping of the peace is a police function."

His final appeal was against the concerted attempt to suppress *Birth of a Nation*, which he objected to on constitutional grounds. "We only ask the constitutional right of free speech. The motion picture is a form of speech, as important, as powerful, and as clean and decent as any form we have."

Griffith's long-winded speech won few converts. In the decades that followed, the controversy over the movie continued. Already saddened by the division of people by class, color, religion, and ethnicity in midtwentieth-century America, Harry expected his motion pictures to help close the gap, not widen it. He was, however, bucking a tide in which the prevailing attitude was one of pride and prejudice for or against those perceived as different.

Conspicuous by their absence were other filmmakers such as Laemmle, Zukor, and Goldwyn, who had just as big a stake in thwarting politically motivated censorship as did Griffith, Dixon, and the Aitkens. Of course, unlike the Aitkens, these studio heads were not linked to two southern firebrands like Griffith and Dixon who brought with them some built-in prejudices against northerners and blacks. Yet, there is no evidence suggesting that Harry and Roy shared these biases or were, for that matter, anti-Semitic, as were so many of their contemporaries in the industry. A backlash against this form of racism may partly explain why the Jewish immigrant moguls neither came to the Aitkens' aid in this matter nor entirely accepted them into the Hollywood community over which they later reigned.

An example of the pride and prejudice of the times that impacted on the Aitkens' empire is found in Budd Schulberg's book *Moving Pictures: Memories of a Hollywood Prince*. Schulberg makes it clear that as a Jewish lad growing up in Hollywood, stars like Tom Mix and Doug Fairbanks held no lustre for him. Only boxers, movie moguls, and others who shared his Jewish heritage stirred his pride.

> The legendary Ty Cobb could break a batting record almost every time he came up to the plate, but no chill came to my skin at the mention of his name. That sensation was reserved for Benny Leonard (undefeated lightweight boxing champion of the world). He was doing with his fists what the Adolph Zukors and William Foxes, and soon the L. B. Mayers and the B. P. Schulbergs were doing in their studios and their theaters, proving the advantage of brain over brawn, fighting the united efforts of the goyische establishment to keep them in their ghettos.

Schulberg's example shows how ethnic and racial controversies nearly always involve a mixture of conflicting aspects that leave one group or the other with a basic distrust. Stereotype thinking of this sort, however, seems to be absent in the Aitkens' case, because these patterns have no roots in their background and upbringing.

No less an authority, the late Dr. William K. Everson, New York University leading lecturer-author on silent films, illustrated this point when he attended a film festival sponsored by the Aitken brothers' hometown newspaper on April 16–17, 1982. Everson gave the keynote speech at this event honoring Harry and Roy posthumously and offered commentary in an article that appeared in the Waukesha County Historical Society's publication, *Landmark*. Waukesha has a notably small black population and no record of racial problems at all, according to Everson. From this, he concluded that *Birth of a Nation* could be shown at a subsequent film festival in the Aitkens' hometown without the usual hostility so often attendant on its public showings. He added, "In view of the Aitkens' financial backing of it [*Birth*] and the fact that the sponsoring *Waukesha Freeman* started life as an abolitionist newspaper, it is certainly an entirely appropriate film to use in 1983" (vol. 25, no. 3/82, p.18).

Originating from an area with such a benign perspective toward the worth of the individual, regardless of race or creed, the Aitkens probably were caught off guard by the controversies that surfaced and took center stage amongst their contemporaries during the silent movie era. However, despite racial protests over *Birth of a Nation* and ethnic overtones in the motion picture industry, the Aitken empire flourished. Riding a tide of publicity sparked by public curiosity in both its controversy and innovation, *Birth of a Nation* continued to interest Americans in great numbers between 1915 and 1919. The public spotlight once again focused on this superpicture from 1922 to 1925 when *Birth* was distributed nationally and internationally by United Artists in a joint venture with Aitken-controlled Epoch Producing Corporation.

Epoch held election of officers yearly, and Harry and Griffith alternated in the office of president. This practice continued even after Griffith left the brothers to make his own pictures in 1917. The now famous director always took a deep interest in Epoch and *Birth of a Nation*—as well he should: it paid him dividends. Griffith was president of Epoch in 1922 when minority groups again organized against the showing of *Birth* in New York City.

Following Epoch's initial successes, however, Harry and Roy had already embarked on still another motion picture–producing venture. Triangle Film Corporation had the potential to be the best company in their entire portfolio, with Harry as president and Griffith, Ince, and Sennett serving as vice presidents of production.

19

Triangle Sets Pattern
for Movie Industry

After the smashing success of *Birth of a Nation* in 1915, the Aitken brothers had 51 percent ownership in Epoch Producing Corporation and another 65 percent of stock ownership in Majestic Film Company. Plus, they still held stock in other holdings, such as Mutual after the takeover by John Freuler. As Harry stated, they rode a crest of stock collateral with which to negotiate bank loans. Like leaders of any other growing business, they sometimes needed capital to meet production, salary, office, and other expenses.

The Aitken business philosophy was simple: forget the high interest rate on loans as long as the new enterprises brought more business, more control of film exchanges, theaters, directors, actors, actresses, cameramen, and other skilled personnel needed to operate a silent motion picture empire. With this approach, it is little wonder that, at any given time, a large portion of stock in one or more of the Aitkens' movie companies was in bankers' hands to secure loans. But the financiers followed success, and the growth possibilities of the Aitken holdings made them willing to advance sums from $25,000 to $200,000 at a time.

Roy was constantly concerned about the number and size of outstanding loans. He often complained to his older brother as they sat alone in their New York apartment. "Sometimes when I think about all the money we owe, I can't go to sleep. Don't you worry about it?" he asked one evening.

Harry looked at him for a moment before answering. "I don't worry as long as I can see our movie companies expanding and doing more business. Certainly, we have to pay out large sums for salaries, rents, and equipment before we can take in sizable returns. But so long as those pictures are showing in theaters and bringing in large gross receipts, we'll eventually get our cut from each production and also a slice from the distribution profits. Then we can pay up loans."

Unforeseen by Harry was the cut in distribution profits that Freuler engineered as president of Mutual Film Corporation. In retaliation for Harry's move in bypassing Mutual for distribution of the *Birth* film, Freuler began to make things miserable for his former Wisconsin partners. He ordered a slowdown in Mutual's distribution of Aitken-owned properties from Majestic, Reliance, Thanhouser, and New York Motion Picture Films, while speeding up productions of North American Film Corporation, Freuler's own producing unit. Harry and Roy chafed under such harassment, since it reminded them of the treatment they had received from another Wisconsin transplant, Carl Laemmle. As he had done earlier, Harry found a way around the blockade raised by a former partner.

One July night, the senior Aitken returned to the apartment out of breath and started packing. "Roy, I'm going to La Junta, Colorado, tomorrow with Kessel and Bauman. Griffith, Sennett, and Ince will meet us there. I want to see if they'll join in a new distribution company I plan— Triangle. If they will, we won't have to worry about Mutual any longer. We'll have a new and better organization than Freuler and his associates. Don't mention this to anyone until all details are concluded."

Within a week the movie world reeled from the news that Harry Aitken had organized Triangle Film Corporation, a new, tightly knit production and distribution organization. The officers included the top names in motion pictures: Harry Aitken, president, and D. W. Griffith, Thomas Ince, and Mack Sennett, vice presidents of production. Adam and Charles Kessel, as well as Charles Bauman, were named to the board of directors.

Harry also borrowed a management tool from Bauman and Kessel that he himself had used successfully in luring D. W. Griffith away from Biograph. Aitken gave his three directors/vice presidents sizable amounts of free stock in Triangle, and he established a profit-sharing opportunity for them on special pictures. He also provided each their own production unit under the Triangle umbrella: Fine Arts for Ince, Keystone Comedies for Sennett, and Master Pictures for Griffith. Harry himself had selected the name for the latter as a way to tout his most successful director in the wake of *Birth of a Nation*. Little wonder that Griffith, Ince, and Sennett snapped up the chance to sign with Triangle. It was simply the best deal any of them had had to date. Each owned stock in Triangle, and each had his own film production studio. The Kessel brothers and Bauman appeared satisfied, too, because they were now part of a combine with the capacity to produce and distribute its own pictures.

The motion picture journals of the day did not miss the significance of the landmark deal. As one publication reported:

> Triangle Film Corporation is probably the most comprehensive film-producing corporation in existence. The new concern will participate in every branch of the motion picture business.
>
> It will not only write its own stories and produce them, but will maintain agencies in every large city which deserves such services. It is also said that a chain of theaters wherein will be shown features made under the Triangle name will be owned and operated by Triangle.
>
> The United States, according to our information, will not be the only field, for the plans of Triangle are to have distributing companies in the principal cities of England, France, Germany, Russia, Italy, Australia, Latin and South America.

What the news accounts failed to do, however, was distinguish between plans and accomplishments. Triangle Film Corporation needed additional funds to bring any of this to fruition, since the size of the Aitken brothers' bank account had dwindled significantly after the $200,000 allocated for Griffith's ill-fated *Intolerance* and the hundreds of people who siphoned away assets through the weekly payrolls.

But typical of Harry's courage, first developed in a Waukesha schoolhouse, he was not about to let lack of funds deter him. He immediately went to the bank in New York that carried the profitable *Birth of a Nation* account. He pleaded his case to the bank officers, explaining Triangle's tenuous situation in an honest and forthright manner. They should know, he told them, the Aitkens had stock in other companies—namely, Majestic, Thanhouser, Reliance, and New York Motion Picture Corporation—but it all lay in the hands of Wall Street bankers as collateral for loans to operate these production units.

"I'll need some money until we can properly finance this new corporation," Harry pointed out.

The bank president reflected on the large *Birth of a Nation* deposits entering his bank every day. "How much will you need?" he asked cautiously.

"About $100,000 to start," Harry said softly.

"What collateral have you got?"

"We haven't any that isn't tied up." Harry's voice barely rose above a whisper.

The banker considered for a moment, pursed his lips, then said, "Well, you are carrying a very fine account here, and you have a good reputation. We'll lend you $100,000 on your personal note. Later, perhaps more."

After securing this loan, Harry and Roy now moved swiftly to set up Triangle-owned exchanges in key cities. To head this venture, they hired J. R. Naulty, who at one time had handled distribution for the Trust's General Film Company. Naulty was very capable, and it did not take him long to persuade many exchange owners to sell to the Aitkens and stay on as managers, as well as owning minority stock. Naulty used as a selling point Harry Aitken's reputation as the man who had financed the famous *Birth of a Nation*, and, along with his brother, had simultaneously built a widespread silent movie empire. "Better to get in on a good deal when the opportunity was offered," Naulty advised the exchange owners.

Within a short period following incorporation, Triangle placed its stock on sale at $5 per share. Because of the past successes of the Aitkens and their three directors, demand for the stock moved at a brisk pace. It rose to $9.25 in no time.

Less sanguine about risking someone else's money than his own, Harry took out newspaper advertisements that sold Triangle stock but also warned applicants not to buy unless they realized that it was a gamble in a new enterprise.

The sale of stock eased the brothers' financial pinch for a while, but a great deal of the new flood of capital went into stepped-up film production, so that they would have enough pictures to supply their many exchanges and theater accounts.

A friend later confided to Roy, "Even when Harry had large sums of money coming in from picture grosses, it was already spent before it reached the brothers' bank account." Rather than an alien situation, this procedure was modus operandi for two young men who refused to turn away from an alluring profit-making opportunity once it caught their eye. The Aitkens were like the captain and first mate of a ship pressed against the shoals yet sailing on in hopes that a clear passage was just around the bend. Harry seemed far more susceptible to the vagaries of life's currents than Roy, who knew and accepted his human limitations.

The proven talents and filmmaking reputations of Griffith, Ince, and Sennett served to balance Triangle's overzealous promotional ventures. Harry and Roy, along with millions of Americans, thought at this point that these three men possessed more artistic and picture-making genius than any trio of directors in the world. The Aitkens were certain that, whatever threat inadequate financing posed to them, their famous directors and talented stars represented a secure financial bridge to the future.

Some saw the Aitken brothers as mere dream merchants peddling a fanciful illusion that had no sustaining power once the dawn broke. Others, including many prominent business and theatrical magnates, viewed the future of Triangle Film Corporation through the same lens as did the Aitkens, a sure bet. The talent cards were stacked in their favor. Divine Providence had given each of their three great directors a different talent, and this diversity enabled the Aitkens to reach millions of people with film productions of considerable variety.

D. W. Griffith, of course, was the director on whom the brothers relied the most. They believed he would continue to demonstrate the creative possibilities of the art of motion pictures through his innovative direction and technical touches. He had already perfected so many techniques—the dissolve, the close-up, night filming, panoramic shots and others, which have been copied and expanded by directors the world over since 1915.

Whatever Thomas H. Ince lacked in artistic skills, he more than made up for in his orderly and systematic approach to filmmaking. Griffith had the wandering genius. Ince had the precision of an assembly line over which he presided as director in chief. He demanded from his subordinates fast action and tight dramatic construction. His scripts and shooting directions were worked out to the last detail. Even when he produced for Carl Laemmle at IMP and later for Bauman and Kessel, he displayed an uncanny ability to recognize a dramatic story in one glance and, more important, to transport it from his mind to a motion picture screen. By the time he joined the big three at Triangle, Ince had set the accepted pattern for standardized movie production.

Mack Sennett, on the other hand, worked with Griffith at Biograph where his trademark sense of humor first surfaced only to be quashed and later rejuvenated under the visionary banner of Bauman and Kessel's Keystone comedies. Sennett looked for the ridiculous in every situation and created many of the hilarious episodes in his Keystone pictures as the production of his movies went along.

The big Irish former boilermaker also created havoc in his private life. He and Mabel Normand had a tempestuous relationship that ended when she caught him in an uncompromising position with her screen rival Mae Busch. This was after Sennett had broken Normand's arm in one of their many fights. Unlike Griffith or Ince, Sennett believed that life was too short to devote it to a single pursuit like moviemaking. This also put him on a collision course with Harry Aitken, who devoted his whole life to his vision. Yet, the two men had a grudging respect for each other, although Harry lamented Mack's inattention to detail unless it wore a skirt. Until late in his career, Sennett eschewed detailed scripts, but by then he and the Aitkens had chosen separate pathways.

Contracts that Griffith, Ince, and Sennett signed with Triangle called for production of one feature per week by Griffith and one by Ince, while Sennett was to produce two double-reel comedies per week. Thus, Triangle was able to offer theaters a Griffith feature and Sennett comedy for half a week and an Ince feature and another Sennett comedy for the last half of the week. Harry brainstormed this simple yet quality-type program. He knew the competition could not match it, because the Aitken directors and their stars had the clout to produce pictures on almost an assembly-line basis and still retain big box-office appeal.

To acquire the Triangle weekly product, theater owners had to contract with Triangle to accept all pictures required for their weekly programs. Their reaction was predictable. A large number of theater owners were willing to come under the Triangle banner, because the magic of Griffith, Ince, and Sennett meant huge box-office grosses. Within three months after the organization, Harry was quoted in a newspaper interview as saying that Triangle had signed contracts with six hundred theaters in the United States to use Triangle products exclusively. In another three months, he was quoted as stating that Triangle now served 1,500 theater owners and had also made large sales of the corporation's films to foreign firms.

Of course, the minute Harry organized Triangle Film Corporation, film supplies to his former distribution company, Mutual Film Corporation, began to dry up. All that was left to Freuler were the pictures of North American Film Company, plus whatever other independent film he could pick up in the United States and Europe. But most U.S. companies had their own distribution channels, and few were inclined to give Freuler any product.

"I'm sorry for Freuler," Harry said one day, "but he made it impossible for us to stay with Mutual. He was so certain that Griffith, Ince, and Sennett would not desert Mutual."

But Harry Aitken expressed no such sentiment for the General Film Company (the Trust), which was also on its last legs. Every new independent company organized by the Aitkens and their colleagues drove a nail deeper into the coffin of the once powerful Motion Picture Patents Company. Although the court victories over the Trust went to Carl Laemmle and Adolph Zukor—who, unlike the Aitkens, had the capital to fight a protracted legal battle—the Aitkens had already won in the court of public opinion. The moviegoing public had voted with its pocketbook. After the twelve-reel *Birth of a Nation* success, the clumsy one-reel products of the Trust lost their appeal. And the Supreme Court of the United States under Chief Justice Charles E. Hughes of New York declared the patents of the Trust invalid. The 1916 decision opened the door of freedom to independents that, in this last battle, broke the Trust's domination of the tools of their trade: the motion picture camera and the projection machine.

As sweet as the victory was for Harry Aitken, it was even tastier for Adolph Zukor, who had been humiliated by the Trust and forced to sign onto its polices to survive. The tenacious little Hungarian had exacted his revenge, and Harry, too busy with his Triangle financial problems, failed to see how thoroughly Zukor and Laemmle had driven this foe from the field.

Harry was always concerned with making quality pictures, no matter what the cost. The brothers had invested heavily in *Intolerance*, an introspective analysis of the absurdities of prejudice down through the ages, which Griffith was making with time out to produce Triangle shorter-reel program movies. Harry was confident, too, that *Intolerance* would be a quality picture and a profitable one, although he did worry about whether profits would match Griffith's fantastic spending on costuming and scenery.

For example, the great director was using four different casts—one for each of the four stories introduced in *Intolerance* by a woman endlessly rocking the cradle of humanity, holding out hope for life eternal in Babylon, Jerusalem, Paris, and New York.

The cost of costumes for the mob of actors as they followed the betrayal of Babylon to the Persians, the injustice against Christ in Jerusalem, the slaughter of the Huguenots in France, and finally a modern story of treachery and love in New York City was only exceeded by the extravagant scenery. For the Babylon scene alone, Griffith created a gigantic set of ancient temples and statues. Costs rose to $12,000 a day, but Harry stuck by his master director.

"We're leading the field," Harry beamed over lunch one afternoon. "Now I think it's time to fortify our position and get some more top-flight actors, perhaps a number of stars from vaudeville, the legitimate stage and musical comedy."

"Who, for instance?" Roy asked with that same uneasiness that always dogged him when Harry spoke of expansion plans.

The older brother then proceeded to name not one but five, then ten or more stage stars. The younger Aitken was astonished at the number, but Harry said, "Well, Frank Keenan is doing well in Ince pictures; so are Douglas Fairbanks and De Wolfe Hopper with Fine Arts."

"But these stage stars will want big salaries. Look at what Fairbanks is getting from us now. Do we have to take this step?"

"Griffith's for it," Harry came back. "These stage celebrities will add prestige to the Triangle program. People will flock to theaters to see them. Just think, Roy, they will bring the glamour of the stage to the movie screen for untold millions to see and enjoy, millions who might otherwise never set foot inside a legitimate theater."

As Roy well knew, there was no dissuading Harry once he had decided to pursue a course of action. He was like a bull elephant charging toward his favorite water hole, and anything or anyone in the way had better step aside or go along for the ride.

So, it came as no surprise to Roy that shortly thereafter Harry mounted a campaign to sign prominent stage stars. He joined his brother, and the Aitkens hired Arthur Klein, a well-known New York theatrical agent, to solicit his clients on behalf of Triangle.

At first approach, many stage stars were hesitant. They were uncertain about the future of silent movies. But the salaries Triangle offered, $1,000 to $2,500 per week, finally won over many of them. The actors were not receiving that sort of pay in the legitimate theater, and they yearned to experience prosperity.

When so many of their stars signed with Triangle, it brought panic to the Schuberts, Al Wood, Erlanger, Sam Harris, and other theatrical producers. Despite the success of *Birth of a Nation*, these leaders remained convinced that the flickers had no lasting future. This attitude caught them off guard, and when their leading stars signed with the Aitkens, the theatrical producers had to scan their reserve supply of actors and actresses seeking those best qualified for starring roles. Of course, this did not engender fondness toward the Aitken brothers, who now could add theatrical producers to the growing list of people who wished them ill will.

Meantime, Harry and Roy were ecstatic at the number and quality of stage stars eager to sign contracts with Triangle. Unmatched by any of the Aitken brothers' rivals, it was an impressive list:

Sam Bernard, Mary Boland, Billie Burke, Frank Campeau, William Collier, Julia Dean, Elliot Dexter, Marie Dore, Dustin Farnum, Lew Fields, Eddie Foy, Jane Grey, Raymond Hitchcock, Taylor Holmes, Joe Jackson, Thomas Jefferson, Orrin Johnson, Wilford Lucas, Willard Mack, Tully Marshall, Frank Mills, Polly Moran, Trudy Shattuck, William H. Thompson, Sir Herbert Beerbohm Tree, Sarah Truax, Helen Ware, H. B. Warner, Joe Weber, and Harry Woodruff.

Onto the Triangle movie lots in California tromped this vast array of stage stars, who appeared to be a second gold rush. They came from England, New York, and other eastern cities. One historian claimed that Harry hired sixty actors from the legitimate stage before his campaign subsided. But Roy had his doubts.

However, since the younger Aitken traveled back and forth from New York to England, he did not bear witness to this stage star invasion. Although he had no firsthand account of the numbers, Roy did have privy to the enormous salaries Harry told him he had to pay to lure the actors to California. And when his brother said that Sir Herbert Beerbohm Tree of England had signed a six-month contract for $100,000, Roy had his second worst attack of nervousness, exceeded only by Harry's near-death experience in Texas. Roy became even more disturbed as he tried to determine what the stage star salaries averaged in a single month.

To add to the problem, Triangle actors and actresses who had been with the brothers since the founding of the corporation in 1915 naturally were upset by the news of the big salaries paid to the stage performers. They registered their anger to a sympathetic Roy, who had seen many of them rise from the ranks by virtue of talent and hard work, only to feel slighted and cast aside on payday. Most of them were later considered the greatest stars in film history, and their names are inscribed in Hollywood and in the hearts of their devoted fans. On the Aitken payroll as longtime regular players were the following:

Spottiswoode Aitken (not related to Harry and Roy), Mary Alden, Roscoe "Fatty" Arbuckle, Bessie Barriscale, Mae Busch, Jewel Carmen, Chester Conklin, Josephine Crowell, William Desmond, Minta Durfee, Louise Fazenda, Dorothy and Lillian Gish, Louise Glaum, Mildred Harris, Robert Harron, Walter Long, Fred Mace, Enid Markey, Mae Marsh, Mabel Normand, Seena Owen, Eugene Pallett, Charles Ray, Wallace Reid, Mack Swain, Constance Talmadge, Norma Talmadge, Henry B. Walthall, and Clara Williams.

There were also many younger actors and actresses who had yet to gain widespread public attention.

Sadly enough, the stage star program did not prove profitable for the Aitkens. They would have been better off sticking with their established movie stars. Most of the stage personalities had acting skills but were often not very photogenic or nearly as smooth and slender as the movie stars the public had been accustomed to seeing on the screen. Indeed, a number of the stage stars were elderly and overweight, and on film a few even looked ridiculous, especially in romantic scenes. The widespread recruiting program also brought too many of them to Hollywood, at too high a cost, too fast. Harry Aitken and D. W. Griffith had always predicted which way movie trends would go. But they were far off the mark on the stage star program. It proved a very costly mistake.

At the same time stage performers were leaving New York in droves for the riches of Hollywood, Harry had other elements of his campaign searching for theaters to lease for showing movies. The Aitkens auspiciously opened the Knickerbocker in New York and presented former stage star Douglas Fairbanks in his first picture for Triangle, *The Lamb*. Ince's picture *The Iron Strain* was also shown, as was Mack Sennett's *My Valet*, starring Raymond Hitchcock and Mabel Normand. Rental for the leased Knickerbocker cost the Aitkens $65,000 per year.

The Aitkens and their partners expected the stage star pictures to draw well. For two weeks, the ones starring Fairbanks, Hitchcock, and an actor named Orrin Johnson did pull in reasonable-sized audiences. Then attendance began to dwindle. At first the brothers thought this was a New York City phenomenon, but the reaction in other cities where stage star pictures were shown confirmed the truth. The public definitely did not like pictures of this type or the stars.

Surveying the results, Harry had only one option: fold the venture as cheaply as he could. So, regretfully, he canceled the contracts of all stage stars, except a few, paid up like a good soldier, and bade them farewell.

The whole stage star campaign turned into a fiasco that cost Triangle several hundred thousand dollars and, perhaps more important, damaged the Aitken image among many exchange and theater owners. The film enterprise so enthusiastically spun began to unwind like the reel on an out-of-control projector.

Luckily, Triangle, undercapitalized from the beginning, had the cash to pay off the stage stars. Only a few months earlier, Harry had been able to obtain loans up to $500,000 from F. S. Smithers and Company, New York. This was the result of a trip to the Aitkens' California studios made by Herbert Smithers, accompanied by Harry and Roy. Smithers, a man in his mid-forties, enjoyed watching movies being produced. Upon his return to New York, he arranged loans to keep Triangle production levels on schedule. He confided to the brothers that he thought Triangle had a promising future.

Later, when Harry began firing the expensive stage stars, Smithers and Company changed their tune. The bankers became alarmed and began to tighten the purse strings. Other bankers financing competitors like William Fox, Carl Laemmle, Adolph Zukor, and Sam Goldwyn used the Aitken difficulties to circulate rumors and put out feelers that movie companies should consolidate. The financial institutions applauded the idea since they felt this step was needed in an industry where fierce competition threatened ruin for many.

"There are too many companies in the field," one banker told Roy Aitken. "Consolidation would create more profitable markets and greatly reduce administrative and other expenses."

Hearing these rumblings from his brother, Harry initiated an idea to placate the bankers and win their support. He designed a plan for the merger of Triangle with the Zukor and Goldwyn interests. It was a bold step, and trade papers began to report that Harry Aitken was often seen in the company of Goldwyn, Cecil B. De Mille, and others. Rumors spread quickly that a big movie merger was in the making.

At dinner one evening, Harry was in high spirits. "Everything is ready, Roy. Our attorneys and Zukor's have drawn up the papers, and the bankers are willing to finance a merger. When it is effected, it will strengthen Triangle and also the Zukor-Goldwyn companies." Then he added almost wistfully, "This merger should make the industry less volatile, eliminate much competition, and put Triangle on a stable keel."

The following week, Harry and his attorneys boarded a train to Los Angeles to meet Zukor and his group. He invited Sam Goldwyn to accompany the Aitken party and even brought his butler along to give Goldwyn the red carpet treatment. Goldwyn seemed to like the attention.

At the conference of the movie chieftains on the West Coast April 16, 1916, Harry, perhaps because he was so confident of his merger plan, committed what in hindsight can only be regarded as a costly mistake. In his enthusiasm for the merger, Harry opened his books and his heart to his would-be collaborators. Zukor and Goldwyn perused in detail Triangle's policies, programming, salary schedules, and other important matters. The Jewish immigrants turned movie moguls on the other side of the table were uncharacteristically silent.

Zukor, Goldwyn, and De Mille listened with polite interest, but only after hours of negotiations did they finally demur and ask for a few days to think the matter over. Back in New York, Zukor maintained his silence. Then he notified Harry that he would not go through with the merger. Goldwyn and De Mille announced their rejections in the same manner. Now that these competitors knew Triangle's exact financial and operating status, they apparently had plans to continue without Triangle or, as some have suggested, wait until they could pounce on its remains should it self-destruct.

The latter possibility gained credence when, shortly after the meeting with Harry, Goldwyn's Paramount and Zukor's Famous Players announced a merger, snubbing Triangle. "It was the greatest switcheroo in motion picture history," said Roy.

Oddly enough, Harry first took the rejection of his merger plan in stride, passing it off as Zukor's way of evening the score for the Aitkens' refusal to join his stage play film production plan in 1913. Harry was only partly right, for Zukor had not finished with the Aitkens, and Harry was soon to reap the consequences of the failed merger.

Some movie writers claim that the merger plans between Paramount (Lasky/Goldwyn/De Mille), Famous Players (Zukor), and Triangle (Aitkens) floundered because Harry and Zukor vied for leadership of the proposed company. One writer asserted that Harry's refusal to put Epoch Producing Corporation and Western Import Company, Ltd., into the combination aroused the distrust of the other participants.

Whatever the reason, the failure of the merger negotiations dealt a body blow, more powerful than any thrown by boxing great Benny Leonard, to Triangle and Harry's carefully worked-out plan. From initial denial that the setback was little more than a personal vendetta, Harry allowed reality to settle in. "There are rough times ahead for us, Roy," he said sadly. "We'll have to find some other way."

Roy had never seen his brother so perplexed. But there was never any bitterness displayed, even when the Aitken brothers realized that the merger of Paramount and Famous Players posed a tremendous threat to Triangle in its exposed, weakened condition.

Zukor and his new partners did not take long to act. Within weeks, they began a raid on the Aitkens' stock of movie stars, offering them salaries that they knew Triangle could not match. Douglas Fairbanks, the legitimate theater star who had been urged to make movies at Triangle by the Aitken brothers, was the first to accept Zukor's offer. From the outset, Fairbanks often spat with D. W. Griffith, who assigned the acrobatic actor to other directors to get him out of his hair. It was in this practice that Fairbanks found wiggle room to break his contract with Triangle. The handsome star claimed that Griffith had violated the terms of the contract by not supervising all of his Triangle pictures.

"I'm sorry, Roy," Fairbanks explained. "But Zukor offered me $10,000 per week. I could not refuse that kind of money."

This move especially hurt the younger Aitken. He was close to the dashing actor socially and had often lent Fairbanks two of his foreign cars, a Leon Bollee and a Renault.

On the heels of Triangle's merger fiasco and star defections, dissension among Griffith, Ince, and Sennett increased. Each began clamoring for more attention, better scripts, more production money, increased publicity, and additional advertising. Each was also quick to point out to the Aitkens that the other two directors were favored at Triangle. But the root of the problem was professional jealousy combined with unchecked egos.

Ince and Sennett were envious of the rise to high stardom of the saturnine Griffith. They constantly quarreled with Harry and Roy, trying to get larger shares of the Triangle picture budget. Sennett managed to make a superpicture, too, through the New York Motion Picture Corporation. It was called *Mickey*. The financially savvy Charles Bauman and Adam Kessel, who ran New York Motion Picture Corporation, under Triangle management, did not like *Mickey's* serious theme. They put it on the shelf, where it remained until 1918. Sennett actually fell ill after this action, but both he and the picture revived when *Mickey* later became a hit and financial success.

Ince had problems of a different sort with his superproduction, *Civilization*. The picture's pacifist theme did not draw well in the United States, which was being guided toward a war psychosis by the turn of events against the Allies.

While the failure of *Mickey* and *Civilization* added to the discontent of Sennett and Ince, it had far greater effect on the Aitken brothers when taken together with all their financial and distribution problems.

News of the movie directors' dissatisfaction at Triangle reached the bankers' boardroom with the speed of a ticker tape. Investors learned that Griffith was irritable because he could not surpass his artistic achievements attained in *Birth of a Nation* and *Intolerance* when, in fact, he had been pampered and spoiled by the Aitkens. They heard how a highly disappointed Ince felt like he had been shot by one of William S. Hart's six guns when word came that *Civilization* failed to win critical acclaim. But news that the always reliable Sennett had turned out his first flop, when his humorous Keystone pictures were the backbone of Triangle, sent the Wall Street bankers into apoplexy.

Predictably, the financiers showed their uneasiness by urging Harry to reduce operating expenses and to make less costly pictures. An ardent advocate of quality motion pictures, Aitken refused to compromise, maintaining that cost and quality were two sides of the same coin.

Alone, however, the brothers could not stem the troubles that now beset them. With many of their top stars having already left to accept higher offers elsewhere, the Aitkens were forced to use many minor actors in picture roles, and so they had to bend on picture quality, which further alienated their three gifted directors. Some film historians mark this moment as the nadir of Triangle pictures, which began to lose some of their formal appeal. Other, more zealous devotees of silent movies indict Harry Aitken as the chief culprit; some even go so far as to accuse him of mismanagement of the company and its funds.

As with so much in the course of human events, the truth lies somewhere between these two extremes. Relative to the appeal of Triangle pictures, it should be noted that in this instance both Griffith and Ince had attained their highest level of artistic achievement before they joined Triangle. And while it is true that their early Triangle pictures did attract substantial numbers of movie patrons, historians holding this view point out that both directors were trading on their past reputations and not the quality of the pictures they filmed for Triangle. Sennett was an exception. His humorous Keystone pictures sold well before, during, and after his Triangle days.

As for the zealots, their position is untenable and unproved either by facts or logic to suggest that Harry deliberately shipwrecked his greatest creation through mismanagement and misappropriation of funds. He and Roy had worked too hard at every level of the movie industry to suddenly allow even one great jewel in their vast empire to slip away without a fight. Were it not for Harry's vision and genius, there would be no cash box in the first place for either operating expenses or stockholder dividends.

As for shifting funds from one company to the next to keep them all afloat, Harry's gamble is described by one of his severest critics as the unpardonable crime of getting caught doing what everyone else applauded if done successfully: manipulating stocks to increase their value. Unfortunately, with Triangle the Aitkens had other forces in play, including their own shortcomings.

Harry had a twofold fault, neither of which had anything to do with crookedness. He moved too fast with his promotional ideas and, like the field general oblivious to all but a far-off objective, Harry out-marched his support and supply train. Therefore, he was unable to consolidate his gains before moving on. This gave his enemies an opening to come in from behind and interdict his lifeline. How Harry had loved to set the pace in the industry, but with the failure of Triangle's stage star system, the tide of his genius was stemmed, and he was forced to begin his retreat.

Harry shared his second shortcoming with his younger brother. The two men had a heavy dose of midwestern naiveté. In their meteoric rise to power and influence, they trampled on a lot of toes—Laemmle's, Freuler's, and Zukor's, to name a few. These individuals and their contemporaries all had the farm boys from Wisconsin in their sights. Harry, as the Aitken leader, should have known that one who gives no quarter need not expect any when the tables are reversed, especially in the case of bitter rivals like Laemmle and Zukor. These two scrappers had fled Eastern Europe at the height of Jewish persecution, and they weren't about to accept the anti-Semitic fervor they found in America. Everyone's motives, unless he or she was part of the nineteenth-century Diaspora, were suspect until proven otherwise. Once crossed, Laemmle and Zukor, so representative of their community, didn't allow themselves the luxury of anger when getting even paid higher dividends.

Another criticism leveled at the Aitkens implies that their egos and enjoyment of the good life guided them. In other words, they lived like successful entrepreneurs. Part of this was because Harry and Roy believed they had to uphold a certain image to close the next deal when the stakes got higher. But none of this is extraordinary in a business still inventing the rules. Harry Cohn, the iron-fisted head of Columbia studios from 1920 to 1958, said of movie production, "It's not a business—it's a racket." Nonetheless, a racket perhaps more suited to fur, glove, and junk merchants (Zukor, Goldwyn, Mayer) than to farm boys from Wisconsin.

John Freuler, like his fellow Wisconsin natives, had the same naiveté. Had he, Harry, and Roy been able to reconcile their differences and join the fourth major movie pioneer produced by Wisconsin, Carl Laemmle, the history of motion pictures in America would have had a far different orientation. For that matter, if the deal with Goldwyn, Zukor, and De Mille had gone through, Triangle would have been saved. As it was, Triangle had ignited the spark that led to not only eventual consolidation but also more fierce competition among the survivors. Roy summed it up years later in a letter to a friend when he wrote, "We did not know how to protect our companies like Goldwyn, Laemmle, and Zukor did."

In his book *Dreams for Sale*, author Kalton C. Lahue observes:

> While Harry and Triangle could not claim direct credit for the consolidation which affected the industry in 1915–17, certainly the threat of Triangle

and its potential influenced and even hastened the combination of Zukor and Lasky into the soon-to-be-all-powerful Paramount Pictures, indirectly setting the stage for Sam Goldwyn to cut the umbilical cord and move in his own direction. In doing these things, Triangle could consider itself one of the prime factors which helped to set the stage for the fantastic competition in the twenties when Paramount, M-G-M and Fox raced to gain a monopoly in production, distribution and exhibition. Yes, Triangle had made its impact felt, but what of Harry Aitken? (197–98)

With all the defections, dissatisfactions, and outright desertions reported in the Aitkens' ranks, it was inevitable that Triangle's problems impacted on the rest of the brothers' empire. First to feel the shockwaves were the theater owners who had signed contracts to rent and show Triangle pictures exclusively. They wanted to obtain pictures by other producers, but under terms of their contracts with Triangle, they could not.

Consequently, theater grosses began to slip, as competition for patrons grew fierce. While Triangle did less business, the corporation's expenses continued to rise. It was a gloomy situation for the thirty-nine-year-old Harry and his thirty-four-year-old brother Roy.

Finally, in late 1916, Harry was forced to sell twenty-five Triangle film exchanges for $600,000 to William W. Hodkinson, who formed the Triangle Distributing Corporation to distribute only Triangle pictures. Hodkinson had had experience with Paramount before the purchase, and it was felt that he would greatly aid in a Triangle comeback. Later, Stephan A. Lynch, owner of a number of southern theaters, bought an interest in the distribution company.

"With someone else worrying about the exchanges, perhaps we can concentrate on production," Harry said hopefully. But Roy knew how badly his brother felt about relinquishing Triangle exchanges.

"It split our carefully conceived Triangle program," said Roy.

With the exchanges gone, the brothers could no longer hold onto the leased theaters that formerly had used only Triangle films. So they disposed of this asset as well. That left them $600,000 in capital to rebuild Triangle. "But was it enough?" Roy asked. And as if in answer to his question, another piece of bad luck struck.

Adam Kessel and Charles Bauman decided to sell New York Motion Picture Corporation. Kessel was ill and wanted some cash instead of an interest in a movie company. Harry faced a dilemma: let Kessel and Bauman sell to a rival movie company, or have the Aitkens buy out their partners.

He took the latter course. This meant parting with $400,000 of the $600,000 received from Hodkinson. "We had to do it, Roy," Harry explained. "We just can't afford to lose Ince and his westerns or Sennett with his Keystones."

Roy had difficulty sleeping that night. He had a recurring dream. All around him cards with stars' faces painted on some of them fell from an endless deck, and when he awakened in the morning, he feared the nightmare of a crumbling silent movie empire had yet to run its course.

20

Triangle's Loss a Boon to Paramount and MGM

Stripped of its theaters and exchange systems, the Triangle Film Corporation battled on in a field marked by relentless competition in early 1917. However, two lights still burned brightly in the once vast Aitken Movie Empire: Epoch Producing Corporation and Western Import, Ltd. As majority stockholders in these two organizations, Harry and Roy continued to reap profits.

Epoch's receipts came from road show company showings of *Birth of a Nation*. Meanwhile, Western Import supplied hundreds of European theaters with films regularly and had expanded its operations to cover London, Copenhagen, Berlin, Paris, and Rome.

As Triangle's difficulties drained away their assets left and right, the brothers had no choice but to use Epoch and Western dividends to keep Triangle from dying. Although they did stem the hemorrhaging through 1917, the amount of money Epoch and Western provided was not enough to sustain operations, so Harry sought loans elsewhere. He ran into a wall of opposition. For the Aitkens, at least, loans had become almost impossible to attain. Still, Harry and Roy pressed on, determined to save Triangle, the first American motion picture corporation to produce its own pictures, first to distribute them through their own chain of film exchanges, and first to exhibit the pictures exclusively in Triangle-owned or -leased theaters. They wanted to return Triangle to its pinnacle as a motion picture empire with more than forty film exchanges, numerous theaters, and ten production units. With the theaters and exchanges gone, the Aitkens clung desperately to their trump card—the production units supervised by Griffith, Ince, and Sennett.

At the height of the Triangle crisis, Griffith suddenly yielded to offers by Zukor and left the Aitkens in May 1917 to produce pictures on his own through a marketing agreement with the Hungarian movie mogul. A month later, on Roy's thirty-fifth birthday, Ince departed, and finally in July, Sennett pulled out. Each contracted for better deals producing for other companies.

Surveying their losses, the Aitken brothers felt betrayed. They had nurtured these three directors to maturity and given them the opportunity to become rich and famous, only to see them panic and turn heel in the face of Triangle's financial dilemma, to which they had contributed.

Ever analytical, Harry outlined for Roy other reasons why the trio of directors jumped ship when they did. Griffith had alienated himself from the Aitkens by his own financial problems relating to *Birth of a Nation* and the even more extravagant *Intolerance*. Similarly, the failure of *Mickey* and *Civilization* added to the discomfort of Sennett and Ince, respectively. They blamed the Aitkens for not pouring in the resources they had allocated to Griffith's special pictures.

As Harry explained the rationale, all Roy could think of was his dream of the falling deck of cards. Suddenly he had faces to go with the blank ones. He told his brother that they now stood alone.

"There're other good directors," Harry said determinedly. "We'll develop our younger men."

He set out to do just that and promoted Edward Dillon, Allan Dwan, and others from Triangle's neophyte ranks as replacements for Griffith, Ince, and Sennett. Then, this crop left, too, for greener pastures, and the Aitkens retained the services of Hal Davis in July 1917. He had been with Carl Laemmle's Universal for several years, and he brought three other directors with him to Triangle. Davis's crew made more than one hundred westerns and Keystone comedies, as well as some dramatic love stories, at reduced costs.

On the other hand, Zukor, Lasky, Goldwyn, Fox, and Laemmle, all shrewd, practical producers, were able to finance and produce quality, colorful motion pictures that rated high with theater owners and movie fans. With an eye on the competition, and long accustomed to the Griffith extravaganzas, Harry thought Triangle's low-cost pictures were inferior. The senior Aitken completely ignored Davis's demonstrated ability to produce low-cost, budget pictures that pleased the public while trimming Triangle's debts by more than $1 million in one year's time. The two did not work well together, and when Davis's contract expired in July 1918, Harry stubbornly refused to renew it. He dismissed the general manager, who might have brought Triangle back from the brink of bankruptcy. This action did not set well with Roy or a number of Triangle investors.

At this point, Harry himself took over the active management of picture production at Triangle. He worked hard with the young directors who remained, hoping to develop another Griffith, Ince, or Sennett. Yet, progress moved too slowly for the forty-one-year-old Aitken. So, when his younger brother arrived in Los Angeles from England one day, Harry had a proposition ready for him.

"Roy," he said with more enthusiasm than their finances merited, "I want you to call on Mary Pickford to ask her if she would be interested in joining Triangle at a salary of $10,000 per week."

Roy was startled. "Me—see her? Why not you, Harry?"

He shook his head that was just beginning to show streaks of gray. "You have a way with the ladies, Roy. And you know Mary, her mother Charlotte, her sister Lottie, and her brother Jack much better than I do. I hear you are a regular at the same parties and dances they attend."

"But $10,000 per week! How can we afford that now?"

"Mary's name is magic at the box office, " Harry insisted. "I've heard she's not happy with her present connection. Let's try. If we sign her, we can always get loans to produce her pictures."

"Well, all right," Roy said reluctantly. "I'll do my best. But don't expect a miracle."

So, once more the brothers looked to Mary Pickford to rescue their fortunes, notwithstanding the disaster of seven years earlier when all but one of her seven pictures made for Majestic Film Corporation were technical failures.

Pickford was very sweet and gracious. "I'm sorry, Roy, but I can't join your company," she said. "I'm planning something else. It's a secret."

Later, the secret was revealed. In an effort to gain artistic control of their films and obtain the profits from their top movies, Mary Pickford, Douglas Fairbanks, Charles Chaplin, and David W. Griffith formed United Artists in 1919.

Roy saw Mary many times after that, and they chatted amiably about movie affairs. She explained her action on the United Artists business. "With all due respect to you and your brother," she said, "why should we toil for producers who make all the profit? Why can't we be our own bosses?"

A year later, when the Beverly Hills Hotel weekly Saturday night dance approached, Roy happened to mention to the manager that he knew many movie stars, including Mary Pickford. "Let's invite her," he suggested eagerly. "Won't you get in touch with her?"

Young Aitken didn't think that the busy Mary, now an executive in her own production company, would attend, but when he phoned, she said she would be glad to come and told him to call for her.

Since the mission-style establishment near the intersection of North Crescent Drive and Sunset Boulevard served as the brothers' West Coast headquarters, the Beverly Hills Hotel manager informed all the other guests that Pickford would attend the Saturday night dance, as the guest of Roy Aitken. The manager was so excited he even decorated the ballroom and acres of fragrant gardens surrounding the hotel with bunting especially for the event.

So on the appointed evening, Roy, decked out in formal attire, directed his chauffeur, Matt Hosely, to park the polished Rolls-Royce at the front door of America's sweetheart on Wilshire Boulevard.

The Rolls was Roy's third foreign car after the Leon Bollee and a Renault. The sporty yellow Bollee had caught the eye of both D. W. Griffith and Douglas Fairbanks. Fairbanks often borrowed the car from Roy to drive around New York and loved it so much that he made Aitken promise to sell it to him when Roy was ready to part with it. Fairbanks bought the Bollee in 1918 two years before his secret marriage to Mary Pickford.

In 1914, Roy bought a Renault car in France and had quite a time getting it out of that country. He used it in England a while and then brought it to New York. The Aitkens' chauffeur, Matt Hosely, whom the brothers had brought from Waukesha to work for them, was quite proud of the stable of foreign cars under his care.

After the Renault, Roy bought the Rolls-Royce with right-hand steering that was the only one he had driven to California for just such an occasion as his date with Mary Pickford. In 1919, he purchased a Vauxhall automobile and used it considerably in the British Isles for trips to Brighton and other resort areas.

With so many foreign cars in the Aitkens' New York garage, life became confusing for Hosely. Sometimes Roy would phone him from the office and ask him to bring around a car to take him to the West Fifty-seventh Street apartment. "Which car, Mr. Roy?" he would say. "Which car?"

And Roy would answer, "The one with the best polish job." This response further confused Hosely, for he kept all of them highly polished.

Harry disapproved of Roy having so many cars, but he knew how his younger brother loved machinery, even as a young boy in Goerke's Corners, so he indulged him. Moreover, there were times when Harry, too, enjoyed being chauffeured around New York and California or wanted to impress a client.

Movie officials, actors, and actresses rode in the foreign cars, and Roy noted that the men especially would examine the engines, upholstery, and gadgets. At parties and other social events the Aitkens attended, the cars were always a good icebreaker for getting conversation started. "Oh, you're the Aitkens who have all those foreign cars," people greeted them.

On the drive back to the Beverly Hills Hotel with Mary Pickford seated beside him in the Rolls-Royce, Roy put the Aitkens' financial misfortunes out of mind. As they passed Gloria Swanson's secluded three-acre estate, Roy thought how Mack Sennett's star had refused his offer to take a ride in the very same car. When he confronted Swanson a year or so later at the Culver City studios, she said apologetically, "Roy, I wanted so much to ride in that Rolls-Royce, but I was afraid the rest of the girls wouldn't like it."

Of course, Roy did not relate this story to Mary, for she might think she was his second choice as a date for the dance. Instead, he told her how he and his brother had recently purchased a dairy farm near their home in Waukesha, Wisconsin. She seemed impressed that the Aitken hobby farm was to be stocked with registered Holstein cattle in an effort to build a quality herd.

Mary Pickford and Roy Aitken were the center of attention. Whenever they approached the dance floor, the other couples drifted away to leave them center stage like a royal court enraptured by the king and queen whom they were content to watch.

Pickford was a perfect dancer, and Roy was thankful he had taken lessons in Waukesha many years ago and had practiced over the decades by dancing with southern belles and some of America's most graceful and beautiful actresses.

Suddenly the hotel manager appeared at the ballroom entrance waving his arms frantically over the heads of spectators. As music stopped between numbers, he called, "Telegram for Mr. Aitken."

Roy turned to Pickford and asked to be excused for a few moments while he went to the front desk. "Oh, I'll go with you," she said.

They hurried into the lobby, and he picked up his telegram. It read, "Mary Ellen just gave birth to a daughter. Mother and daughter are doing fine. Fred Klussendorf."

Roy explained that Fred was his dairy farm manager in Waukesha. Mary laughed delightedly. The manager then took the telegram to the ballroom and read it to the other guests. "One of the Aitkens' prize cows has given birth to a calf," he announced to cheers and applause.

Meanwhile, Harry grappled with Triangle's desperate financial situation. He tried to secure loans from whomever he could, even those offered by complete strangers. S. A. Lynch, a southern film distributor who played both sides of the fence handling Zukor-Paramount and Triangle releases came forward. But it was too little, too late. Finally, the bankers from whom the Aitken brothers had obtained loans stepped in and took over active management of Triangle in May 1919. This development devastated the Aitkens. Now, except for their votes as board members, they had little power to influence Triangle's affairs.

The bankers installed Percival L. Waters as Triangle's new president and general manager. Since early 1918, he had represented investors such as Felix Kahn in their various interests in Aitken operations. Waters had had extensive experience with the old Edison Company and General Film Company, the Trust's once powerful arm. He also had substantial social ties with Zukor.

Waters's chief task was to try to pay some of Triangle's debts. Therefore, at the bankers' urging, he quickly sold Triangle's Culver City studio complex to Samuel Goldwyn. The former glove salesman from New York and his brother-in-law, Lasky, now had the best production facilities on the West Coast. Next, Waters terminated Triangle's picture production and dismissed most of its personnel. Then, he began to release many of the old silent films made by the Aitken movie companies since 1912.

As large stockholders in Triangle, Harry and Roy constantly urged the general manager to get back into movie production at least until they had time to develop the younger directors. But Waters told Harry that the bankers he reported to, including Kahn, who had also raised millions of dollars for Zukor, had denied the Aitkens' request.

At last it dawned on Harry that Zukor's influence was still being used to wreck Triangle. Together with his lawyers, Harry prepared a petition claiming conspiracy on the part of Lynch, Zukor, Kahn, and Waters. He alleged that the four had deliberately forced Triangle into bankruptcy although fully aware at the time that the actual indebtedness of the company, outside tax liens, was only a matter of some $4,500. Harry lost.

Ironically, the decision came in the same year that the German Tri-Ergon sound system and Phonofilm sound system of Lee De Forest, an American inventor, led to sound being photographically recorded on film.

Harry had also tried to forestall the Triangle receivership action in a 1923 letter that he prepared to plead his case to the stockholders of Triangle Film Corporation. While it is unclear whether Harry actually sent it to Triangle stockholders, this amazing document does show his determination to salvage the Aitken empire in 1923. It also counters the speculative analysis engaged in and the conclusions drawn by Aitken critics, who were not privy to Harry's thinking.

> Are you willing to throw away a million dollars?
> That is what you are doing if you vote for the dissolution of Triangle:
> It is eight years since Triangle was formed. In 1915 the moving picture business was in a state of chaos. Most of the pictures being made were unspeakably poor. The shining exceptions were the dramas being made by Griffith and Ince and Sennett's Keystone Comedies. Distribution was as chaotic as production: advertising and exploitation were even worse.
> Triangle brought their three great producers together; it provided an adequate and effective sales and distribution organization. Back of Triangle was

an idea or rather an *ideal:* the making of better pictures than had ever been seen before. Which meant the use of greater *people,* more careful directors, and better management.

In all three things Triangle succeeded. Succeeded far beyond the hopes of its most enthusiastic well wishers. In a very few months Triangle, a wholly new institution, was among the best known producing companies in the world. Its pictures were famous from London to Calcutta and from Portland to Dallas. Triangle was the originator of $2.00 moving pictures—the first company that had made pictures good enough to justify high prices, and to take the business forever out of the ten-cent class.

Then why, you ask—and properly—didn't Triangle make large profits from the beginning? Because of an error in judgment for which I take full responsibility.

Not in excuse, an extenuation I ask your attention to the great numbers of other men—many of them handling large enterprises that had been well established for years—who made mistakes at that time. In conditions such as the world had never known before, it was not possible to foresee what was coming. A period of inflation and rapidly rising costs followed by war regulation, restriction and taxation was for us, as it was for others, unprovided for. A capital that should have been ample was utterly inadequate to carry the volume of business we were doing, with costs doubling almost over night.

In the mistaken belief that this condition was temporary, loans were made— *temporary* capital was supplied for a *temporary* emergency. For these loans a very high price was paid. It had to be. In the condition of the money market at that time, the management did what was *possible* to do; not what it *wanted* to do.

And the life of the company was saved.

Meantime, as stockholders, you had not been asked to step in and save your property, though men in the management time and again came to its rescue.

How many motion picture companies then looked upon as old, established and prosperous are alive today?

Loans did not mean cost alone. They meant control. And in a final effort to save your property, to safeguard your interests, the men who had organized Triangle and put it on its feet, stepped aside and the banking management took hold.

Now film men are not bankers; and bankers are not film men. It is not unnatural that those who assume the responsibility of management in order, mainly, that the loans to the banks might be liquidated, should devote their energies to liquidation.

How well the work of *Liquidating* Triangle was done has been outlined to you in a statement put out by the management sometime ago.

The only debts of any amount that remained were:

1. An unsettled claim of the government on account of 1917 taxes.
2. A judgment arising out of an old contract with some of the original owners of the New York Motion Picture Corporation.

For the past five years your company has been virtually *out* of the film business. You own thousands, literally, of negatives, covering some of the best-known and most popular pictures ever made. No one knows how much money could be made from the *active* sale and exploitation of these pictures. Last winter, when the management of Triangle threatened a receivership for lack of money, the writer and some of his friends bought a few of these negatives, paying for them some $200,000 cash—about $150,000 of which went to Triangle directly, the remainder having been paid for the rights Triangle wished to acquire. These negatives are now owned and are being exploited by an organization known as Tri-Stone Film Corporation, and there is clear evidence from the experience of the past six months that these pictures are easily saleable to theaters at fair prices, and—what is more important—that the public wants and goes to see.

The writer is the largest single owner of Triangle stocks. No one has at stake so large an interest. To no one is it so important that the *assets* of Triangle be made to realize for *stockholders* the largest possible value.

Realizing, after years of patient waiting, that the present management contemplates no active step looking toward a profit for the stockholders, he has for sometime been endeavoring to perfect a plan by which the great assets of your company might be made actively productive—for you—and for him.

Suddenly—the company was thrown into Bankruptcy.

It is not the purpose of this letter to undertake any explanation either of the inactivity of the past few years, the recent attempt to secure your consent to the liquidation of the company, and the consequent scrapping of the whole value of the Triangle trademark and good will, or the unexplained and perhaps unnecessary proceedings in Bankruptcy.

It is the purpose of this letter to ask your co-operation in rehabilitating your property. It is suggested that a committee of stockholders be formed for the purpose of studying the situation and of formulating and laying before you some plan by which the great property which is yours may be conserved and made active for your interest.

There is no time to lose. The motion picture business never showed healthier conditions; there never was a time when the opportunity was greater than *now.*

The writer has an option on the complete ownership of the negatives recently purchased from Triangle Tri-Stone. He is ready to put these into any sound place of reorganization that may be decided upon. And to co-operate in lifting the receivership and taking over the Triangle business, or buying the negatives and starting anew.

The names already suggested for the stockholders' reorganization committee are as follows. . . . Will you express your wishes about these and some such others, as you may think desirable?

Very truly yours,
H. E. A.

Harry's letter demonstrates that the ever enthusiastic promoter was still trying to move ahead in making the best of the situation for all concerned, even after an earlier Triangle stockholder's suit had been instituted against Harry and Roy. In the litigation, the stockholders claimed the Aitkens' extensive financing procedures had weakened Triangle unnecessarily. Other defendants named were Joseph Simmonds and Hyman Winik. Simmonds was the president of Tower Film Corporation and W. H. Productions. Hyman Winik was associated with the Reserve Film Corporation, Western Import Company, Inc., and Western Import Company, Ltd.

According to the public record in the archives of the New York Supreme Court, the complaint brought by Arthur Butler Graham, acting for the Triangle Film Corporation, alleges three separate suits totaling $3 million against the Aitkens and their associates. These actions were alleged to have taken place between February 16, 1916, and December 27, 1917. In the first complaint, it is alleged that the Aitkens, by virtue of their affiliation with Triangle (as directors of the corporation) and their stock interest, caused a board of directors to be elected over which they held the dominating sway. Through this alleged control, the Aitkens were alleged to have sold Triangle shares of stock for $99,950, when the stock was worth $1,500,000, to the Lothbury Syndicate, Inc., in which the Aitkens also held control. In this manner, it was charged that the Aitkens derived great profit at the expense of Triangle when they transferred the assets to other companies they held.

The other allegations followed the same pattern throughout the remaining suits. The Aitkens and codefendants Hyman Winik and Joseph Simmonds, along with the corporations they controlled, were charged with selling Triangle stock and other assets to these corporations profiting from the discrepancy between value claimed and selling price.

Mickey, Mack Sennett's masterpiece, and the deal made by the Western Import Company, Inc., to acquire rights to the film, demonstrate how the scheme was alleged to have worked relative to Triangle movie assets. It was alleged in court that the Aitkens caused Triangle to sell rights to the picture to Western Import Company for $175,000, when they were worth $500,000. Damages of $325,000 were sought.

In the second action, along with Harry and Roy, defendants Winik and Simmonds were assessed $200,000 in damages for an alleged conspiracy to defraud Triangle as part of the deals mentioned in the first suit.

Added to the actions already mentioned, the third suit alleged that capital stock of the Western Import Company, Inc., the Western Import Company, Ltd., and the Reserve Film Corporation. allowed these corporations to accrue the profit in the various deals with Triangle. Again, the problem was that the Aitkens or their codefendants controlled the corporations cited.

With no allies left, the brothers fought hard, denying the allegations, and the legal battle lasted for months in the New York courts. In the end, the judgment went against the Aitkens, and it took practically all their assets, except the Epoch Producing Corporation (*Birth of a Nation*), to settle the stockholders' claims for $1,375,000.

Battered but unbowed, the brothers had planned ahead for such a contingency. They thought if they could keep their old films in their hands long enough, they might be able to mount a comeback.

Their first opportunity for this kind of insurance came shortly after Triangle went into receivership. The bankers organized a company called Tri-Stone, and this firm began buying up Triangle's important film assets, including films and scenarios.

For some months, Tri-Stone began selling these assets and even reissuing some of the old films. When Tri-Stone could not make enough profit to suit the bankers, they then decided to sell all Triangle assets outright.

Patrick Powers, once associated with Universal pictures, bought many of the Tri-Stone offerings, and Harry and Roy approached him with an offer to buy back some of their pictures. To do this, the Aitkens organized Triumph Pictures Corporation, whose stated purpose was to produce motion pictures and also to reissue older silent films.

They were able to buy many pictures and scenarios from Powers, and so once again they had legal possession of many Triangle and Keystone films.

Following the lawsuit and with a sizable stock of these negatives in hand, Harry and Roy retreated to Waukesha and started to release the films. Although Waters and Tri-Stone had extensively exploited some of these films, the Aitkens used their skills developed earlier to find additional markets throughout the United States.

In the midst of their Triangle frustrations in 1922, there came a bit of serendipity to lighten up their otherwise bleak prospects. Hiram Abrams, who now headed United Artists, called Harry and Roy with an offer. United Artists (Pickford, Chaplin, Griffith, et al.) proposed to take over the distribution of *Birth of a Nation* to movie theaters on a national and international scale. United Artists had a well-trained organization for extensive distribution as well as advertising and promotional facilities. Previously, *Birth of a Nation* had played largely in legitimate theaters at high prices. Now, under the United Artists proposal, it would be offered to all theaters at lower prices. Abrams enthusiastically predicted a profit of $1 million split between United Artists and Epoch Producing Corporation.

"We'd like to have you travel and publicize the film, Roy," suggested Abrams. "Especially in Europe, getting bookings. You've had a great deal of experience with European film men, and this should prove helpful in promoting the picture at this time."

Thrilled by this interesting assignment, Roy accepted.

Through the United Artists contract, the dividends to Epoch shareholders went up considerably between 1922 and 1925, due entirely to the United Artists promotions. Although nobody made $1 million from the deal, as Hiram Abrams had predicted, the returns were quite substantial. After the mid-1920s, however, Epoch Producing Corporation never declared dividends, because promotion expenses remained high and showings became infrequent. The Aitken contract with United Artists terminated in 1926.

At last, after eleven years, the famous silent film that had revolution-ized motion pictures had fallen on deaf ears at the box office. The same fate that befell *Birth of a Nation*, however, struck its competitors and cham-pions with equanimity as studio chieftains set aside rivalries, albeit briefly, to fortify themselves against a new revolution.

21

Enter Sound, Exit an Old Era

In 1927, Harry and Roy Aitken, like their former New York and Holly-wood associates, watched the screen in disbelief as singer Al Jolson stretched out his arms and belted out a folksong. The world had its first full-length talking picture. *The Jazz Singer* became the toast of the nation.

"Sound had burst into the realm of silent movies and changed every-thing," Roy said.

Meanwhile, Harry dared to think about getting back into the produc-tion of motion pictures after the loss of Triangle. But perhaps for only the second time in his life, he hesitated before plunging headlong into a new opportunity.

Harry decided that the call of the new siren song, offered by talking pic-tures, must go unanswered until he and Roy could build up their de-pleted financial resources. Then, too, since their mother suffered from chronic heart trouble, the Aitkens decided to launch their comeback from as close to home as possible.

Except for the United Artists deal, the only substantial contact Harry and Roy had with Hollywood was through an exchange of correspon-dence between the former stars and their employers. For example, they heard through the grapevine that David W. Griffith had fallen on hard times as well. After 1925, Griffith's pictures faded in box-office appeal, and he lost the moviegoing public's respect. Sensing the master's decline, his major players deserted him just as he and the actors and directors at Triangle had done to the Aitkens. But the brothers held no malice and took no joy in the great director's downfall. In fact, they marveled at how his deft film techniques had stayed with him so long. Yet, the word was out that Griffith's story themes belonged to another era. He could not adapt to the bold new cinematic presentations ushered in by the talkies.

More cheerful news surrounded Aitken-Griffith protégé Mary Pickford, who was named best actress by the Motion Picture Academy for her role as a young, unwed mother in *Coquette* in 1929. The Aitkens sent a message congratulating her on winning an Oscar in the sound picture category. They also noted that the best picture for 1928–1929 was an MGM musical, *Broadway Melody*. This gave Harry an idea for the reissue of *Birth of a Nation* with a soundtrack added.

Sarah Hadfield Aitken did not live to see her sons plan their comeback in the motion picture industry in 1929. Her heart gave out on March 6 that year at age seventy-eight. She did, however, live to see them rise to the pinnacle in motion pictures, and although they returned home to her nearly penniless, she was proud that they had handled success and defeat with equanimity. The one had not made them pompous and arrogant and the other had not left them bitter and disparaged. This was an answer to a mother's prayers, she told them, and then near the end she made them promise again to attend church regularly.

As one of two girls in a family with nine brothers, Sarah Jane Hadfield Aitken's epitaph was written by the time she was three years old, growing up on a farm in Waukesha County. This excerpt from a poem entitled "Farmers' Girls" from the 1854 issue of the *Waukesha Plain Dealer* summed up their mother's rural life for Harry and Roy. Yet, it also brought into sharp focus the unforgiving muse they had followed on a pathway so different from the one that the rest of the Aitken family had chosen.

> Starching the "fixins" for Sunday, churning the snowy cream,
> Rinsing the pails and strainer down in the running stream,
> Feeding the geese and turkeys, making the pumpkin pies,
> Jogging the little one's cradle, driving away the flies.
> Grace in every motion, music in every tone,
> Beauty of form and feature thousands might covet to own,
> Cheeks that rival spring roses, teeth the whitest of pearls,
> One of the country maids is worth a score of city girls.

Harry and Roy put their personal plans aside as they laid their mother beside their father Elvin and an infant brother Bertie, who died the year Harry was born. As lifelong residents of Waukesha, they paid only a nominal fee to cover "perpetual care" and to have Sarah interred in Prairie Home Cemetery. This was a privilege they once thought they would never use.

The two brothers looked at each other across Sarah Aitken's modest marker and without a word knew what the other was thinking. First came a flood of memories of their mother seated at the piano playing Christian hymns while her flock sang songs guaranteed to win her approval. Her wealth was in her family. Now at fifty-two and forty-seven, respectively, Harry and Roy were older, grayer, practically broke, and struck by the contrast of their mother's simple, peaceful life against their own glory days of 1915 and 1916 when they were taking in millions of dollars annually—and spending them, too.

They talked about the lessons learned and believed they were now wise enough to mount a comeback without repeating past mistakes, such as living on the extremes rather than striving for balanced moderation as the rest of their family had done, following Elvin and Sarah Aitkens' gentle example.

But first they had to find allies who themselves needed a boost up from poor circumstances. So, a year after Sarah's death, Harry Aitken, Thomas Dixon, and David W. Griffith got together in Hollywood by mutual consent. "Now's our chance to put sound on *Birth*," Harry told his former partners. "With sound dubbed in on the film, we could reissue *Birth* and bring in heavy grosses. With the profits we can get back into film production."

Griffith and Dixon were excited about the prospect, and so was William H. Kemble, a former theater owner who once purchased films from Mutual and Triangle. He contracted with the partners to put sound (music) on the *Birth*. Enthusiastic and a hard worker, Kemble raised $150,000 for the project. This was splendid progress, and, overjoyed, others on the team worked diligently to accomplish the task. Griffith spent days editing the silent film and making suggestions for music. In fact, General Electric afterward received a citation for the excellent sound work.

Nevertheless, when *Birth of a Nation* with dubbed-in sound was released, the partners knew immediately it could not compete with the newer sound pictures. More important, the public knew it, too. Movie patrons grew uneasy watching the jerky and rapid action produced by a combination of different film speeds that made the soundtrack too fast for action shown on the screen. The older film systems were out of synchronization with newer projection machines developed for sound.

The failure of the *Birth* sound version dashed the hopes of the Aitken brothers, Griffith, and Dixon. They had confidently expected so much of the venture. Out of the failure, however, came a new idea: refilming an entirely new *Birth of a Nation* picture and eliminating some of the scenes and titles that had previously raised racial objections. Harry as usual played a key role, as the success of the venture rested on raising money.

An aging Dixon went back to his North Carolina home to rest and to await results of Harry's attempt to resurrect *Birth*. Griffith went into virtual retirement, hoping to be called if financing became available. He was almost pitifully eager to cooperate and looked forward to directing a new *Birth* film.

Calling on many of his former New York and Hollywood associates, Harry worked hard to raise money for the remake of *Birth*. He did manage to raise meager amounts, but unlike 1914 when America was highly excited about motion pictures, stock market turmoil and a depression in 1930 poisoned the business climate against such a risky venture.

To help defray Harry's expenses as he traveled the nation, Roy established a fountain syrup business in Waukesha on a small scale. He made his own syrups and traveled the familiar towns and cities of Wisconsin selling his products just as he had pedaled insurance and films nearly three decades earlier. Later, in a letter to a friend, Roy described the process as follows:

> I am sure Harry must have told you about the strawberry syrup that a friend of ours, Charles James, concocted. I made it out of pure strawberry juice and added an ounce to a six-ounce container, and it made a swell strawberry drink. Just like chocolate milk. Then when the war came on, the dairies decided to use the juice, so I was out of biz [business]. However, I had sugar rationing, so the same James sent me a cola syrup, and I used the sugar to make a cola drink. Hired a bottling plant and made a good living for us during the war when Coca Cola could not get sugar enough. With an occasional booking from the *Birth*, we kept going. But it took a lot of traveling money as well. Harry kept going as you know.

Harry and Roy made slow progress but got so far as paying Dixon $10,000 to write a new *Birth of a Nation* script, one that probably would be acceptable to black leaders. However, after five years of fruitless effort, Harry finally decided the brothers would not try to finance a new picture on their own. Instead, they would continue renting the thirty-five-millimeter version of the *Birth* upon request, along with some Keystone pictures they owned. In the meantime, they would try to interest other movie producers to remake *Birth of a Nation* and let them bear the financial responsibility.

Time was running out on the original producers of America's greatest motion picture. Griffith, a lonely old man, died on July 23, 1948, in a second-class hotel. He had come full circle from cheap rooms as a struggling actor to the same kind of roof over his head in his seventy-third year. Dixon and William S. Hart, the cowboy actor, preceded Griffith in death. Dixon, like Griffith, was in debt in his last years. Hart, however, left an estate valued at $1,170,000. Griffith was bitter over this fact until the end.

In an interview with Walter Monfried of the *Milwaukee Journal* in 1951, Harry reflected on the death of Hart a few years earlier. "William S. Hart started making westerns for us at $300 per week. After he became immensely popular, he came to me one day and told me apologetically and said he had been offered $8000 per week" (2).

According to Harry, Hart added that he knew he was not worth that amount, but that he could not refuse it. Harry immediately matched the offer and the two men signed a two-year contract that Hart later broke.

Unlike Griffith, Harry was not one to hold grudges. Nonetheless, he was relieved when Hart confided shortly before his death that he regretted leaving the Aitkens, saying that he had been misled.

Eight years later, Harry collapsed in the Chicago office of a theater owner. He never regained consciousness from a heart attack and died on the sales firing line August 1, 1956, shortly before his seventy-ninth birthday. To the last, Harry was trying to promote a remake of *Birth of a Nation* as the first step toward regaining the brothers' lost empire. Dennis Leslie said he was with Harry when he passed away at the Newberry Theater in Chicago, and he later wrote Roy to express his sense of outrage that the movie industry had failed to recognize their contributions. "Without the Aitken Brothers," said Leslie, "there would not have been the film industry in California as we know it today. . . . I believe there should be some sort of memorial set up here in Hollywood in memory of you, your brother and D.W."

Roy thanked Dennis Leslie for his sentiments and replied, "The winds will never blow and the stars will never shine upon a gentler, kindlier, purer soul than Harry's."

Roy brought his brother's body back to Waukesha by train, and the only official memorials Harry received were the tears of his surviving sisters and brother. In subsequent years, however, tributes were forthcoming from Jack Warner and Anita Loos. The former had sent a telegram, dated March 12, 1959, on the occasion of the Wisconsin Idea Theater's Conference Convention in Waukesha honoring the Aitken achievements. "I feel privileged to salute a genuine motion picture pioneer who helped create the first great feature film. The *Birth of a Nation* has a secure place in screen history and in the gratitude of myself and others who found it an inspiration for a picture making career. My warm congratulations and good wishes to Roy Aitkin [*sic*] on this occasion. Jack L. Warner, President, Warner Brothers Pictures."

Screenwriter Anita Loos's praise came in 1974 when she, Lillian Gish, Gloria Swanson, and others sent telegrams and made phone calls to Roy on the occasion of a historical marker being raised at the Aitkens' birthplace. Said Loos in her congratulatory telegram to Roy, "The farm where you and Harry grew up was certainly a cradle for the entire film industry." The most substantial tribute to Harry came in 1965 in Roy's account of their odyssey in *The Birth of a Nation Story*, the book he wrote in collaboration with Al P. Nelson.

At the Prairie Home Cemetery, Harry was finally at peace. Roy stood by the grave long after the other mourners had left. He recalled Harry's words about the huge kaleidoscopic, fantasy-laden, grotesque, incredible journey they had taken through life. It had been all those things and more.

Harry had led a zestful life before going out vibrantly when the time came. Since few men have so enriched the motion picture industry more

than Harry, who made it his whole life, the anonymous poet need look no
further for a model for his poem than the senior Aitken brother:

> A master in the art of living
> Draws no sharp distinction
> Between his work and his play,
> His labor and his leisure,
> His mind and his body,
> His education and his recreation,
> He hardly knows which is which.
> He simply pursues his vision
> Of excellence through whatever
> He is doing and leaves
> Others to determine
> Whether he is working or playing.
> To himself he always seems to be doing both.

A t the time of Harry's death, Roy was seventy-four and the sole survivor of the Majestic, Fine Arts, and Triangle executives. He lived in a
Waukesha home near his widowed sister Gladys, who occupied the Aitken
family home and kept an eye on him. He had spent more than fifty years in
motion pictures but still did not talk of retirement. With Harry gone, Roy
was more determined than ever to carry on the work they had started. "The
courage to go on must be stronger than the power of failure; besides, I
wanted to postpone the rocking chair for as long as I could," he said.

To stay busy, he picked up where Harry had left off and tried to market
the *Birth of a Nation* thirty-five-millimeter version to theaters. He found
minimal interest. Racially, the picture was too controversial to show in
public theaters. However, the sixteen-millimeter format moved quite well
to colleges and universities, where it was shown to many motion picture
study groups, and so he spent his time shipping prints to campuses across
the United States.

He also marketed a few Keystone films that he owned. Then, with the
help of Kent Eastin of Blackhawk Films, Davenport, Iowa, *Birth* was issued in an eight-millimeter version, and it sold well, especially to the ever
increasing numbers of movie buffs.

Roy made room in his schedule for visits or calls to friends from his
silent movie days to exchange birthday or holiday greetings or just to
catch up on the latest news. After one such contact with Anita Loos and
Lillian and Dorothy Gish in New York, Loos (the famous Aitken screenwriter) responded by letter, dated April 3, 1957:

> In reply to your request that I send you a record of the telephone conver-
> sation we had just before you left New York, I have dictated the following
> which, incidentally are not only my views, but also those of Lillian and

Dorothy. We feel that your basic story is that of farm boys who came from the hinterlands with no equipment except your ideals and dreams, and at a time when films were of a vulgarity only to be endured in Nichelodeans, unaided and with everything against you, you two developed the art of the motion picture to a point where, in "The Birth of a Nation" [*sic*] it reached a peak that has never been surpassed.

Lillian, Dorothy and I were entranced at hearing your complete story for the first time and we feel that the general public would be even more so. In the early days of the movies, when we were working for you, we thought of you and Harry as two men of solid financial background who deigned to give Hollywood a little of your attention, apart from your many business and social activities in the great capitols of the world. Only at this late day do we find out that your financial standing was nil; that you had no training at all in worldly matters and that the aura of elegance which hovered about you . . . your immaculate chic . . . your four (count 'em, four) custom built foreign motor cars were only a part of a painfully achieved camouflage. In fact, no Horatio Alger story is more incredible than your account of the financing of "The Birth of a Nation" which was done piece-meal with blood, sweat and tears.

The stories of the countless prominent people who worked for you in the old days have been told many times, but the account of your early struggles and precarious adventures in promoting capital, has never been written and it is one of the most important and interesting in the entire history of the motion picture.

Following the triumph, both financial and artistic, of "The Birth of a Nation," came the debacle, when a new element of commercialism entered the movies . . . a sad comment on what happened when materialism overran Hollywood.

In the old days, we who worked for Griffith, were told that there must always be a "run to the rescue" at the end of every story. I think that the "run to the rescue" in your story should be your book. I do believe that all of us who worked for you should have a part in this "run to the rescue," but our stories are old and have been dished up innumerable times. Your story has never been told. Even those of us who were a part of it never knew that the truth, in all its amazing details, was more incredible and fascinating than any of us ever dreamed. I hope, dear Roy, that we may meet with the writer of your book and supply him with any details he may wish, concerning our own part in your careers.

It was wonderful seeing you here in New York, and Lillian, Dorothy and I look forward with greatest pleasure to your next visit.

Best love as always.

Devotedly,
Anita

In the early 1960s, two of Roy's sisters passed away, Jessie Fetters on December 20, 1960, at age eighty and Mabel Griswold on August 4, 1963, at seventy-eight. Within seven years, Roy had lost three of his siblings. Nevertheless, Roy did not slow down, except that in 1966 at age eighty-four, he

finally disposed of his Keystone films and his interest in *Birth of a Nation*.
He thought that Harry would understand that he had been nursemaid
long enough to the greatest and most controversial silent motion picture
ever produced. But the muse of entertainment would not release the grand
old man of movies that easily. He continued to field hundreds of letters
and phone calls from old-time theater owners and young movie buffs.
They all wanted to know if he had any silent films for sale or rent. Several
invited Roy to speak before their groups and recall for them the golden
days of the silent screen.

Through the years, Roy was constantly amazed at the growing interest of
so many Americans in the memorabilia of the silent screen days, which for
him were more than fifty years in the past. He was also astonished at how
easily interest in silent movies of yesteryear bridged the generation gap.

Roy hit it off well with movie buffs that he believed constituted the art
phenomenon of the age. The respect for the era refused to die, and he was
pleased to see that practically every major city, and even smaller towns,
had one or more movie buff clubs. Boasting five, ten, or more members,
they met periodically in each other's homes to show and discuss silent
movies. Larger clubs would often rent a hall and exhibit silent movies to
members and friends.

Aitken watched a growing side-industry take shape as well. The silent
movie appeal spilled over into collectibles. High premiums were paid for
old-time, colorful movie posters, handbills, programs, movie projectors,
and other paraphernalia. He wished Harry had lived to share in the
growth of the movie buff trend, or at least in the lively correspondence
and reading associated with their days in the trenches.

Many of the movie enthusiasts wrote to Roy regularly, as did a number
of bookstore owners. He also read all the publications pertaining to the
movies and in this way took a trip down memory lane, reviewing silent
and sound movies as only he could. It was a special treat to see mass-
circulated movie magazines feature stars who had worked for the Aitkens.

Roy was always on the lookout for movie stars who visited Milwaukee.
If his schedule and health permitted, he wanted to be on hand to greet
them. One of his fondest memories dates back to the time when he and
Harry went to see Gloria Swanson, who appeared as the guest at a leading department store in Milwaukee. Although no longer in the movie production business, the Aitken brothers were given front-row seats at the
Swanson promotion. A smiling and still beautiful Gloria introduced the
Aitkens to her audience as "her first movie employers," and she mentioned why she had not accepted Roy's invitation to ride in his Rolls-
Royce many years earlier. Later, Enid Markey, also one of the Aitken stars,
stopped in town and called Roy for a pleasant chat.

At one point, Roy got in touch with Miriam Cooper, who had starred in *Birth of a Nation* and had written about her movie life in a book, *The Dark Lady*. He was told by a movie buff friend that Miriam was in a Virginia nursing home and phoned her. In earlier years, Harry and Roy had attended many parties at the home of Cooper and her husband Raoul Walsh in Hollywood. After Roy's phone call, he and she phoned each other quite often and exchanged letters until her death in 1975.

Roy's files and briefcase were jammed with letters received over the years from Joseph Henaberry (who played Abraham Lincoln in *Birth of a Nation*), director Raoul Walsh, Julian Johnson, James Montgomery Flagg, Frank Newman (the Aitkens' St. Louis theater partner), actor Chester Conklin, and many others.

In addition, Roy's schedule would find him in the home of Clark Wilkinson several times a year at Baraboo, Wisconsin. Wilkinson, an insurance man, spent a great deal of time on his hobby collecting movie memorabilia. Roy was astounded to see the size of Wilkinson's collection of movie props, posters, flyers, and pictures. Perhaps the largest and most complete in the United States at that time, the movie museum occupied most of the basement in Wilkinson's home, and Roy was glad to see that the man's patient wife did not object, although one section of the display contained posters from famous horror movies.

To spend a day with the Wilkinsons was pure pleasure for Roy Aitken, as was his contact and later association with the Cinephiles, a group of movie collectors from all parts of the United States. In their eyes he was forever young. And from his standpoint, he considered himself lucky to count so many interesting business and professional people, theater owners, even farmers, as his friends.

22

The Cinephiles

In 1966, Clark Wilkinson hosted the Cinephile convention at Baraboo and invited Aitken to attend as speaker and guest of honor. In his speech, Roy traced his and Harry's careers in the movie business from nickelodeon operators to one of Hollywood's top producers during the silent film era.

Roy commended the group on the work they were doing to further the study and enjoyment of the silent movies and for their preservation of motion picture relics. He noted that quite a number of these men and women had invested from $1,000 to $15,000 and even more in projectors, old movies, and basement theater rooms. Roy contrasted this with the $100 investment Harry, John Freuler, and he had used to get started. He praised the Cinephiles for their enthusiasm and devotion to silent films. "It reminds me of the eagerness which movies inspired in Harry and me and others in those decades so long ago," he told the two hundred Cinephiles gathered for their semiannual meeting.

When he had finished, the Cinephiles presented Roy with a beautiful trophy. It was a replica of the camera that Griffith's cameraman, Billy Bitzer, had used in filming *Birth of a Nation* in 1915. In his acceptance remarks, Roy said that only one camera had been used in filming *Birth*. "I shudder when I think of what might have happened if that one camera had failed or been destroyed," Aitken said. "Nowadays, of course, motion picture producers use many cameras when shooting films. They don't want to waste costly scenes and time because of camera failure."

The following year, the Cinephiles met at Chicago and honored actress Colleen Moore, who at one time worked for the Aitken companies. Since his own speech, however, Roy had begun a lively correspondence with many of the Cinephiles who wanted to share their enthusiasm with someone they admired as a movie pioneer.

One particular relationship developed between Aitken and a Cinephile named Sam Rubin, who operated a furniture store in Indiana, Pennsylvania. Rubin published a mimeographed periodical for movie buffs known as the *8 mm Collector*. Next it was retitled the *Classic Film Collector*, and then it became *Classic Images*.

Whatever the name over the masthead, the periodical contained the same content: news about silent and sound film companies, movie buffs and their collections, reminiscences of movie pioneers, and other film matters. Of course, Rubin asked Roy to write a lengthy recollection of his and his brother's long and distinguished movie career. After the article was published, Roy received a number of letters from old silent movie friends he had not heard from in years, and he made some new friends. It seemed that Cinephiles everywhere wanted to correspond with Roy Aitken of Waukesha, Wisconsin.

Roy had his favorites among the group. One was Mike Kornick, a customs official from Campbell, Ohio. He had perhaps the most complete collection of silent movie serial material and star obituaries in the nation. Kornick and his wife spent their vacations traveling across America visiting old-time movie stars, some in nursing homes and others in private residences or hotels. He had autographs and pictures of many of these stars.

"My wife and I have a wonderful time attending Cinephile meetings and looking up and interviewing old time movie stars," Kornick wrote to Aitken.

Another movie buff cornered Roy at a Cinephile conference and confessed his affinity for the silent movies. "I exhibit some of these films for my farm friends and relatives," said the Missouri farmer. "Sometimes, if no one comes to see the pictures, I run them anyway for my own enjoyment."

Testimonials like this raised Roy's curiosity, and to find out the level of interest in the old silent films, he interviewed Kent D. Eastin, president of the Eastin-Phelan Corporation, distributor of Blackhawk eight- and sixteen-millimeter films. Eastin reported from his office in Davenport, Iowa, that there are more movie enthusiasts in the United States than most people did realize. For example, he said Blackhawk's active list of people interested in movie lore topped a hundred thousand names in 1967.

"This list would exclude customers who have not purchased from Blackhawk for years or more," Eastin explained to Aitken. He then provided a profile of Blackhawk customers:

> Ninety percent of the individuals on our list are interested, in varying degrees, in the collection of motion picture data. The word buff relates to degrees of enthusiasm. Some are hard core buffs, and they belong to clubs and associations

such as the Cinephiles, which have several hundred members. Then there are 500 to 2,000 in a slightly cooler circle around this nucleus. But there are thousands of individuals who are working on modest collections in foreign countries. I do know many movie buffs in the United States who have several thousand dollars or more invested in films and equipment. And, as time goes by, many may well get into the most enthusiastic and committed group.

Blackhawk does an extensive business outside the United States and our Bulletin helps to keep them in touch with what is offered in films. More than 5,000 copies of each issue also go to collectors in other countries. Blackhawk films in 8-mm and 16-mm entertain people all over the world likely to become avid movie buffs.

Armed with a list of local names supplied by Blackhawk, Roy made contact with movie buffs in the Milwaukee area and kept a log on their activities. He found that Raymond Plopper not only collected silent films but also had built a nickelodeon theater in his West Allis, Wisconsin, home. It seated ten persons, had dual projectors in the projection booth, and featured stereo background music.

"I have about $9,000 tied up in my movie project," Plopper admitted to Roy, "but I still feel I'm a novice in my hobby. During the past year [1967], we set up a regular winter program to show these films and invited many people to view them. My wife buys films for me as birthday and Christmas gifts from time to time."

Plopper was proud to report that *Birth of a Nation* held a prominent spot at the top of his feature film list. Also included were *Last of the Mohicans* with Wallace Beery, *The Grand Duchess and the Waiter* with Adolphe Menjou, Charlie Chaplin's *City Lights*, *The Lost World* with Wallace Beery and Lewis Stone, and *The Black Pirate* with Douglas Fairbanks Sr.

A number of people told Roy that by collecting old films, they had the pleasure of viewing what they had missed years ago. "I am now enjoying movies as they should be enjoyed, and I can bring back to life all these great stars at the press of a button," said one movie buff who wished to remain anonymous. The same man told Roy that he had five scrapbooks of movie star pictures, magazines, stills, magic lanterns, projectors, slides, and theater props to go with what he considered the largest collection of full-length eight-millimeter silent movies in his city.

"I don't collect any old nitrate type films," he said, "because I don't want this beautiful collection to go up in smoke." Roy related his own experience in Chicago in 1905 with nitrate film and fire.

But the real fire this time was kindled in the old man's soul as he sat in the Holiday Inn at Goerke's Corners with the briefcase across his lap. He wished his brother Harry had lived to see the phenomenon they had started grow into dreams and fantasies for so many people. Harry would have liked the Cinephiles and the book that Roy wrote to set the record straight on making *Birth of a Nation*. The ninety-two-year-old former movie mogul lifted his red-rimmed eyes heavenward. He seemed to be addressing Harry as he asked, "How can interest in silent movies ever die when there are numerous Cinephiles, young and old, and other movie enthusiasts, who are so dedicated to the memory of those glorious days of the cinema?"

He opened his briefcase and removed a copy of *The Birth of a Nation Story*. A smile pushed the wrinkles aside on his cheeks as he remembered that day in the spring of 1968, when he had presented a copy of the book to actor Paul Newman, an Aitken screen favorite.

Newman had come to Waukesha County in March of that year on a campaign swing for Senator Eugene McCarthy, a presidential candidate. Roy heard about the visit and thought how nice it would be to meet the handsome Hollywood idol. He felt that they would have a great deal to talk about because he was a pioneer, and Newman was the epitome of a personable, modern actor with a gift for making high-quality movies.

On a cold day, not unlike those he and Harry spent milking cows, Roy was home reading newspaper accounts of Newman's Wisconsin tour when the telephone rang. It was his longtime friend, Mayor Robert Collins of Delafield, a small city thirteen miles west of Waukesha.

"Paul Newman is going to give a talk at the Delafield Square in an hour and a half," Collins said, "and I'm on the welcoming committee. Why don't you give Newman an autographed copy of your book *The Birth of a Nation Story*? I'm sure he'd like to own it. I'll drive over and pick you up in a half an hour."

Collins and his family drove Roy to a parking place a few spots down from one reserved for Newman's limousine. The mayor said he would bring Newman over to meet his family and Roy at the appropriate time.

"Nobody minded the cold wind blowing off the lake," said Roy. "Everyone was excitedly waiting for Newman to arrive. It was like anticipating one of Uncle Bert's circus parades or a performance by Buffalo Bill."

Soon Newman appeared and the crowd cheered. He began speaking from the steps of a local drugstore, and Roy had a perfect view. He could see the actor's uncovered head and broad shoulders above the crowd.

Then Mayor Collins came to his car. "Paul Newman wants to meet and talk with you, Roy," he said. "And he'd also like to have you ride with him to our next stop at Mukwonago. If you want to go along in his car, my wife will drive behind the Newman limousine and pick you up at Mukwonago."

"Yes, yes!" Roy said.

With the help of the local police officers, Roy made his way through the crowd to Newman's car. The door opened and a very attractive woman greeted Aitken with a handshake and introduced herself as Sally Johnson. She motioned for the eighty-six-year-old man to sit down by her side in the backseat, which he was glad to do since she reminded him of the girls he and Charles Welch used to drive around these same roads. But when Newman emerged from the crowd, the woman moved to a front seat and the actor sat down beside Roy.

Newman shook Aitken's hand warmly and heaved a sigh of relief that he was finished with his speech. Soon the car moved away, with squad cars in front and at the rear. As the actor and the movie mogul drove along the streets of Delafield, Newman remarked what a lovely village it was. "It reminds me of my home town in Connecticut," he said.

When they got to the open highway, Roy gave him an autographed copy of his book, which Paul opened with interest and began reading, looking at the many pictures.

"Why, here's Gloria Swanson!" he exclaimed. "I saw her in California some weeks ago. We were working on the same project."

While the actor was intent on perusing the book, Roy enjoyed the fine scenery as the caravan sped along. Newman, too, stopped reading frequently to admire the beautiful countryside where the Aitkens had grown up.

As the actor continued reading, he peppered Roy with questions about the cost of movie productions in the silent film days. Roy told him about the difficulty he and Harry encountered in raising money for anything that resembled a movie. "People thought the movies a very unpromising business in the pioneer days of Hollywood," said Roy.

"I'm going to enjoy reading this book," Newman said. "It looks great!"

The actor was very attentive when the old man told him the Aitken movie companies, under Harry's leadership, had produced some 2,500 films from 1911 through 1922.

For Roy, reminiscing about his and Harry's odyssey ended all too briefly. He felt that there was a great deal more to discuss with Newman relating to the beginnings of the great motion picture business. Not often did he get the ear of such a distinguished modern spokesman.

But the limousine came to a halt in Mukwonago, and immediately there came a pounding at the window. Roy looked up and saw an eager, young woman with her hair hanging over one eye and part of her face. She was trying to take a picture. The old man inched forward to see whether it was he that she wanted, but "No! No!" she kept motioning for Roy to lean back, out of the way. She wanted Paul Newman. Roy slumped back against the car seat thinking that perhaps this might be the appropriate time to buy that rocking chair.

But, of course, he did not until six years later after he had visited the old homestead at the Holiday Inn site one more time. On his way out the front entrance of the motel with his sister Gladys, Roy E. Aitken touched the marker honoring the Aitken brothers. "It's been a colorful, exciting career," Roy recalled. "I wouldn't have missed it for anything."

Harry E. Aitken, the chief Cinephile if ever there was one, would have approved, Roy decided. The Aitken brothers had left their mark not only on history but also on the land of their forefathers. In his mind's eye, he once again saw the old stone farmhouse and his hardworking father who had tended the farm so patiently.

"In all he built, love was understood," wrote Wisconsin writer August Derleth in an "Elegy to My Father." While the original poem applies to every farm father like Elvin Aitken, a few italicized modifications provide a fitting elegy to Harry and Roy as well:

> The echo of his whistling at work
> Stalks the rooms of this house [*empire*] he built
> Like a ghost never to be laid . . .
> He loved the feel of wood [*film*] in his hands
> He built to last
> In all he built, love was understood
> As tangible as wind's rune
> In the aspen tree
> The saw's [*projector's*] song cutting through wood [*darkness*]
> Against his knee [*For all to see*].

Epilogue

Roy E. Aitken died on October 28, 1976, in a Waukesha nursing home, followed by sister Gladys's death in 1980. He was ninety-four and had outlived most of his major contemporaries. He had witnessed the rise and fall of other movie moguls like Sam Goldwyn and Louis B. Mayer who, like he and Harry, were eventually stripped of their power and fought unsuccessfully to make a comeback. Roy had seen the ever clever Carl Laemmle avoid this fate by turning his Universal City over to his son Carl Jr., in 1936. Then the Aitkens' erstwhile competitor retired to enjoy the fruits of his labor. But three years after relinquishing the reins of Universal, Carl Laemmle died on September 24, 1939. He was seventy-two.

Only Adolph Zukor survived Roy Aitken. Zukor was pushed into retirement in March 1949 and died thirty years later at age 103 at his fabulous estate in New Jersey.

Louis B. Mayer, Jesse Lasky, Goldwyn's former brother-in-law and partner, Harry Cohn, and Cecil B. De Mille died within six months of each other between 1957 and 1958. All left sizable estates except Lasky who, like the Aitkens, died practically broke. Mayer bequeathed more than $7 million to his daughters, and Goldwyn left more than $16 million to his heirs upon his death at age ninety-four on January 31, 1974.

While each movie pioneer shared the common fate of men and women everywhere, their reputations, legacies, and places in history are what set them apart. Unlike the Goldwyns, Mayers, Zukors, and others of the immigrant community, here, too, the Aitken brothers were shortchanged.

To unravel this puzzle let us begin with reputations. In Budd Schulberg's book *Moving Pictures: Memories of a Hollywood Prince*, he summa-

202

rizes and distinguishes his own Jewish family from the "cliched foibles of such Hollywood boss-families as the Mayers, the Warners and the Laemmles." Schulberg adds, "L. B. was a tyrant, Jack Warner was a loud-mouthed vaudevillian and Uncle Carl Laemmle—although one of Hollywood's original 'mound builders'—pretty much a joke for the way he surrounded himself with boatloads of relatives from Laupheim, his birthplace in Bavaria" (292).

Similarly, Goldwyn biographer A. Scott Berg makes a very revealing statement about Harry Cohn, who had run Columbia Pictures since its creation in 1920 until his death in February 1958. "When a member of the Wilshire Boulevard Temple asked Rabbi Magnin if he could not think of 'one good thing to say about' the deceased [Cohn]," Berg writes, "the rabbi paused and said, 'He's dead'" (484).

Goldwyn himself pinned an epitaph of sorts on Zukor, according to Berg, when he once referred to the Hungarian as the man who "stole more money from this business than anybody who ever lived" (447).

By contrast, without a full-length published chronicle of their visionary accomplishments in building America's first movie empire, the Aitkens' reputation barely has extended beyond Wisconsin borders since the dissolution of Triangle, except among movie buffs and Cinephiles. If they were tyrants, no one has come forward to say so, and only one rabid Triangle devotee has labeled Harry a manipulator with floating ethics for allowing his empire to crumble. It is worth noting that the comments against Mayer, Goldwyn, Cohn, Zukor, et al., come from within their community of commonalty or, as Schulberg says, "the Hollywood boss families." These elite individuals could be at each other's throats one minute and in the next borrowing money to set up a rival company or winning the hand of their competitor's daughter in marriage.

As outsiders, the Aitken brothers did not have these kinds of connections. For example, Carl Laemmle searched for a suitor for his daughter Rosabelle, but, regardless of the moderate disparity in ages, he obviously never gave thought of marrying her to Harry or Roy and creating a new dynasty with his former partners. Yet, several other contemporaries married starlets half their ages after divorcing their Jewish wives. Closed out of the mainstream of Hollywood social life, the Aitkens were never able to establish a reputation acceptable to the other moguls who mistakenly thought the farm boys' ambition bordered on hubris and not on the hard work of their own experience.

Relative to legacy and place in history, the Aitkens will eventually emerge to take a seat at the Hollywood banquet of "royal" pioneers. Their accomplishments are far too significant to go ignored for another century. They are like historian Daniel J. Boorstin's genuine hero versus the celebrity—the one known for achievements, the other for his or her well-knowness. True genius needs but a short span to take root. Mozart turned out his masterpieces at an early age, and Jefferson wrote the Declaration of Independence while still in his thirties. The Aitken brothers were cut from the same cloth, as their greatest accomplishments came early and peaked at ten to fifteen years into their careers. Yet, to those who know the story, the achievements of the Aitken brothers are already legendary and an indisputable part of motion picture history. For example:

- As early as 1911, several years ahead of their contemporaries, the Aitkens formed a national movie distribution company. Their Mutual Film Corporation, held in partnership with John Freuler and others, was instrumental in breaking the back of a monopoly of film producers called the Trust and in turn paved the way for independent filmmakers and distributors.
- Harry and Roy Aitken produced the first superpicture, artistically and technically speaking. Although controversial, *Birth of a Nation* established Hollywood as the entertainment capital of the world. Moreover, Roy lived to see a panel of two hundred movie critics selected by *Variety* magazine name *Birth* "the greatest picture of all time because of its historical accuracy and its introduction of new filming techniques."
- They were the first American movie company to establish branches in London, Berlin, Copenhagen, Paris, Rome, and other cities.
- Before the Aitkens used full-page ads and public relations skills to promote the movies directed by D. W. Griffith, Thomas Ince, and Mack Sennett, no other producer had used this medium. In addition, their movie company produced a weekly news and style show viewed by millions and later developed into the newsreel format, made famous by Fox's Movietone.
- Stars such as Douglas Fairbanks Sr., Mary Pickford, Gloria Swanson, Charlie Chaplin, Norma and Constance Talmadge, William S. Hart, Hedda Hopper, Lillian and Dorothy Gish, Wallace Beery, Roscoe "Fatty" Arbuckle, and many others owe their illustrious movie careers to the Aitken brothers, who developed them into celebrities.
- Harry Aitken was the first top studio head to insist on family-oriented movies and exercised self-censorship to achieve this goal. The Aitken credo was "Clean Pictures for Clean People," and the brothers stuck to this policy in the face of opposition because it reflected their small-town values, which they were unwilling to compromise.
- With Triangle the Aitkens formed a motion picture company that controlled its product from production to distribution to exhibition. In this way they revolutionized the industry for control by later movie moguls such as Loew (Metro), Goldwyn, and Mayer

(MGM), Fox, Cohn (Columbia), Laemmle (Universal), and Zukor (Paramount).

- Single-handedly, the Aitkens catapulted the movies into respectability by persuading Wall Street bankers to invest in the new phenomenon and at the height of their careers produced 2,500 silent films.

Despite this unmatched record, there are those who would still deny the Aitkens their rightful place in movie history. Some nominate for first-among-pioneer status cameraman Edwin Porter, whose *Great Train Robbery* inspired a number of future producers such as the Aitken brothers and Goldwyn to get into movies. But one great film does not make an empire. If that were the case, then David W. Griffith's claim as "the man who had invented Hollywood" would have validity on the technical and artistic merits of his directorship of *Birth of a Nation* alone. Porter and Griffith were great disciples of great innovators such as the Aitkens, who could take an idea and disseminate it to millions, creating a whole industry in the process. Substantial as their contributions were, the accomplishments of Porter and Griffith are on a different tier than the men who led them and others into greatness. Likewise, Goldwyn, Zukor, and Laemmle benefited from the Aitkens' leadership as the brothers repeatedly broke new ground for later movie empire builders to follow. For the most part, other moguls became celebrities as imitators of, or were spurred on by, the Aitkens' early achievements, and in this way were able to bridge the gap between silent films and sound. Like pupils of great teachers, the survivors of the silent era had learned their lessons well and applied them in new situations.

Of course, none of this explains why the Aitkens' place in film history has been either lost or ignored. However, intriguing clues call for speculation. Between Harry, the visionary and planner for an entire industry, and Roy, the loyal foot soldier, the Aitkens needed a chief of staff. Laemmle and Mayer both exhausted the talents of the sickly Irving Thalberg in this role at Universal and MGM, respectively. Charles Hite was being groomed by Harry to assume chief-of-staff duties for the Aitkens, but like Thalberg, he died tragically in the prime of his life. Had Hite lived to translate Harry's genius into operational functions and provide order to Roy's field campaigns so that they meshed with the overall mission, the brothers' achievements and those of the empire they built might have been protected and thus survived.

Survival aside, the Aitken legacy suffered an even more unkindly cut at the hands of their rivals' biographers, film historians, and critics. Whether intentionally or by accident these scholars have, for the most part, ignored the Aitken role in Hollywood's formative years, treated the brothers with indifference, or revised the record. Rarely have Aitken accomplishments been placed in true perspective. Even those considered the most authoritative sources on the silent movie era portray the Aitkens in diminished light, if they portray them at all.

Another pattern was to shed more or less light on the Aitkens depending on whether the expert was writing or speaking to a local or national audience. This point is illustrated in the ambiguity shown by the late William K. Everson, author of *American Silent Film* and a recognized arbiter on questions relating to motion picture history. First, in a newspaper interview in the *Milwaukee Journal*, April 28, 1957, Everson credits the Aitken brothers as being the financial genius behind *Birth of a Nation* for which D. W. Griffith got the glory. "They did it on a shoestring," he said. The same article quoted Everson relative to Harry and Roy's struggle to create Triangle, "It [the story] would be a fabulous book."

Unfortunately, when the authority on silent cinema wrote his own account in 1978, twenty-one years later, he skimped on the Aitkens' contributions or, as did most of his fellow writers, relied on the biographies of Aitken contemporaries who had an ax to grind.

The most common slight, however, is to treat Harry and Roy as bit players, mentioning the great companies established, the moving pictures produced, and the directors and stars assembled without linking them to the brothers per se. For example, one reads about Majestic, Reliance, Bison, Thanhauser, Mutual, Keystone, Fine Arts, and Triangle without learning that each of these great companies was founded or nurtured by the Aitkens. Similarly, one is left with the erroneous impression that Griffith, Ince, and Sennett formed Triangle, and not Harry and Roy following their triumphant world tour with *Birth of a Nation*.

As for the classic and pacesetting Aitken-produced pictures such as *Birth*, *Intolerance*, Keystone comedies, and Bill Hart westerns—featuring Gish, Normand, Swanson, Fairbanks, and others—each is inextricably linked in film history to Harry and Roy Aitken. As enthusiastically as Zukor, Goldwyn, Mayer, and other Aitken rivals were in driving the brothers from the field, they were equally sanguine in their efforts to discredit their quarry. Zukor and his colleagues not only divided the spoils among themselves or their offspring, they saw to it, through rumor and innuendo, that the same Wall Street bankers who had once backed the Aitkens dropped them. Of course, this tactic prevented Harry and Roy Aitken from mounting a credible comeback. It also led to acceptance of an incomplete picture of their great struggle since the survivors—not the vanquished—get the last word.

Information filtered through three-quarters of a century of opinions after the fact can also present an unclear picture of how and why the Aitkens lost their empire. William K. Everson attributed the fall in part to the Aitken trademark slogan. "Clean pictures for clean people" translated to "dull pictures for dull people" in the public's eye, Everson asserted, again tying the slogan to Triangle without mentioning that it was Aitken philosophy in its simplest form (page 120 in paperback edition).

Everson leaves little doubt in his readers' minds that the preferred advertisements of the time were those promoting racy pictures. Zukor's Famous Players, the forerunner of Paramount, led the field in lasciviousness in the silent film era. Nonetheless, the film historian seems to excuse this mocking of ethics on the grounds that it was good for business. In other words, one was obliged to enter the abyss of bad taste in order to survive, according to the mogul's mantra.

Alone, the Aitkens fought such growing cynicism until they, too, were forced to capitulate and seek a merger with Zukor and Goldwyn. But here as well, they received no accolades for attempting to raise motion picture standards for as long as they could hold out. Instead, praise, however reluctantly given, went again to Triangle the company as if no connection existed between this entity and its founders from Wisconsin. Everson himself missed an opportunity to secure the link and give proper attribution. His quoted words, especially those italicized in his reference to the "clean" slogan, are given emphasis to show the absurdity in placing too great a gap between creation and creator. "Cognizant of the fact that the movies were still considered not quite respectable, *Triangle* lost no opportunity to stress *their* concern to earn that respect by citing whenever possible, the endorsement of ministers and teachers concerning the spiritual or educational values of *their* films" (page 120 paperback edition).

A few short years after Triangle lost its assets with the Aitken empire in ruins, the brothers' philosophy on self-censorship was vindicated. Following a public outcry against sex, murder, and drugs in 1922, Hollywood established its own censorship board to oversee on- and off-screen morality.

While the war against Hollywood's unchallenged influence on public morality rages on in a new century, past skirmishes over self-censorship exact a toll. In hindsight, Harry and Roy Aitken, as the guiding geniuses behind a policy that advocated decency in this cause, combined with their lifelong struggle against intolerance, remain among the war's first casualties and its first champions. Granted, this fact is hard to discern by a cursory look at the Aitken record as it stood at the close of the twentieth century. But so are many of their other achievements.

Yet, if historian Daniel Boorstin is right, and time is an ally of the achiever and foe of the celebrity whose well knowness fades, then we can expect the legend of the Aitkens to get better, or at least more accurate, with every passing year. Placing history aside, can Hollywood, the world's dream factory, forever ignore a home-grown story right under its nose? The Aitken odyssey is familiar to everyone with a dream: how to face up to challenges boldly and either triumph or go down gallantly. Harry and Roy did both and in doing so showed a new generation what made life worthwhile in the past.

But they did more. They added their unique brand of ambition, style, learning, work relations with people, and awareness of right or wrong actions as they followed the song of a silent siren that called to them throughout their lives. Only at the end of their movie careers did the Aitkens discover that the brightest light is projected from within.

Bibliography

Aitken, Roy E. *Landmark,* "War on Woodchucks," vol. 10, no. 4/67; "Bringing in the Sheaves," vol. 10, no. 4/68; "Breaking Horses," vol. 11, no. 2/68; "It's Nutting Time Again," vol. 12, no. 4/69; and Special Aitken Brothers Issue, vol. 25, no. 3/82. Waukesha, Wis.: Waukesha County Historical Society, 1967–1982.

Aitken, Roy E., and Al P. Nelson. *The Birth of a Nation Story.* Middleburg, Va.: Denlinger, 1965.

Anonymous. "Farm Girls" (poem). *Waukesha Plain Dealer.* Waukesha, Wis.: 1854.

Anonymous. "Master in the Art of Living" (poem).

Barry, Iris. *D. W. Griffith: American Film Master.* New York: Museum of Modern Art, 1940.

Behlmer, Rudy, ed. *Memo from David O. Selznick.* New York: Viking, 1972.

Berg, A. Scott. *Goldwyn: A Biography.* New York: Knopf, 1989.

Bitzer, G. W. *Billy Bitzer: His Story, The Autobiography of D. W.Griffith's Master Cameraman.* New York: Farrar, Straus & Giroux, 1973.

Carey, Gary. *All the Stars in Heaven: Louis B. Mayer's MGM.* New York: Dutton, 1981.

Chaneles, Sol, and Albert Wolsky. *Movie Makers.* Secaucus, N.J.: Derbibooks, 1974.

Croy, Homer. *Star Maker: The Story of D. W. Griffith.* New York: Duell, Sloan & Pearce, 1959.

Derleth, August. "A Little Elegy for My Father." *Collected Poems, 1937–1967.* New York: Candlelight, 1967.

Ellis, Mel. *Notes from Little Lakes.* Waukesha, Wis.: Cabin Bookshelf, 1996.

Everson, William K. *Landmark,* "Waukesha, Home Burg of Aitkens, Who Backed Griffith and Triangle, Takes the Shoestring Fest Path." Special Aitken Brothers Issue, vol. 25, no. 3/82. Waukesha, Wis.: Waukesha County Historical Society, 1982.

———. *American Silent Film.* New York: Oxford University Press, 1978. Paperback edition, New York: Da Capo Press, 1998.

Finch, Christopher, and Linda Rosenkrantz. *Gone Hollywood: The Movie Colony in the Golden Age.* Garden City, N.Y.: Doubleday, 1979.

Franklin, Joe. *Classics of the Silent Screen.* New York: Citadel, 1959.

———. "Silent Movies of Early Years Became a Powerful Art Form" (Hollywood, Calif.—NANA—1961 dateline). *The Milwaukee Journal,* Greensheet, Nov. 20, 1961.

Gard, Robert E., and L. G. Sorden. *Wisconsin Lore.* New York: Duell, Sloan & Pearce, 1962.

Gish, Lillian. *Dorothy and Lillian Gish.* London: Macmillan London, 1973.

———. *Lillian Gish: The Movies, Mr. Griffith, and Me.* Upper Saddle River, N.J.: Prentice-Hall, 1969.

Hart, James, ed. *The Man Who Invented Hollywood: The Autobiography of D. W. Griffith.* Louisville, Ky.: Touchstone, 1972.

Henderson, Robert M. *D. W. Griffith: His Life and Work.* New York: Oxford University Press, 1972.

Johnson, Jean Lindsay. *Illustrious Oconomowoc.* Milwaukee: Franklin, 1978.

Journal Special Correspondence. "Silent Movie Days Memories Bubble." *The Milwaukee Journal,* April 28, 1957.

Kerr, Walter. *The Silent Clowns.* New York: Knopf, 1975.

Ketchum, Richard M. *Will Rogers: His Life and Times.* New York: American Heritage, 1973.

Lahue, Kalton C. *Dreams for Sale: The Rise and Fall of the Triangle Film Corporation.* Cranbury, N.J.: A. S. Barnes, 1971.

Lahue, Kalton C., and Terry Brewer. *Kops and Custards: The Legend of Keystone Films.* Norman: University of Oklahoma Press, 1968.

Lee, Raymond. *The Films of Mary Pickford.* New York: Castle Books–Barnes, Inc., 1970.

Lockwood, Charles. *Dream Palaces: Hollywood at Home.* New York: Viking, 1981.

Macrone, Michael. *It's Greek to Me!* New York: Cader Books, HarperCollins, 1991.

Monfried, Walter. "All Early Film Stars Worked for Two Wisconsin Brothers." *The Milwaukee Journal,* Greensheet, July 18, 1951.

Randall, Richard S. *Censorship of the Movies.* Madison: University of Wisconsin Press, 1970.

Scherman, David E., ed. *Life Goes to the Movies.* New York: Time-Life Books, 1975.

Schickel, Richard. *D. W. Griffith: An American Life.* New York: Simon & Schuster, 1984.

Schulberg, Budd. *Moving Pictures: Memories of a Hollywood Prince.* New York: Stein & Day, 1981.

Swanson, Gloria. *Swanson on Swanson: An Autobiography.* New York: Random House, 1980.

Torrence, Bruce T. *Hollywood: The First Hundred Years.* New York: Zoetrope, 1982.

Wells, Robert W. *Fire at Peshtigo.* Madison, Wis.: Northword, 1983.

Widen, Larry, and Judi Anderson. *Milwaukee Movie Palaces.* Milwaukee: Milwaukee County Historical Society, 1986.

Wisconsin Library Association. *Wisconsin: A Guide to the Badger State.* New York: Hastings House, 1954.

A

Aitken Brothers
Selected Filmography

Note: a number of 1915 Keystone Comedies, featuring Fatty Arbuckle, Mabel Normand, Edgar Kennedy, Harold Lloyd, Polly Moran, and other Aitken-KB-Sennett players are available on Video Film Classics, Volumes 1–7, from Kartes Video Communications, and at some video stores.

This sampling of films produced and distributed by the Aitkens demonstrates the vastness of the brothers' empire during their peak years. Between 1913 and 1922, Harry and Roy developed, produced, and promoted motion pictures at a pace exceeding modern movie-making conglomerates such as Walt Disney (Buena Vista), Fox (20th Century), Sony (Tri-Star), and Paramount (Viacom). In addition to this list of titles, the Aitkens produced more than two thousand other films. Like modern studio heads they selected and bought scenarios; hired writers, directors, actors and extras, and cinematographers; and built studios, leased equipment, and met a huge payroll, supervising the product from start to finish, including promotion. To place the undertaking in perspective, note that the Aitkens directed and managed, under various company logos, some of the early movie industry's most distinguished brands. Included were Bison, Bronco, Epoch, Equity, Fine Arts, Kay Bee, Keystone, Komic, Majestic, Master, Mutual, Reliance, Thanhouser, Triangle, and other film production and distribution companies, as well as theaters.

Unfortunately, less than fifty percent of the total film output generated during the silent era survives today. Countless film negatives were lost by the Aitkens themselves in a warehouse fire on Long Island, N.Y., despite the film's storage in a vault and in fireproof containers. Fortunately for genealogists, film collectors, researchers, and other devotees of Hollywood's Golden Era, Harry and Roy inventoried what documentation they could assemble and placed it in the Aitken Brothers' Papers (Boxes 1–27) at the Wisconsin State Historical Society (WSHS) in Madison. This filmography and the actors' list that follows in appendix B were compiled, for the most part, from this inventory of materials, some of which was handwritten. Outside sources were checked to confirm dates and other details relating to the films and actors who appeared in them. Other repositories for Aitken documents and films that have survived include the Academy of Motion Picture Arts and Sciences in Los Angeles (Keystone material), the Museum of Modern Art in New York City (Griffith papers), and the Waukesha County Historical Society in Waukesha, Wisc. (documents donated by Roy Aitken and Al Nelson).

Film titles are grouped by their release year and arranged alphabetically, followed by the releasing company and number of reels. Unless otherwise noted, assume the film was the standard length of two-reels. If black and white still photographs were taken during shooting or for publicity purposes, the Aitkens indicated the number available. For many of the movies they made, the Aitkens also preserved other data and rare documents such as synopses, subtitles, production reports, etc. As indicated these are noted below. An asterisk after a title indicates a film pictorially presented in *A Silent Siren Song*. Obviously Harry and Roy Aitken wanted to share this information with succeeding generations. Why else painstakingly catalogue films, directors, stars, and other documents unless they wanted to ensure that this great legacy survived as an example of what a talented team can accomplish, wherever, whenever, or whoever gets the credit.

1913

A Desperate Lover (Mutual-Keystone—1 reel)
A Doctored Affair (Keystone—1 reel). See Aitken papers for press release.
A Fishy Affair (Keystone—1 reel)
Bougainvillea Police (Keystone—1 reel)
Gypsy Queen (Keystone—1 reel)
The Great Leap (Majestic). Directed by William Christy Cabanne with "part-time supervision" by D. W. Griffith after he joined the Aitken organization on October 1, 1913.

1914

The Avenging Conscience (Reliance-Majestic—6 reels). Directed by D. W. Griffith and opened at the Strand, New York, August 2. Suggested by Edgar Allan Poe's *The Tell-Tale Heart* and *Annabel Lee*, *Conscience* featured Spottiswoode Aiken, Lillian Gish, Robert Harron, Mae Marsh, Blanche Sweet, Henry Walthall, and others who would make dozens of pictures under the Aitken banner. Griffith and cameraman Billy Bitzer developed the camera techniques used to shoot this picture.
The Battle of the Sexes (Majestic-Mutual—5 reels). Directed by D. W. Griffith and based on *The Single Standard* by Daniel Carson Goodman. Opening at Weber's Theatre, New York, on April 12, it was probably the first Griffith picture released by the Aitkens, since *The Escape* was on hold while Blanche Sweet recuperated.
Caught in a Cabaret (Keystone). One of many films directed by the versatile Mabel Normand. Synopsis and titles are on file.

The Deadly Glass of Beer (Mutual). Synopsis is filed with Aitken Papers at the Wisconsin State Historical Society (WSHS).

*Dough and Dynamite** (Mutual-Keystone). One of thirty-nine films Charlie Chaplin made for the Aitkens. Synopsis and titles are on file.

The Escape (Reliance-Majestic—7 reels). Directed by Griffith, based on a play by Paul Armstrong, this film opened at the Cort Theatre, New York, on June 1. Griffith complained that the Aitkens weren't promoting *Escape* adequately.

The Floor Above (Reliance-Majestic). Directed by James Kirkwood and based upon the E. Phillips Oppenheim novel *The Mystery of Charlecot Mansions*. *Floor* was one of dozens of Aitken films starring Dorothy Gish.

His Trysting Place (Mutual-Keystone). Another film directed by Charlie Chaplin with synopsis and titles available.

Home, Sweet Home (Majestic—6 reels). Directed by D. W. Griffith with scenario by Harry Aitken from lyrics composed by John H. Payne. *Home,* based on the popular ballad of the day, opened May 17 at the Strand, New York.

The Idler (Reliance—1 reel). The Synopsis is on file at WSHS.

The Raiders (Mutual-Kay Bee). Continuity instructions, fifteen photos, and cutting sheet are available.

The Sisters (Majestic-Mutual). Directed and written by Christy Cabanne, *Sisters* is one of several Aitken films in which the Gish sisters appeared together. Dorothy gives up her man to Lillian and marries another. The two women reconcile after their babies are born. Dorothy sacrifices again for her sister's happiness.

1915

Above Par (Reliance). Titles and fourteen still photographs are on file.

Added Fuel (Reliance). File contains titles and twenty-nine photos.

The Baby (Reliance—1 reel). Directed by Sidney and Chester Franklin. Synopsis, eleven photos, and titles are on file.

*Birth of a Nation** (Majestic-Epoch—12 reels). Directed by D. W. Griffith who wrote the script with Frank G. Woods, based on the novel and play, *The Clansman* by Thomas Dixon Jr., with additional material from the same author's story *The Leopard's Spots*. Renamed *Birth,* the film opened at the Liberty Theatre, New York, on March 3. This pacesetting film epic is available on home video through Allied Artists Entertainment Group.

Buried Treasure (Reliance—1 reel). Titles and eighteen photos are on file.

Checkmate (Majestic—1 reel). Titles and nine photos.

The Comeback (Majestic). Directed by Raoul Walsh. Synopsis, sixteen photos, and titles are on file.

A Costly Exchange (Komic—1 reel). Titles and seventeen photos are in the Aitken Papers.

The Double-Crossing of Slim (Reliance—1 reel). Titles and thirteen photos are included in the Aitken Papers.

Father and Son (Mutual/Reliance—3 reel). Synopsis, fifty-seven photos, and titles are available.

A Game Old Knight (Keystone). Directed by Richard Jones. Synopsis, five photos, and story are on file.

The Girl and the Mummy (Triangle). Directed by DeWolfe Hopper. Synopsis and one photo are listed.

Her Grandparents (Majestic—1 reel). Directed by Frank Powell. Titles, fourteen photos, and a press release comprise the Aitken file.

The Iron Strain (Kay Bee—6 reels). Directed by Thomas H. Ince. Synopsis, twelve photos, story, titles, and press release.

Jordan Is a Hard Road (Triangle-Fine Arts). Written and directed by Allan Dwan. Adapted from the novel by Gilbert Parker.

The Lamb (Triangle). Directed by Christy Cabanne with a scenario contribution by Granville Warwick, a pseudonym used by Griffith. Harry Aitken featured *The Lamb* to catapult Douglas Fairbanks into film stardom when he introduced his latest production company to New York audiences on September 23. Filling out the Triangle triple-feature bill was Ince's *The Iron Strain* and Raymond Hitchcock in *My Valet*. Top tickets sold for $2 at the Knickerbocker Theatre. *The Lamb* remains a favorite at film festivals everywhere.

The Little Match Makers (Majestic—1 reel). Press release and sixteen photos are on file.

The Martyrs of the Alamo (Fine Arts—5 reels). Synopsis, one hundred photos, titles, and press report are filed with the Aitken Papers.

Matrimony (Kay Bee—4 reels). Check WSHS for synopsis, fourteen photos, story, titles, continuity, and cutting sheet.

Minerva's Mission (Majestic). Directed by Paul Powell Synopsis, twenty-two photos, titles, and press release are in the Aitken Papers.

Old Heidelberg (Triangle—5 reels). Directed for the Aitkens by John Emerson from a novel by W. Meyer-Forster. As war clouds gathered on the horizon, the Aitkens had the courage to use the entertainment media to mount a personal plea for the avoidance of war, which is major theme in *Old Heidelberg*.

The Penalty (Mutual/Reliance). File contains twelve still photos.

The Stolen Magic (Keystone). Directed by Mack Sennett. Synopsis, two photos, and production report are on file.

A Submarine Pirate (Keystone—3 reels). Directed by Charles Avery and Syd Chaplin. Syd's "Gussle" series rivaled brother Charlie's "Little Tramp's" adventures during Syd's sojourn with the Aitkens. Synopsis and five photos of *Submarine* surface in the Aitken Papers.

A Temperance Lesson (Majestic—1 reel). Aitken Papers include titles and nine photos.

The Turning Point (Reliance—1 reel). Synopsis and nineteen photos are extant.

*Victorine** (Majestic). Directed by Paul Powell and adapted from Julian Street's story *The Goings on of Victorine,* the film has Dorothy Gish playing a carnival girl who thinks she loves the strong-man who throws knives at her as part of his act. When he turns up drunk to hurl the blades, Victorine has second thoughts and looks more favorably on the carnie-worker who rescues her. File includes synopsis and twenty-one photos.

The Winged Idol (Kay Bee—4 reels). File contains synopsis, three photos, titles, press release, and continuity sheet.

1916

Ambrose's Cup of Woe (Keystone). Directed by Fred Fishback and Herman Raymaker. Mack Swain turned his Ambrose characterization into a regular series that delighted Keystone devotees. The Aitken file includes synopsis, one photograph, and production report.

Ambrose's Rapid Rise (Keystone). Directed by Fred Fishback—synopsis and two photos.

The Beckoning Flame (Kay Bee—5 reels). C. Gardner Sullivan wrote the scenario. File includes synopsis, five photos, titles, continuity sheet, production and expense reports, and copyright material.

An Artist's Wife (Majestic—1 reel). Aitken Papers contain titles and twenty-three photos.

Bath Tub Perils (Keystone). Directed by E. H. Frazee. Titles, three photos, and production report are on file.

Better Late than Never (Keystone). Directed by Frank Griffin and Jean Havez. Synopsis, two photos, press release, and production report on file.

Black Eyes and Blue (Keystone). Synopsis, three photos, and production report are available.

Bride of Hate (Kay Bee—5 reels). Synopsis, twenty-one photos, story, titles, and continuity are in the Aitken Papers.

Bullets and Brown Eyes (Kay Bee—5 reels). J. G. Hawks wrote the screenplay. File includes synopsis, four photos, titles, annotated continuity sheet, and production and expense reports.

By Stork Delivery (Keystone—1 reel). Directed by Fred Fishback. File includes synopsis, twelve photos, titles, letters, and memorandums relating to removal of objectionable material from the film for Pittsburgh audiences.

Cinders of Love (Keystone). Directed by Walter Wright. Synopsis and production report are on file.

The Corner (Kay Bee—5 reels). Directed by Thomas H. Ince. Synopsis, four photos, titles, continuity sheet, press release, and expense reports comprise the file.

A Dash of Courage (Keystone). Charles Chase directed this film. On file are synopsis, ten photos, and a production report.

Dollars and Sense (Keystone). Documentation in the Aitken Papers consists of a synopsis and two photos.

The Great Pearl Tangle (Keystone). Directed by Dell Henderson. Synopsis, three photos, and production report on file.

Gypsy Joe (Keystone). Directed by Clarence Badger and William Campbell. File contains synopsis, seven photos, and production report.

Hay Stacks and Steeples (Keystone). Another picture directed by Clarence Badger, this time with Bert Lund. Gloria Swanson was the lead actress. Synopsis, eight photos, and production report are part of the Aitken legacy.

*He Did and He Didn't** (Keystone). Synopsis, press release, production report, and seven photos in addition to the one appearing in this book are on file in the Aitken Papers.

Hell's Hinges (Triangle—5 reels). Directed by William S. Hart from a script by C. Gardner Sullivan, this film was shown at the Waukesha festival honoring the

Aitkens April 16–17, 1982, on the Carroll College campus. Festival speaker and movie buff Paul Killiam said *Hell's Hinges* stands as "one of the Aitkens' contributions to the history of film" in that they recognized and encouraged Hart's tremendous talent not only as an individual western star but as a director. The Aitkens saw to it that Ince gave Hart the "freedom to make his strong, adult westerns his way."

His Auto Ruination* (Keystone). Directed by Fred Fishback, this was another of the many Keystone two-reel comedies to showcase the talents of stars Mack Swain, Harry Gribbon, Julia Faye, May Wells, Harry McCoy, and Bobby Dunn. The Aitkens introduced larger casts and higher production values at Keystone in order to place more emphasis on characterization and less on the fast and furious pacing that Mack Sennett had relied on prior to Aitken leadership.

His Bitter Pill* (Keystone). This satiric and merciless Mack Sennett (he played the heroic sheriff) spoof of Bill Hart's movie plotting and cowboy character traits continues to draw audiences at film festivals. It was one of the favorites shown in Waukesha to honor the Aitkens, April 16–17, 1982. Mack Swain headed an all-star cast. The Aitken Papers contain a synopsis, nine photos, and a production report of *Pill*.

His Last Laugh (Keystone). Directed by Walter Wright, this was another comedy featuring Keystone regulars Harry McCoy and Julia Faye. Synopsis, seven photos, and production report constitute the Aitken file.

His Last Scent (Keystone). Directed by Charles Avery. Synopsis, nineteen photos, and production report.

His Lying Heart (Keystone). Versatile Ford Sterling teamed with Charles Avery to direct one of many pictures he made for the Aitkens as either director or actor. Synopsis, eleven photos, titles, and production report are on file.

Hoodoo Ann* (Triangle-Fine Arts—5 reels). Directed by Griffith, who also wrote the scenario, this film showed the Aitken shrewdness for star building. Harry and Roy "suggested" that Griffith pair Mae Marsh and Robert Harron in the leading roles. The stars innate chemistry clicked and they became a famous romantic duo. This was another feature shown at the Aitken Film Festival in 1982 at Harry's alma mater in Waukesha.

Intolerance* (Majestic-Wark—14 reels). With both scenario and direction by D. W. Griffith, *Intolerance* cost the Aitkens $200,000 to produce, twice their investment in *Birth* while drawing far less at the box office. Griffith was making overtures to switch allegiance to Harry's rival Zukor while spending Aitken money on this film, which was artistically acclaimed but a public failure. Despite using many of the same players that he had featured in *Birth*, Griffith seemed perplexed when audiences found it hard to follow *Intolerance's* four separate episodes. Between each part, Lillian Gish endlessly rocked the "cradle of civilization." Ironically, in a tribute the Aitken-Griffith team would have thought impossible eighty-six years ago, young people today leave a showing of *Intolerance* with the sense that they have seen "the most exciting film of their lives" according to Griffith biographer Robert M. Henderson (Henderson 1972).

The Judge (Keystone). Synopsis, five photos, and production report are in the Aitken Papers.

The Love Comet (Keystone). Directed by Walter Wright. File consists of production report and three photos.

A Modern Enoch Arden (Keystone). Directed by Clarence Badger—not to be confused with *Enoch Arden,* the 1915 Reliance-Majestic picture directed by Christy Cabanne in which Griffith played a minor role as Annie Lee's (Lillian Gish) father. Alfred Paget played Enoch; Wallace Reid played his childhood friend (Phillip) who eventually marries the twice-wed Annie. Badger's *Modern Enoch,* released on January 16, 1916, features comedy stars Joe Jackson, Mack Swain, Hank Mann, Dora Rogers, Betty Marsh, and Vivian Edwards. Although both *Enoch* versions were Aitken productions, only the Keystone synopsis with three photos and a production report are retained in their papers.

The Village Blacksmith (Keystone). Directed by Hank Mann. Synopsis and one photo are filed in the Aitken Papers.

The Waiter's Ball (Keystone). One of many Aitken productions starring Roscoe "Fatty" Arbuckle. He also directed this film, assisted by Ferris Hartman. Appearing with Arbuckle were Al St. John, Corrine Parquet, Kate Price, Joe Bordeau, and Alice Lake. File contains synopsis and production report.

Wife and Auto Trouble (Keystone). Directed by Dell Henderson, who made greater use of plot in accordance with the Aitken theory that this works better than one farcical incident following another, the technique used in previous Keystone comedies. The plot here was simple. A henpecked husband (William Collier) wins the allegiance of his secretary (Mae Busch) by buying a car for her that the wife thinks is hers. Keeping both the secretary and the wife in the dark until he can find a solution is the lead character's goal. But plans are ruined when his brother-in-law spills the beans and the car chase begins. Synopsis, one photo, titles, and production report provide a summary of the story.

1917

An Iceman's Bride (Keystone). In one part of the Aitken Papers this is also referred to as *Icelandic Bride* although the inventory list shows a synopsis, three photos, titles, and continuity sheet under *Iceman.*

An Officer's Mess (Triangle—1 reel). By early 1917 Harry Aitken directed his producers (where possible) to return to the one-reel comedy as a measure to get more film into the hands of Triangle exhibitors. But Mack Sennett balked at the plan, arguing that Keystone facilities in Edendale were geared to two-reel format. Synopsis, six photos, titles, and continuity sheet show the typical one-reel that Aitken wanted.

A Bachelor's Finish (Triangle—1 reel). File consists of synopsis and two photos.

Back of the Man (Kay Bee—5 reels). There is a discrepancy regarding this title as well. This film with synopsis, two photos, and titles on file is referred to as *Back of the Moon* in one handwritten reference.

Because He Loved Her (Keystone). Synopsis is the only document in Aitken Papers.

The Betrayal of Maggie (Keystone). Features Charles Murray and Louise Fazenda. File contains synopsis, ten photos, press release, continuity sheet, and correspondence on censorship.

Blood and Thunder (Keystone). Synopsis, three photos, story scenario, continuity, production report, copyright material, and cutting sheet are filed.

Blood Will Tell (Kay Bee 5—reels). File contains synopsis, two photos, story, continuity, production report, and copyright material.

A Boomerang Frame-up (Triangle—1 reel). Synopsis, two photos, titles, continuity, and cutting sheet are on file.

Cactus Nell (Keystone). Another Fred Fishback directed movie that showcased the talents of Polly Moran and Wallace Beery among others. Synopsis, one photo, and titles are on file.

The Camera Cure (Triangle—1 reel). Synopsis and two photos in the Aitken Papers.

The Clodhopper (Triangle—5 reels). Screenplay written by M. J. Katterjohn with synopsis, seven photos, story, titles, annotated continuity, and production report.

Dad's Downfall (Triangle—1 reel). Synopsis and three photos constitute the Aitken file.

*A Dark Room Secret** (Triangle—1 reel). Only the synopsis is on file. But the one extant photo showing the bathing scene is included among illustrations in *A Silent Siren Song*.

Dizzy Heights and Daring Hearts (Keystone). The Aitkens list this picture, directed by Walter Wright, as being released in 1917; others place it a year earlier. A synopsis and four photos are on file.

A Dog Catcher's Love (Keystone). Everyone agrees that this film, directed by Eddie Cline, made its debut in 1917. Synopsis and one photo are in the Aitken file.

Done in Oil (Triangle—1 reel). Synopsis, five photos, and production report are on file.

Fickle Fatty's Fall (Keystone). By now Fatty (as in Arbuckle) needed little introduction to silent film audiences. Synopsis, one photo, titles, and production report show typical episode. Arbuckle teamed with Mabel Normand to form one of Keystone's most enduring couples. Both fell from grace following allegations that they were suspects in separate unsolved murders during their careers.

The Finished Product (Triangle—1 reel). Synopsis and one photo on file.

The Firefly of Tough Luck (Triangle—5 reels). Directed by Thomas H. Ince. File contains synopsis, thirteen photos, titles, continuity sheet, and production report.

The Food Gamblers (Triangle—5 reels). Synopsis, two photos, titles, continuity sheet, and production report on file.

For Valour (Triangle—5 reels). File includes synopsis, three photos, story, titles, and press release.

Framing Farmers (Triangle—5 reels). Directed by Thomas Ince; includes synopsis, fourteen photos, titles, and continuity sheet.

The Girl Glory (Kay Bee—5 reels). Synopsis, two photos, titles, continuity sheet, and expense report are on file.

Haunted by Himself (Keystone). Synopsis, story, titles, and eight photos are on file.

Heart Strategy (Triangle—1 reel). Aitken file contains synopsis, three photos, press release, and production report.

Her Busted Debut (Keystone). Synopsis, thirteen photos, continuity, and cutting sheet are on file.

Her Cave Man (Triangle—1 reel). File contains synopsis, three photos, titles, and production report.

*Her Fame and Shame** (Keystone). Directed by Frank Griffin. In addition to the photo of Louise Fazenda with Charles Murray in the picture section of this book, six other photos of *Her Fame and Shame* are on file.

Her Torpedoed Love (Keystone). Directed by Frank Griffin and featuring Ford Sterling, Louise Fazenda, and Edgar Kennedy. Aitken Papers include titles and eleven photos.

His Baby Doll (Triangle—1 reel). Synopsis and one photo are on file.

His Bad Policy (Triangle—1 reel). File contains synopsis, three photos, titles, and continuity sheet.

His Criminal Career (Triangle—1 reel). Synopsis and three photos are on file.

His Disguised Passion (Keystone). Directed by Robert Kerr. Synopsis, two photos, and continuity sheet are on file.

His One Night Stand (Triangle). Directed by Charlie Chaplin. Synopsis, one photo, and press release.

His Rise and Tumble (Triangle—1 reel). File contains synopsis, five photos, and titles.

His Thankless Job (Triangle—1 reel). Synopsis and six photos are on file.

His Unconscious Conscience (Triangle—1 reel). File consists of synopsis and four photos.

Honest Thieves (Triangle—1 reel). Synopsis, two photos, press release, and production report are contained in the Aitken Papers.

The House of Scandal (Triangle—1 reel). Synopsis and one photo constitute the file.

The Little Brother (Kay Bee—5 reels). Consult file for synopsis, fourteen photos, titles, and production report.

Love or Justice (Kay Bee—5 reels). Synopsis, seven photos, story, titles, and production report are on file.

Madcap Madge (Kay Bee—5 reels). File contains photo composite of thirty-one scenes, synopsis, and ten still photographs.

*A Maiden's Trust** (Keystone). Directed by Harry Williams, the film also starred Ford Sterling. The actor from La Crosse, Wisc., was an Aitken favorite dating from their early Mutual days and throughout his career at Keystone, where he appeared as actor, director, or both in dozens of films. Evidence for this is found in the synopsis, six photos, and titles the brothers filed away for safekeeping.

The Man Who Made Good (Triangle—5 reels). File contains a bonanza—synopsis, fifty-two photos, story, and titles.

The Millionaire Vagrant (Kay Bee—5 reels). Production and expense reports and three photos are contained in this file.

Oriental Love (Keystone). Directed by Walter Wright. Synopsis, titles, and three photos of stars Ora Carew, Joseph Belmont, Joseph Callahan, Nick Cogley, and others in action.

A Royal Rogue (Keystone). Directed by Robert Kerr. Synopsis, six photos, and press release.

Sole Mates (Triangle—1 reel). Synopsis and eight photos are on file.

Souls Triumphant (Triangle–Fine Arts). Directed by John G. O'Brien, this film paired Lillian Gish with Wilfred Lucas, and its theme of a straying husband's return is as popular with movie buffs today as it was in 1917.

*Teddy at the Throttle** (Keystone). Directed by Clarence Badger, who paired Gloria
  Swanson with Wallace Beery, to whom she was married for a month (in real
  life). *Teddy* also starred a canine actor whose company Miss Swanson seemed to
  prefer to Beery's.

The Telephone Belles (Triangle—1 reel). Synopsis, eleven photos, and production report are on file.

Their Domestic Deception (Triangle—1 reel). File contains synopsis and five photos.

Until They Get Me (Triangle). Synopsis, four photos, titles, continuity sheet, and
  production report on file.

War and Matrimony (Triangle—1 reel). Titles, synopsis, one photo, and continuity
  sheet on file.

Without Honor (Triangle—5 reels). Synopsis, twenty-three photos, story, titles, and
  continuity sheet are on file.

1918

Boss of the Lazy "Y" (Triangle—5 reels). Synopsis, eight photos, titles, and continuity sheet on file.

Desert Law (Triangle—5 reels). File includes synopsis, fifteen photos, story, titles
  and subtitles, continuity sheet, review, and production report.

Did She Do Wrong? (Keystone). Synopsis, seven photos, titles, and annotated continuity sheet are on file.

Dimples and Dangers (Keystone). Aitken Papers file includes synopsis, twelve photos, titles, and continuity sheet.

High Stakes (Triangle—5 reels). Synopsis, thirty-three photos, and titles and subtitles are on file.

High Tide (Triangle—5 reels). File contains synopsis, eighteen photos, titles, and
  press release.

His Nimble Twist (Triangle—1 reel). Synopsis, one photo, and titles are on file.

His Punctured Reputation (Keystone). File contains synopsis, seven photos, titles,
  continuity, and cutting sheets.

I Love Charles Albert (Keystone). Synopsis, five photos, and production report.

Innocent Sinners (Triangle—1 reel). File contains synopsis and eight photos.

A Lady Killer's Doom (Keystone). Synopsis, six photos, titles, continuity, and cutting sheets.

The Marriage Bubble (Triangle—3 reels). Titles, sixteen photos, and twenty-
  four–picture composite sheet are on file.

Mr. Miller's Economics (Keystone). Synopsis, five photos, titles, continuity sheet,
  and production report.

Unfaithful (Triangle). Synopsis, two photos, titles, continuity sheet, and expense
  and production reports.

1919

Devil May Care (Triangle—5 reels). Synopsis, four photos, titles, publicity material,
  and correction sheet.

A Discord in A Flat (Triangle—1 reel). Synopsis, one photo, titles, and continuity sheet on file.

The Hushed Hour (Equity). Only a press release is on file.

1920

Bombs and Brides (Keystone). Synopsis, three photos, and production report.

Forbidden Women (Equity). Only the synopsis is on file.

Mid-Channel (Equity—5 reels). Directed by Harry Carson. Synopsis and review on file.

Whispering Devils (Equity). Synopsis and press release.

1921

Charge It (Equity). Only the synopsis is on file.

Hush (Equity). Synopsis, story, and press release are filed in the Aitken Papers.

Straight from Paris (Equity). File consists of synopsis and press release.

What No Man Knows (Equity). Synopsis and story.

1922

For the Soul of Rafael (Equity). Cast list and synopsis on file.

The Worldly Madonna (Equity). Synopsis and review on file.

YEAR UNKNOWN

Ghosts (Majestic—4 reels). Adapted from the play by Henrik Ibsen, the premise of *Ghosts* validates the Biblical canon that the "sins of the father are visited on the children." The Aitken film was true to the play by showing, through subtitles and on-screen conflict, that the roots of this premise run deep.

His Saving Loss (Triangle—1 reel). Synopsis, story, titles, and continuity on file.

Little Dove's Romance (Bison—1 reel). Negative possibly destroyed in fire along with other documents.

A Noble Red Man (Bison—1 reel). Documents and negative possibly lost in fire.

The Struggle (Bronco—2 reels). No further record.

Yellow Flame (Bronco—2 reels). No further record.

B

Aitken Actors by
Representative Screen Credits

Adams, Kathryn:
 Forbidden Women
Adams, Mildred:
 The Great Pearl Tangle
Aitken, Spottiswoode:
 The Angel of Contention
 Avenging Conscience
 Birth of a Nation
 Home Sweet Home
 Intolerance
 A Temperance Lesson
Alden, Mary:
 The Battle of the Sexes
 Birth of a Nation
 The Green-Eyed Devil
 Home Sweet Home
 The Lily and the Rose
Alexander, Ben:
 The Hushed Hour
Alexander, Gerard:
 Hush
 Straight from Paris
Allan, Winifred:
 For Valour
 The Man Who Made Good
Allardt, Arthur:
 Black Eyes and Blue

Allen, Estelle:
 Mabel, Fatty and the Law
 Mabel Lost and Won
 When Ambrose Dared Walrus
Allen, Phyllis:
 Caught in a Cabaret
 Fatty's Plucky Pup
 Fickle Fatty's Fall
 Gentlemen of Nerve
 The Judge
 A Submarine Pirate
Anderson, Andy:
 His Disguised Passion
 Oriental Love
Anderson, Betty:
 Dizzy Heights and Daring Hearts
Anderson, Claire:
 Bathtub Perils
 Cinders of Love
 Dimples and Dangers
 Done in Oil
 Heart Strategy
 His Baby Doll
 His Disguised Passion
 The House of Scandal
 A Temperance Lesson
Anderson, Dave:
 Dizzy Heights and Daring Hearts

Carter, Rose:
  Blood and Thunder
  His Nimble Twist
  A Matrimonial Breaker
Cavender, Glen:
  Because He Loved Her
  A Dog Catcher's Love
  A Submarine Pirate
  The Village Blacksmith
Chaplin, Charlie:
  Caught in a Cabaret
  Dough and Dynamite
  His New Profession
  His Trysting Place
  The Rounders
Chaplin, Syd
  Giddy, Gay and Ticklish
  A Lover's Lost Control
  A Submarine Pirate
Chase, Charles:
  His New Profession
  The Rounders
Churchill, Ruth:
  Her Cave Man
Cianelli, Eduardo:
  The Food Gamblers
Claire, Gertrude:
  Madcap Madge
Clark, Florence:
  His Baby Doll
  Sole Mates
  The Telephone Belle
Clark, Harvey:
  High Stakes
Clarke, Kenneth:
  I Love Charles Albert
Clifton, Elmer:
  An Artist's Wife
  Birth of a Nation
  The Comeback
  Intolerance
Cogley, Nick:
  Dizzy Heights and Daring Hearts
  Dollars and Sense
  Oriental Love
Collier, William:
  Better Late Than Never

Honest Thieves
  Wife and Auto Trouble
Conklin, Chester:
  Betrayal of Maggie
  Cinders of Love
  Dizzy Heights and Daring Hearts
  Dough and Dynamite
  The Great Pearl Tangle
Conway, Jack:
  Added Fuel
Cooley, Hal:
  A Dog Catcher's Love
  A Royal Rogue
Cooper, Dulcie:
  Charge It
  What No Man Knows
Cooper, Miriam:
  An Artist's Wife
  Birth of a Nation
  Home Sweet Home
  Intolerance
Crawford, Florence:
  Buried Treasure
Crisp, Donald:
  Birth of a Nation
  The Escape
  Home Sweet Home
  An Old Fashioned Girl
Crommie, Lige:
  Dollars and Sense
  His Last Laugh
Cronnell, Ben:
  His Nimble Twist
Crosthwaite, Ivy:
  By Stork Delivery
  Fickle Fatty's Fall
Crowell, Josephine:
  Birth of a Nation
  Intolerance
Curtis, Jack:
  The Firefly of Tough Luck
  Until They Get Me

Dagmar, Florence:
  The Marriage Bubble
Dalton, Dorothy:
  Back of the Man
  Unfaithful

Darien, Frank:
  His Criminal Career
Daugherty, Hobo:
  The Double-Crossing of Slim
Davenport, Alice:
  His Last Scent
  A Maiden's Trust
  The Stolen Magic
  Wife and Auto Trouble
Davenport, Milla:
  Forbidden Women
Davidson, Max:
  The Girl and the Mummy
Dawes, Henry:
  Dough and Dynamite
Dean, Julia:
  A Matrimony
DeGrasse, Sam:
  Children of the Feud
  Her Official Fathers
  An Innocent Magdalene
  Intolerance
  The Martyrs of the Alamo
De La Cruz, Juan:
  For the Soul of Rafael
De La Parelle, Marion:
  Gypsy Joe
Delphino, Mildred:
  Framing Farmers
Depp, Harry:
  A Boomerang Frame-up
  A Dark Room Secret
  A Discord in A Flat
  Done in Oil
  Honest Thieves
Desmond, Lucille:
  Mr. Miller's Economics
Desmond, William:
  Blood Will Tell
  Bullets and Brown Eyes
  The Marriage Bubble
  The Phantom's Farewell
Devereaux, Jack:
  The Man Who Made Good
DeWitt, Elizabeth:
  A Dark Room Secret
  Gypsy Joe

Dillon, Edward:
  Home Sweet Home
Dillon, Jack:
  A Bachelor's Finish
  The Comeback
  The Martyrs of the Alamo
Dixon, Henry P.:
  The Man Who Made Good
Dodge, Anna:
  Framing Farmers
  Until They Get Me
  Without Honor
Donnelly, James:
  Dad's Downfall
  His Baby Doll
  An Iceman's Bride
  Innocent Sinners
  The Telephone Belle
Dorian, Charles:
  I Love Charles Albert
Dowling, Joseph:
  Bullets and Brown Eyes
Drew, Cora:
  Minerva's Mission
Dunn, Bobby:
  By Stork Delivery
  His Busted Trust
  Secrets of a Beauty Parlor
Durfee, Minta:
  Fatty's Faithful Fido
  Fickle Fatty's Fall
  The Great Pearl Tangle
  His Wife's Mistakes
  The Other Man
Dwiggins, Jay:
  His Bad Policy
  A Matrimonial Breaker
  An Officer's Mess
  War and Matrimony

Edwards, Aaron:
  Boss of the Lazy "Y"
  The Firefly of Tough Luck
Edwards, Vivian:
  His Lying Heart
  His One Night Stand
  His Rise and Tumble

His Wild Oats
A Modern Enoch Arden
Sole Mates
The Village Blacksmith
Emery, Maude:
For the Soul of Rafael
Emory, May:
Ambrose's Cup of Woe
By Stork Delivery

Fairbanks, Douglas:
American Aristocracy
Double Trouble
His Picture in the Papers
The Lamb
Farley, James:
Desert Law
Farnum, Dustin:
The Iron Strain
Fawcett, George:
The Corner
Fay, Hugh:
Bathtub Perils
His Unconscious Conscience
The House of Scandal
A Maiden's Trust
Faye, Julia:
His Last Laugh
Fazenda, Louise:
Betrayal of Maggie
Bombs and Brides
A Game Old Knight
Her Fame and Shame
Her Torpedoed Love
Felix, George:
Haystacks and Steeples
Fields, Eleanor:
His Thankless Job
Fishback, Fred:
The Great Pearl Tangle
Foote, Courtney:
Home Sweet Home
Foss, Darrel:
The Firefly of Tough Luck
The Girl Glory
Without Honor

Francisco, Betty:
Straight from Paris
Franey, William:
His Punctured Reputation
A Lady Killer's Doom
French, Charles:
The Clod Hopper
The Iron Strain
Love or Justice
Fuller, Dale:
Bathtub Perils
The Camera Cure
Haunted By Himself
Her Busted Debut
His Baby Doll
His Punctured Reputation
A Lady Killer's Doom
Their Domestic Deception

Garcia, May:
Mr. Miller's Economics
Gardner, Reece:
The Village Blacksmith
Garney, Augustus:
The Martyrs of the Alamo
Garwood, William:
The Little Brother
Gaston, Mae:
Victorine
Gastrock, Phil:
Desert Law
Gaye, Howard:
Birth of a Nation
Her Mother's Necklace
Intolerance
Gaye, William:
Daphne and the Pirate
George, Maud:
The Marriage Bubble
Gilbert, Billie:
His Rise and Tumble
Gilbert, Jack:
The Millionaire Vagrant
Gilmore, Barney:
The Man Who Made Good
Gish, Dorothy:
Granny

Harris, Lecretia:
  Mr. Miller's Economics
Harris, Mildred:
  Little Matchmakers
  The Phantom's Farewell
Harron, Robert "Bobby":
  The Battle of the Sexes
  Birth of a Nation
  Home Sweet Home
  Intolerance
  A Lesson in Mechanics
  The Newer Woman
  The Rebellion of Kitty Belle
  Sands of Fate
Hart, Lallah:
  Dimples and Dangers
  The Escape
  Heart Strategy
Hart, William S.:
  The Apostle of Vengeance
  The Captive God
  The Dawn Maker
  The Gunfighter
  Hell's Hinges
  The Patriot
Hartford, David M.:
  Blood Will Tell
  Bride of Hate
Haver, Phyllis:
  His Unconscious Conscience
Hayes, Frank:
  The Stolen Magic
Hazleton, Joseph:
  Heart Strategy
Headley, Josephine:
  The Little Brother
  The Millionaire Vagrant
Henabery, Joseph:
  Birth of a Nation
  Her Official Fathers
  The Turning Point
Henderson, Jack:
  Black Eyes and Blue
  A Discord in A Flat
  A Dog Catchers Love
  A Royal Rogue

Herring, Aggie:
  Madcap Madge
  The Millionaire Vagrant
Hickman, Howard:
  Blood Will Tell
  Matrimony
Highby, Wilbur:
  The Turning Point
  Until They Get Me
Hill, Thomas:
  The Double-Crossing of Slim
Hinckley, William:
  Victorine
Hitchcock, Raymond:
  The Stolen Magic
Holmes, Lois:
  Cinders of Love
Hooper, De Wolf:
  The Girl and the Mummy
Hope, Gloria:
  The Hushed Hour
  The Phantom's Farewell
Horning, Bob:
  A Dark Room Secret
Howles, R. J.:
  The Penalty
Hughes, Eunice:
  His One Night Stand
Hunt, Irene:
  Added Fuel
Hunt, Jack:
  The Telephone Belle
Hunt, Mrs. J.:
  Bride of Hate

Irving, William:
  His Unconscious Conscience
  A Matrimonial Breaker

Jabson, Edwin:
  Framing Farmers
Jackson, Joe:
  Gypsy Joe
  A Modern Enoch Arden
Jackson, Julia:
  High Tide

Lewis, Ralph:
  The Avenging Conscience
  The Comeback
  Intolerance
  The Turning Point
  Victorine
Lewis, Vera:
  Intolerance
Lincoln, Elmo:
  Intolerance
Lind, Myrtle:
  Dimples and Dangers
  A Maiden's Trust
  A Matrimonial Breaker
Linden, Clarry:
  A Boomerang Frame-up
Livingston, Jack:
  The Back of the Man
  Madcap Madge
Lloyd, Harold:
  Court House Crooks
  Miss Fatty's Seaside Lovers
Lockney, J. D.:
  The Girl Glory
Long, Walter:
  Birth of a Nation
  Buried Treasure
  Intolerance
  Jordan is a Hard Road
  Out of Bondage
  Sold for Marriage
Lorraine, Leotta:
  Desert Law
Lowery, W. E.:
  Checkmate
  The Tear That Burned
Lucas, Wilfred:
  The Food Gamblers
  The Hushed Hour
  Souls Triumphant
Luther, Anna:
  The Marriage Bubble
Lynard, Lenore:
  Whispering Devils
Lynd, Myrtle:
  Did She Do Wrong?
Lyndon, Larry:
  Dad's Downfall

Mace, Fred:
  Bath Tub Perils
  His Last Scent
  A Lover's Might
  The Village Vampire
MacGuire, Earnest:
  Caught in a Cabaret
Mack, Fred:
  Blood and Thunder
Mack, Willard:
  The Corner
Mackinnin, John:
  Forbidden Women
MacQuarrie, Frank:
  Boss of the Lazy "Y"
Manly, Marie:
  Boomerang Frame-up
  His Nimble Twist
Mann, Hank:
  A Modern Enoch Arden
  The Village Blacksmith
Markey, Enid:
  Blood Will Tell
  The Iron Strain
Marsh, Betty:
  Gypsy Joe
  A Janitor's Wife's Temptation
  A Modern Enoch Arden
Marsh, Marguerite:
  The Turning Point
Marsh, May:
  Avenging Conscience
  Birth of a Nation
  Home Sweet Home
  Intolerance
Marshall, Tully:
  The Deadly Glass of Beer
  Intolerance
Martin, Alatia:
  His Saving Loss
  An Iceman's Bride
Martin, Edward:
  Framing Farmers
Mason, William:
  Cinders of Love
  A Dash of Courage
  Dizzy Heights and Daring Hearts

Matthews, Dorcas:
  The Little Brother
  Love or Justice
  Madcap Madge
  The Millionaire Vagrant
Maxam, Louella:
  His Bitter Pill
  His Lying Heart
Maxmillian, Robert:
  The Waiters Ball
McCoy, Harry:
  Because He Loved Her
  Caught in a Cabaret
  The Great Pearl Tangle
  His Last Laugh
  A Movie Star
  Perils of the Park
McDiarmid, G. V.:
  The Double-Crossing of Slim
McGuire, Paddy:
  A Discord in A Flat
McKim, Robert:
  The Phantom's Farewell
  The Raiders
  Unfaithful
McKinnon, Al:
  His Criminal Career
Merritt, Paula:
  For the Soul of Rafael
Mestayer, Harry:
  High Tide
Millais, Warren:
  Whispering Devils
Miller, Charles:
  The Corner
Miller, Elda:
  The Food Gamblers
Miller, Jane:
  High Stakes
Milliken, Robert:
  His Disguised Passion
Mitchell, Rhea:
  The Beckoning Flame
Moon, Arthur:
  His Saving Loss
  Without Honor

Moore, Owen:
  The Battle of the Sexes
  The Escape
  Home Sweet Home
  Susan Rocks the Boat
Moore, Vin:
  By Stork Delivery
Moran, Polly:
  By Stork Delivery
  Cactus Nell
  Her Fame and Shame
  His Naughty Thought
  Vampire Ambrose
Morante, Melbourne:
  Did She Do Wrong?
Morris, Reggie:
  Done in Oil
  A Finished Product
  Haystacks and Steeples
Morrison, Lewis:
  The Betrayal of Maggie
  Bombs and Brides
  A Game Old Knight
  Gypsy Joe
  Her Fame and Shame
Murray, Charles:
  The Beckoning Flame
  The Betrayal of Maggie
  The Great Vacuum Robbery
  Her Painted Hero
  His Hereafter
  The Judge

Normand, Mabel:
  Caught in a Cabaret
  He Did and He Didn't
  His Trysting Place
  The Stolen Magic
  Wished on Mabel
Northrup, Harry:
  The Hushed Hour

Opperman, Frank:
  Better Late Than Never
  Her Fame and Shame
  His Savings Loss

Owen, Seena:
  Bred in the Bone
  Intolerance
  An Old Fashioned Girl

Paget, Alfred:
  Enoch Arden
  Intolerance
  The Martyrs of the Alamo
  Pathways of Life
Pallette, Eugene:
  Gretchen the Greenhorn
  Intolerance
  The Penalty
Parker, Gladys:
  Dad's Downfall
Parquet, Corinne:
  The Waiter's Ball
Pavis, Yvonne:
  High Tide
Payson, Blanche:
  Dollars and Sense
  Haunted By Himself
  His Nimble Twist
  His Punctured Reputation
  An Iceman's Bride
  Oriental Love
  Wife and Auto Trouble
Pearce, George:
  Desert Law
Pearce, Peggy:
  A Dog Catcher's Love
Perkins, Walter:
  Without Honor
Perrin, Jack:
  Haunted By Himself
  Her Busted Debut
  His Unconscious Conscience
Perry, Vester:
  Added Fuel
  An Artist's Wife
  Checkmate
Perry, Walter:
  Until They Get Me
Persse, Tom:
  His Unconscious Conscience

Peters, House:
  The Winged Idol
Pette, Graham:
  Boss of the Lazy "Y"
  High Tide
Phelps, Lee:
  Framing Farmers
Pickford, Jack:
  Home Sweet Home
  The Mysterious Shot
Pickford, Mary:
  Courting of Mary
  Dan's Reward
  Fudge
  Kleptomaniac
  Magic Vase
  Red Riding Hood
  Rose of Yesterday
Pierce, George:
  Framing Farmers
Pierson, Leo:
  Desert Law
  High Tide
Pike, Wallace:
  His One Night Stand
Portel, Victor:
  His Last Scent
Porter, Dave:
  A Bachelor's Finish
Porter, David:
  Honest Thieves
Price, Kate:
  The Waiter's Ball
Pringle, Della:
  A Bachelor's Finish
  A Finished Product
  Haystacks and Steeples

Ralston, Ester:
  Whispering Devils
Rankin, Caroline:
  Dad's Downfall
  His Bad Policy
  A Matrimonial Breaker
  An Officer's Mess
  War and Matrimony

Rawlinson, Herbert:
Charge It
Ray, Charles:
Back of the Man
The Clod Hopper
The Millionaire Vagrant
Rea, Alice:
The Girl and the Mummy
Reeves, Myrtle:
Mr. Miller's Economics
An Officer's Mess
Reid, Wallace:
Arms and the Gringo
Birth of a Nation
The City Beautiful
Down the Road to Creditville
Reisner, Charles:
His Lying Heart
Reynolds, Vera:
His Criminal Career
Richardson, Jack:
Desert Law
Love or Justice
Ridgeway, Fritzi:
I Love Charles Albert
Ring, Sutherland:
His Last Laugh
Rishell, Myrtle:
High Stakes
Mr. Miller's Economics
Robinson, Eileen:
Mid-Channel
Rodgers, Dora:
Did She Do Wrong?
Gypsy Joe
His Disguised Passion
His Nimble Twist
An Iceman's Bride
A Modern Enoch Arden
Rodney, Earl:
A Bachelor's Finish
His Bad Policy
An Officer's Mess
War and Matrimony
Rollens, Jack:
High Tide

Ross, Milton:
The Phantom's Farewell
Rossen, Dick:
High Stakes
Rowe, James:
His Disguised Passion
Royce, Cora:
His Trysting Place
Rubens, Alma:
The Firefly of Tough Luck
Ruggles, Wesley:
A Submarine Pirate
Russell, Raymond:
A Royal Rogue

Salmon, Nate:
A Discord in A Flat
Salter, Thelma:
Matrimony
Sampson, Teddy:
The Deadly Glass of Beer
Schade, Fritz:
His Disguised Passion
His Last Scent
Schiller, Carl:
Devil May Care
Schiller, Kate:
Devil May Care
Sears, A. D.:
The Martyrs of the Alamo
Sears, Laura:
Framing Farmers
Without Honor
Sedgwick, Josie:
Boss of the Lazy "Y"
Sennett, Mack:
The Stolen Magic
Seville, Gus:
A Discord in A Flat
Seymour, Clarissa:
Straight From Paris
Shattuck, Thuly:
Back of the Man
High Stakes
Love or Justice
Madcap Madge

Sherman, Lowell:
  What No Man Knows
Sherry, J. Barney:
  The Beckoning Flame
  The Iron Strain
  The Millionaire Vagrant
  What No Man Knows
Siegmann, George:
  The Angel of Contention
  The Avenging Conscience
  Birth of a Nation
  Intolerance
Sills, Milton:
  The Hushed Hour
Simpson, Russell:
  The Food Gamblers
Sims, Milt:
  His Punctured Reputation
  A Lady Killer's Doom
Singleton, Joe:
  Desert Law
  His Lying Heart
Smith, L. R.:
  His Rise and Tumble
Smith, Sid:
  Oriental Love
Snyder, Jack:
  The Food Gamblers
Somerville, George:
  A Game Old Knight
Sotchell, Lola:
  The House of Scandal
Southern, Sam:
  Whispering Devils
Spencer, James:
  His Criminal Career
St. Clair, Mal:
  A Boomerang Frame-up
  The Camera Cure
  Did She Do Wrong?
  Dollars and Sense
  His Baby Doll
  His Nimble Twist
  An Iceman's Bride
  Their Domestic Deception
St. John, Alfred:
  Fatty's Faithful Fido

Fatty's New Role
Fickle Fatty's Fall
He Did and He Didn't
Her Cave Man
The Waiter's Ball
Standing, Wyndham:
  The Hushed Hour
Stanley, Maxfield:
  Birth of a Nation
Starke, Pauline:
  Until They Get Me
Starr, Jane:
  The House of Scandal
Steers, L. T.:
  The Hushed Hour
Sterling, Ford:
  Court House Crooks
  Her Torpedoed Love
  His Lying Heart
  His Wild Oats
  A Maiden's Trust
Stewart, Ethel:
  Devil May Care
Stewart, Roy:
  Boss of the Lazy "Y"
Storm, Jerome:
  Bride of Hate
Strong, Porter:
  Victorine
Sullivan, Helen:
  For the Soul of Rafael
  Mid-Channel
Summerville, Slim:
  Cinders of Love
  A Dog Catcher's Love
  Dough and Dynamite
Sutherland, Edward:
  Dad's Downfall
  Heart Strategy
Swain, Mack:
  Ambrose's Cup of Woe
  Ambrose's Rapid Rise
  By Stork Delivery
  Caught in a Cabaret
  His Bitter Pill
  His Trysting Place
  A Modern Enoch Arden

Swanson, Gloria:
   A Dash of Courage
   Dangers of a Bride
   Haystacks and Steeples
   The Sultan's Wife
   Teddy at the Throttle
   Whose Baby
Sweet, Blanche:
   Avenging Conscience
   The Escape
   Home Sweet Home
   The Hushed Hour
Swickard, Joseph:
   Ambrose's Cup of Woe
   Haystacks and Steeples

Talmadge, Constance:
   Betsy's Burglar
   Girl of the Timber Claims
   Intolerance
   The Microscope Mystery
Talmadge, Norma:
   Children in the House
   The Devil's Needle
   Fifty-Fifty
   Going Straight
   Martha's Vindication
   Missing Links
   The Social Secretary
Tearle, Conway:
   Forbidden Women
   Whispering Devils
Teddy, Keystone:
   A Dog Catcher's Love
Thatcher, Eva:
   Haystacks and Steeples
Theby, Rosemary:
   The Hushed Hour
   Whispering Devils
Thomas, Olive:
   Madcap Madge
Thompson, Margaret:
   Back of the Man
   Blood Will Tell
Thurman, Mary:
   The Betrayal of Maggie
   Bombs and Brides

Her Cave Man
His Last Laugh
Tincher, Fay:
   A Costly Exchange
   The Quicksands
Toncray, Kate:
   Little Meena's Romance
   The Little Yank
   Old Heidelberg
Trask, Wayland:
   Bombs and Brides
   Cactus Nell
   Her Cave Man
   Her Torpedoed Love
   The Judge
Trick, Martha:
   Black Eyes and Blue
   A Royal Rogue
Tucker, Richard:
   The Worldly Madonna
Turner, Fred A.:
   Atta Boy's Last Race
   The Girl and the Mummy
   Her Mother's Daughter
   The Hunchback
   Intolerance
   The Lost House
   Out of Bondage
Turpin, Ben:
   A Clever Dummy
   Lost—A Cook
   Sole Mates

Ullman, Carl:
   The Little Brother

Vermont, Charlotte:
   Unfaithful
Vernon, Bobbie:
   A Dash of Courage
   Haystacks and Steeples
Vroom, Frederick:
   High Tide

Wagner, Carolyn:
   The Millionaire Vagrant

Walsh, Raoul:
The Angel of Contention
The Availing Prayer
Birth of a Nation
The Green-Eyed Devil
The Rebellion of Kitty Belle
Sands of Fate
Walthall, Henry B.:
Birth of Nation
The Floor Above
Home Sweet Home
The Mysterious Shot
The Old Man
Warner, H. B.:
The Raiders
Warters, William:
The Girl Glory
Washington, Ed:
High Stakes
Mr. Miller's Economics
Wayne, Maude:
Haunted By Himself
Her Busted Debut
His Punctured Reputation
Honest Thieves
A Lady Killer's Doom
The Telephone Belle
Weaver, Henry:
For Valour
Webster, Lillian:
The Penalty
Weil, Elvira:
Bride of Hate
The Millionaire Vagrant
Wells, Mai:
Cactus Nell
Honest Thieves
West, Billie:
Above Par
The Comeback
Whitman, Al:
Desert Law
Whitman, Walt:
Boss of the Lazy "Y"
Desert Law
The Firefly of Tough Luck

The Girl Glory
The Millionaire Vagrant
Without Honor
Wilbur, Crane:
Devil May Care
Williams, Clara:
The Corner
The Winged Idol
Williams, Kathlyn:
Hush
Williams, Stanton:
Forbidden Women
Willis, Paul:
Little Matchmakers
Wilson, Hal:
Charge It
Whispering Devils
Wilson, Margery:
Bride of Hate
A Costly Exchange
The Clod Hopper
Intolerance
Little Matchmakers
Without Honor
Wilson, Tom:
The Martyrs of the Alamo
Withey, Chet:
A Costly Exchange
The Lost Lord Lowell
Woodruff, Henry:
The Beckoning Flame
Woodward, Guy:
A Dash of Courage

Young, Clara Kimball:
Charge It
For the Soul of Rafael
Forbidden Women
Hush
Mid-Channel
Straight From Paris
What No Man Knows
The Worldly Madonna
Young, Lucille:
An Artist's Wife

C

Supporting Documents
from the Aitken Papers

Anchored in an era they helped create, the Aitken Brothers, their films, their players, and their contributions to film history may have been lost had they failed to preserve the documents scholars rely upon as primary sources. Nowhere is this more evident than in the papers they left behind relating to production costs, censorship and expansion as viewed from the empire builders themselves.

First, consider the cost. Modern movies cost millions to make. Producers spent $4,500,000 to make *Mahatma Ghandi*. They spent $7,500,000 on the black and white feature *Who's Afraid of Virginia Woolf?* According to the Aitken production/ expense report for *Love or Justice*, made a few decades earlier than *Woolf*, the breakdown is as follows:

Love or Justice	
No. 522	
Director: Edwards	
Camera: Lyons	
Commenced March 5th	
Completed April 7	
Stock, Directors, Actors, etc.	3,536.20
Star: Louise Glaum, 4 weeks, 5 days	483.33
Labor & Operation, Carpenters, etc.	732.01
Auto Expense, Driver's Salaries	37.50
Ranch R & M, Salaries	13.96
Laboratory Operations, Salaries	697.69
Wardrobe, Salaries	9.13
Payroll, Indirect, Salaries	2,530.58
Total Payroll, Salaries	7,557.07
Picture Expense, Direct	383.58
Props, Scenery, Wardrobe, Direct	58.65
Arsenal, Asset	4.25

Scenery, Asset	130.02
Props, Rental	25.00
Laboratory Material	183.43
Auto Expense, Use of Machines	157.50
Film, Positive & Negative	1,101.17
General Picture Expense, Undist.	382.37
General Picture Expense, Depreciation	200.24
Total Picture Expense	$10,183.28

No doubt star salaries today have escalated the cost. Some are estimated to receive $20 million for a single picture. And a half hour television sitcom can earn the co-star one million per episode.

Censorship was another thorny problem for the Aitkens. Each major city empowered its mayor or censorship board to excise offending material from motion pictures before they were shown. As champions for clean pictures, the Aitkens rarely challenged the nitpicking these local officials applied to all films. Unlike "talking pictures," silent films could pass muster by deleting a snippet here or, as was more often the case, changing the subtitles.

On the other hand, entire scenes were lost when a censor modified an offending passage on a sound film. Aitken file documents, relating to *Bride of Hate, Betrayal of Maggie* and *By Stork Delivery*, demonstrate how a raised eyebrow sent censors scurrying for their scissors in the first quarter of the twentieth century:

Philadelphia
Bride of Hate

Eliminate subtitle: "We must be married before it is too late—before Uncle learns."
Eliminate subtitle: "I can't stop now, but don't worry, I won't forget you," and substitute "I can't stop now, but"
Eliminate subtitle: "I can't have you leave me now," and substitute "I never really loved you—we might as well break off our engagement."

New York
Betrayal of Maggie

Eliminate throwing underclothes over screen and corset in man's lap.
Eliminate subtitle: "Everything is off."
Eliminate all views of forcing minister to perform the marriage service at point of gun.
The reasons for the above eliminations are that they are "indecent," "inhuman" and "sacrilegious."

New York
By Stork Delivery

Show Uncle Ambrose telegram relative to sex of coming baby only once.
Eliminate little girl peeping in keyhole during mother's confinement.
The reason for the above eliminations is that they are "indecent."

Pittsburgh ("No matter what was cut in New York, Pittsburgh always scissored (sic) a bit more," the Aitkens noted.)
By Stork Delivery

Eliminate views of clerk poking Ambrose in ribs after Ambrose has whispered in his ear.
Eliminate views of mother fainting, of nurse going to her and lifting her out of chair.
Eliminate views of doctor with bag going into bedroom.

Eliminate subtitle: "Hustle—the stork is on the way," and substitute: "Hustle home at once."

Eliminate views of man pulling drapery off another man riding on bicycle when the man is shown in his underclothes, views of man without trousers lying in street and getting up, and all subsequent views of him without trousers, in the reel. Cut until he has his trousers on.

Eliminate views of father going anxiously to bedroom door with subtitle spoken by the nurse: "Don't go in yet."

The reason for the above eliminations is that they are "indecent."

Undaunted by rising production costs and skirmishes with the censors at home, the Aitkens looked to Czarist Russia and beyond. In one of those strange twists of history, the Wisconsin farm boys led a movie blitzkrieg into territories their Hollywood counterparts had once fled because of persecution.

By letter J. P. Tippett, an Aitken-Mutual employee informs P. A. Powers, general manager of the Aitken controlled production companies in America of his initial efforts to establish motion picture distributorships throughout Europe. The reference to "Mr. John Law" in Tippett's letter shows the risk involved in starting new ventures in a totalitarian state:

St. Petersburg
Russia

February 27, 1914

My Dear Mr. Powers:

Your letter of February 16th forwarded from London. Thanks for same. I came out of London almost three weeks ago. First opened Italian main office at Milan, with a branch at Rome. Then came into Russia. Have been negotiating sometime with a Company here. Closed with them a tentative contract. They buy our film, payment on which is guaranteed by a deposit in our London Bank. They to open six bona fide offices—headquarters in Moscow, then this city, Warsaw, Odessa, Kieff, and Rostow-on-the-Don. This country is as large as U. S. and a closed book even to London film men. No American brands are fairly represented. Return to London next week; then will open an office for Spain and Portugal at Barcelona. After that, go into the Balkan States. Place representatives at Bucharest, Belgrade and Sofia. We then have Europe absolutely covered.

I wish you could see the Cinema Theatres here. Palaces and plenty of them—225 I am told in St. Petersburg. Mr. John Law is very prominent in this country. The other night in the Metropole Hotel in Moscow five secret police accompanied by three dozen detectives tore down the hall my room was on, and into another room. The dogs running over the bed and chairs, sniffing and smelling. I like the country; you can live well, and they have any country in the world beat when it comes to comfort on railroad trains. And as for the M. P. business, it certainly looks promising.

Yours truly,

(Signed) J. P. Tippett

Index

About the Authors

The late Al P. Nelson's writing career spanned six decades and included nine books, seventy-five short stories, and some five thousand articles published. After graduating from Marquette University, Milwaukee, with a degree in journalism in 1926, Nelson worked at various jobs until the Great Depression convinced him to become a freelance writer. Although he taught writing courses for the University of Wisconsin–Madison Extension Division during a sixteen-year period beginning in 1964, Nelson continued to write until age eighty-four. He is the recipient of numerous writing and teaching awards, including one for teaching excellence from Standard Oil in 1970, and another in 1980 when he received the first annual Christopher Latham Sholes Award from the Council for Wisconsin Writers. Al P. Nelson is the author of *Brand of the Outlaw, Gunsmoke, Bullets for Badwater, Writing for Fun and Profit, Writing the Nonfiction Book, Mysterious Malady, The Birth of a Nation Story* (with Roy E. Aitken), and others. Like his son-in-law and coauthor, Nelson shared a passion for literature and philosophy, which he considered twin springboards for lifting the human spirit.

Mel R. Jones started as a cub reporter, college field correspondent, and military journalist. He continued to write throughout a twenty-one-year Army career in the combat arms that dovetailed with his assigned additional military specialty as a public affairs officer. He served two tours of duty in Vietnam, and his military decorations include the Legion of Merit, Bronze Star, Meritorious Service Medal, and Air Medal. His civilian honors include the Wilbur Wright Award from the Aviation Space Writers Association for service during the Cuban Missile Crisis. He also won awards for writing and producing two television documentaries and a book on aerobatic flying. His freelance writing career began in earnest when he married coauthor Nelson's daughter, Marian, and later established M. R. Jones and Associates, Inc., a Wisconsin public relations firm he currently heads. Jones graduated from Florida Southern College and holds a master's degree in international relations (1975) from Boston University. Like his father-in-law, he attended Marquette where he received a master's degree in journalism (1983). Mel R. Jones is author of *In the Eye of the Storm,* "Candle in the Dark," *Public Affairs Handbook, Putting Wings on Dreams, Above and Beyond: Eight Great Aerobatic Champions,* and numerous articles.

The coauthors' specific interest in the performing arts stems from a life-long fascination with its various forms and from living in a Wisconsin community that claims notables such as Alfred Lunt, Lynn Fontanne, and the Aitken brothers.